*ALSO BY RICK PITINO*
Born to Coach

*ALSO BY DICK WEISS*
(with Dick Vitale) Time Out, Baby

# FULL-COURT PRESSURE

▬ ▬ ▬

# *FULL-COURT*

A Year in

Kentucky

Basketball

■ ■ ■

# *PRESSURE*

## Rick Pitino
### with Dick Weiss

**New York**

Library of Congress Cataloging-in-Publication Data
Pitino, Rick.
Full-court pressure: a year in Kentucky basketball / by Rick
Pitino with Dick Weiss.—1st ed.
p. cm.
Includes bibliographical references.
ISBN 1-56282-753-7
1. University of Kentucky—Basketball—History. 2. Pitino, Rick.
I. Weiss, Dick. II. Title.
GV885.43.U53P58 1992
796.323′63′0976947—dc20          92-22087
CIP

First Paperback Edition
10 9 8 7 6 5 4 3 2 1

# Contents

*For Joanne, Michael, Christopher, Richard, and Ryan, who have given me love and support in pursuit of my basketball dreams; and to Cawood Ledford and Bill Keightley, two great friends in Wildcatland.*

*—R.P.*


*For my parents, Dick and Barbara Weiss; and Joan, who was with me every step of the way.*

*—D.W.*

# Acknowledgments

**I** first want to thank Rick, Joanne, Michael, Chris, Rick, and Ryan for opening the door and letting a relative stranger walk into their lives for four months. Joan Williamson for reading the manuscript. Kentucky athletics director C. M. Newton, assistant Athletic Director Gene DeFilippo and Sports Information Director Chris Cameron and his outstanding staff for easing the way. Herb Sendek, Billy Donovan, Bernadette Locke-Mattox, Mike Atkinson, Ralph Willard, Marta MacMackin, Suzetta Yates, Mike Bales, Joe Iracane, Van and Lois Florence, Doug Sizemore, Barb Kobak, Rock Oliver, Jodi DiRaimo, Dave Dibble, JoAnn Hauser, Ilene Hauser, and Jerry McLaughlin for being friends I could count on. Cawood Ledford, Bill Keightley, Seth Hancock, Rena Vicini, and Oscar Combs for helping feel the pulse of basketball in the Commonwealth. Leslie Wells, our editor at Hyperion, for her constant support and positive vibes. Julie

### ACKNOWLEDGMENTS

Watson for her dilligent efforts as our researcher. Jersey Red Ford, Bill Minardi, and Bill Reynolds for providing me with much needed background and insight. Pat Forde, Chuck Culpepper, Rob Bromley, Larry Vaught, Bob Watkins, Dave Baker, Alan Cutler, Tom Wallace, Ralph Hacker, Brooks Downing, Tom Leach, Rick Bozich, and all the members of the Lexington and Louisville media who made me feel at home. Mike Rathet and Pat McLoone of the Philadelphia *Daily News* for allowing me the time to do this project. Larry Donald, John Feinstein, Lesley Visser, Jeff Samuels, Charlie Pierce, Bob Ryan, Malcom Moran, Ken Denlinger, Dick Vitale, Stan Hochman, Jackie MacMullan, Phil Jasner, Dick Jerardi, Diane Weiss, Billy Reed, Joe Cassidy, Rick Troncelliti, Mike Kern, and Mike Flynn for their support, past and present. And a team that wouldn't quit.

—D.W.

# Introduction

While being interviewed for a national magazine last fall, right off the bat I was asked: "What has Rick Pitino done for the Kentucky basketball program?"

"He has taken it from ashes to stardust," I answered.

I don't know how I came up with that line, but that's exactly what Rick has done in his three years at the University of Kentucky—he's taken a once-proud, tradition-rich basketball program, reduced to rubble by an NCAA investigation, and restored it to prominence much sooner than even the most wide-eyed optimist could have imagined.

The simple fact is, what Rick Pitino has done at Kentucky is nothing short of a miracle. To take a shattered program, especially in today's out-of-sight, out-of-mind television age, and rebuild it so quickly is an accomplishment that boggles the mind.

Three years ago, after the NCAA sanctions had been handed down and we were at our lowest point, someone asked me how long I thought it would take before Kentucky could get back on top. I said it would take at least five, maybe six years.

Even as I said it, I'm not sure I really believed my own words. After all, Kentucky got blindsided by the NCAA, hit by a series of sanctions that, in effect, kept the Wildcats out of the spotlight for two years. No postseason play; no live TV, a cutback in the number of scholarships . . . at the time, there didn't seem to be any light at the end of what looked to be an awfully long and dark tunnel.

I couldn't have been more wrong. None of us could have been more wrong. And for that, we all owe an eternal debt of gratitude and thanks to C. M. Newton.

What C.M. did was to take his time, find the coach he wanted, then go after him with every ounce of energy he had available.

And the man C.M. came up with in what has proved to be a stroke of genius was a fiery, aggressive New York Italian-American who was as different from most Kentuckians as night is from day.

Richard Andrew Pitino.

From day one, Wildcat fans fell in love with Rick. Oh sure, we couldn't understand much of what he was saying—he said foreign things like "Rupp Arener" and "Indianer"—but that didn't really matter. Those things we did understand we liked, things like up-tempo style, three-point shot and pressing defense.

We also liked the way Rick almost immediately brought back the dignity and hope that had been lost during that long and turbulent year that preceded his arrival. Rick told us we would win again, and that we would have fun again. And, boy, was he right.

Rick came to Kentucky with the reputation of being a rebuilder. He'd already worked wonders at Boston University, Providence College, and in New York with the Knicks of the

NBA, so everyone knew that he understood what it takes to turn around a struggling program.

Still, none of those situations remotely resembled the one facing him when he arrived in Lexington. Here, he was faced with those sanctions, which was bad enough, along with a depleted roster that included just eight healthy scholarship players.

And staring them in the face was one of the nation's most demanding schedules.

I predicted eight wins for the Cats that season. In fact, I told Rick that if Kentucky could win ten games, he'd get my vote for National Coach of the Year.

Incredibly, that Kentucky team—Pitino's Bombinos, which will always rank among my all-time favorites—broke even with a 14–14 record.

Believe me, though, it didn't take an entire season to realize how fortunate we were to have Rick Pitino as our coach. What he did that year was to take a group of hard-working but limited players and, by the sheer force of his will and his charismatic personality, drive them to overachieve beyond even their wildest dreams.

Then came the 22–6 record in Rick's second year, followed in 1991–92, the Cats' first year off probation, by a 29–7 record and a trip to the NCAA's Sweet Sixteen and a loss to Duke in the final eight. Two years ago, the Wildcats had the best record in SEC play; this year, they captured the SEC's Eastern Division title and won the conference tournament in Birmingham.

Suddenly, the University of Kentucky was back on top again, both on and off the court. Suddenly, we once again could take great pride in being Big Blue fans.

The last three seasons have been three of the happiest, most pleasant I've experienced in my 39 years at UK. Rick Pitino is the reason why. I'm enormously fond of Rick, and I've genuinely enjoyed working with him. In every way, he's been generous, courteous, and professional. Truth is, I simply can't say enough good things about him.

I don't know what the future holds for UK basketball. No one does. But I do know that whatever success the Wildcats achieve down the road can be traced back to one man—Rick Pitino.

Rick once did a book titled *Born to Coach*. If there ever was an appropriate title, that's it.

I'll tell you something else: when it comes to coaching basketball, Rick Pitino is as good as it gets.

    —Cawood Ledford
      April 19, 1992

# Prologue

$O$ne point.

That's how close we came to going to the Final Four.

I thought we would start booking reservations for the championship in Minneapolis when our point guard Sean Woods shook off Duke's Bobby Hurley and shook up the sell-out crowd at the Spectrum.

Woods drove the lane and launched a high arching baby hook that sailed just over the outstretched reach of All-American center Christian Laettner. His magnificent field goal gave us a one-point lead with only 2.1 seconds left in overtime during the NCAA Eastern Regional Final.

But joy turned to massive disbelief in an instant when Laettner, who had not missed a shot all night, took a 75-foot pass from Grant Hill, put the ball on the floor, sighted the basket, and made a 17-foot turnaround jumper just before the scoreboard clock read 0:00.

Laettner's unbelievable shot put the finishing touches on Duke's 104–103 overtime victory. In my mind, it was one of the greatest games ever played in the history of modern basketball.

The Duke players bolted onto the floor in jubilation, swamping their hero under the weight of their bodies.

Our players and staff were in a fog. John Pelphrey, one of our senior captains, just stood there motionless for ten, fifteen seconds, just ten feet from where Laettner took his shot. He had his hand on his head. Sean just lay on the floor, motionless in the chaos swirling around him. Eventually, Junior Braddy went over to pick him up. Sean went searching for Laettner.

When he finally spotted him, he went over and embraced him.

"Great shot," Sean said.

"Great game," Laettner replied.

Then Sean followed the rest of our team into the locker room.

This wasn't the way I had envisioned the season ending. For an instant, I thought we had grabbed the brass ring—then it was taken away.

When I looked around the locker room, I could see all their faces: Jamal Mashburn, Gimel Martinez, Junior Braddy, Dale Brown, Travis Ford, Chris Harrison, Andre Riddick, Aminu Timberlake, Carlos Toomer, Henry Thomas, Jeff Brassow. Mostly, I saw our four seniors—Sean Woods, John Pelphrey, Deron Feldhaus, and Richie Farmer.

This team had come so far in just three years. We had won 29 games. We had captured the SEC tournament. And we had pushed Duke, the 1991 national champion, to the brink. They had done all of this in Kentucky's first year off probation.

I didn't want the players to forget what they had accomplished. I pulled out an aging cover of *Sports Illustrated*, dated May 29, 1989. The headline screamed KENTUCKY'S SHAME.

I showed it to the players.

"From three years ago to now, I couldn't be any prouder of a basketball team. We are not losers," I said. "Don't let two seconds determine your basketball life—because it's worth a lot more than that."

Then, I sent them to the showers. "When you come out, I want you to stop crying and act like men who are proud of their accomplishments."

I wanted to do everything I could to make them stop crying. Instead, they had me crying. That's how much they cared about playing for Kentucky.

The Commonwealth wept for Kentucky that night. They cried for a team that caught time in a bottle. Now whenever a great game is played, fans will always think of Kentucky-Duke. All future Kentucky teams will be compared to this one.

They've set the standard for the amount of heart a team should have.

They are destined to become part of Kentucky folklore, occupying space in the same pantheon as Rupp's Runts or the Fiddlin' Five.

They are the Unforgettables.

# FULL-COURT
# PRESSURE

∎∎∎

# -- 1 --

# *GREAT EXPECTATIONS*

The blue station wagon drove through the unlocked gate into one of the enclosed fields at Claiborne Farm—3,200 acres of rolling countryside in Paris, Kentucky, just outside Lexington.

It was early March and Seth Hancock, the owner of the No. 1 breeding farm in the United States, was off to inspect the mares and their newborn foals. Most of them had royal blood. They were sired by such legendary stakes horses as Nijinsky II, Mr. Prospector, and 49'er.

"We're trying to breed equine athletes here," he said. "The only difference between these athletes and great basketball players is that great players have only two legs."

The state of Kentucky has always been in the business of producing champions, in both horse racing and basketball. The approach to Bluegrass Field in Lexington takes you over the white fenced-in paddocks of Calumet Farm, home of two

Triple Crown winners and eight Kentucky Derby champions.

But really to look at Calumet, you need to drive along Man O' War Boulevard. This is the only state where they name the streets after horses.

A horse is lucky. He has to win only one race to be a Derby winner. But the expectations for Kentucky basketball are much greater. The passion the fans have for Kentucky basketball is more intense than anything else I've ever experienced. If you ask them why, they say they don't know. That's just the way it is.

But it's there, and it runs deep in a rural state where the median income is under $15,000. Basketball has always been a common thread tying together the entire population of three and a half million. Fans are young and old, rich and not so rich, men and women.

Intellectually, I knew this. But nothing prepared me for how much Kentucky basketball is part of their daily lives.

Last year, I received a letter from a John Austin Delpont of Hazard, Kentucky. He sent a picture of his son, who he claimed was blossoming into a good player and wanted to attend Kentucky. I looked at the picture and couldn't make it out. Then I saw the writing on the top.

It was a six-month-pregnancy sonogram.

The father sent me an update this year and enclosed a picture of the prospect, who is now two feet tall and weighs 21 pounds, and has better than average vertical jump and foot speed for a ten-month-old. He will be eligible for recruitment in the year 2009. He just wanted to keep me posted on his son's development.

A woman from Whitesburg, Kentucky, climbed on the bus after our Louisville game last year and told me she named one of her children after me. I was expecting to see a baby. Instead, she showed me her cocker spaniel puppy. His name is Ricky P. Eyster. I just got a letter in December from that dog. That's right. It arrived just before Christmas, with a picture of Ricky P. wearing a Kentucky jersey.

"My mom and dad wanted me to send you this picture because they are very proud of me," it began. "I am so glad they named me for you. I like you a lot. I hope you remember meeting me last year when my mom got on that bus and introduced me to you. (I was kind of embarrassed but you know how parents are.)"

Ricky P. went on to wish my family a merry Christmas, and finished up this way: "Please don't think I am just a silly dog—I am honored to be called Ricky P. 'cause I think you are G-R-R-EAT!" I was surprised he didn't leave a pawprint.

I told Richie Farmer about it on the way over to my television show, and he started to laugh. "Coach," he said, "I've gotten letters from people in prison, people in sanitariums. But no farm animals."

Our team's performance during the 1991–92 season matched the intensity of our fans. We won 29 games, captured the Southeastern Conference championship, finished sixth in the final Associated Press poll and reached the Elite Eight of the NCAA tournament.

Anyone who watched our team play should have been very, very pleased. They could see with their own eyes how much effort our players put forth. But, because Kentucky basketball has had such a grand tradition, current players always raise greater expectations than those of most other teams. Ask our legendary announcer Cawood Ledford. Anytime he is out on a speaking engagement, among the first questions he's asked is "Do we have a chance to win it all this year?"

It seems some fans just expect Kentucky to be in the Final Four every year. To them, it's as natural as competing in the Kentucky Derby. This year, our first off NCAA probation, we came within two seconds of getting there.

My apologies to the local businessman who started manufacturing Final Four shirts in July with the 1-2-3 point shot on the front and Minneapolis Final Four on the back. Maybe he could save them for next year, but he'll have to change the name of the city to New Orleans.

It was nice to be released finally from the prison we occupied for two years. Kentucky basketball crashed and burned Friday, May 19, 1989. A live statewide audience watched as the NCAA sentenced the school to sanctions that included no postseason competition and scholarship limitations for two years, and no live TV for a year.

The investigation began after an Emery Freight package popped open during handling in a Los Angeles terminal back on March 31, 1988. Witnesses claimed the envelope contained a videotape and $1,000 cash in $50 bills. The envelope was addressed to Claud Mills, whose son Chris was a basketball star at Fairfax High in Los Angeles. The return address was marked Kentucky Basketball Office. It culminated in 18 violations and the resignations of beleaguered coach Eddie Sutton, his assistants Dwane Casey and James Dickey, and athletic director Cliff Hagan. Several *Parade* All-America players opted to go elsewhere.

I arrived right after the probation started. It ended the moment the clock struck midnight on March 2, 1991, about two hours after we defeated Auburn to finish our year at 22–6 and clinch the best record in the Southeastern Conference.

Three days later, the Kentucky team and I found ourselves riding in an old-fashioned victory parade, complete with marching bands, cheerleaders, and five fire engines.

There I was, sitting with our captain Reggie Hanson, our starting point guard Sean Woods, and reserve forward Henry Thomas as we made our way through the streets of downtown Lexington, down the Avenue of Champions on the way to Memorial Coliseum. Thousands of fans lined the parade route and we were covered by a snowstorm of confetti. The Commerce National Bank decorated its windows with huge letters that read, SEC #1. Go Cats.

By the time we reached Memorial Coliseum, there were 4,500 fans inside, waiting for the start of a pep rally. Governor Wallace Wilkinson sent a proclamation congratulating the team, and our athletic director, C. M. Newton, officially announced the end of the probation, using the words "Never Again."

When it was my turn to speak, I turned the mike over to the players. They were the ones responsible for this amazing turnaround. The crowd chanted, "Reggie, Reggie, Reggie," when Reggie Hanson got up to speak. Gimel Martinez, our center from Miami, thanked the fans in both English and Spanish. And Sean had written a short speech for the occasion.

"Today, we marched through downtown," he said. "Hopefully next year we can march through New Orleans."

I told Sean later his sense of direction was off by about 1,500 miles. The 1992 NCAA Final Four was to be in Minneapolis.

Technically, we weren't eligible to win the SEC championship, but after the final game of the season, our cheerleaders trotted out an 18-foot-high banner to midcourt that proclaimed us as the SEC's No. 1 team. I know the conference office was very upset with us because, even though we were ranked ninth in the final AP poll, they chose to list us at the bottom of the SEC standings with an asterisk next to Kentucky's name. We weren't trying to rub it in. None of the kids on that team were involved in the probation problems. Most of them never thought they'd be part of a championship season.

The student bookstore across from Memorial Coliseum began selling T-shirts in September with a cartoon of General Douglas MacArthur on the front, accompanied by the words, WE HAVE RETURNED. Everyone assumed it would be business as usual.

Everyone but Louisiana State University coach Dale Brown, that is. Brown claimed it would be impossible to judge the real Kentucky program until after the probation was over and all that pressure on the team was back. He claimed part of Kentucky's relaxed attitude was due to the fact nothing was at stake.

Some time ago, Kentucky basketball crossed the line and became a big business. Ours might have been the only team referred to as the GM of the sport. The fun goes out of basketball when the most important number is on the bottom line and not on the scoreboard.

I'm going to try to reverse that corporate takeover mentality. Our goal here is to change the image of Kentucky basketball. We're going to make this fun again, or somebody else will be coaching the Kentucky Wildcats. Yet the pressure to win that existed in the past will always exist to some degree, anytime you play at this level.

I don't think we're going to change the importance of Kentucky basketball to the fans. I know we're not. And we don't want to. But I think we've changed the fans' attitude when they come to a game. They should come out to enjoy themselves and not carry the game like a weight on their shoulders. We've tried to make it fun for them. But we still have a long way to go.

I thought our fans would have had their eyes opened last year when Reggie Hanson, our best player, wasn't selected in the first two rounds of the NBA draft, even though the senior from Somerset was visible on TV and had played for a championship Kentucky team.

But the fans were blinded by the past.

And what a past it had been!

Kentucky has won five NCAA championships and two NIT titles. Kentucky has been ranked No. 1 seven times by the Associated Press poll since its inception in 1949. Kentucky has finished in the Top Ten 27 times. Kentucky teams have won 36 SEC championships—more than the 11 other conference teams combined. Kentucky has been to the NCAA tournament 33 times, if you count our trip in March 1992.

The late Adolph Rupp created prestige that was unmatched when he coached here. Rupp coached Kentucky to four NCAA championships—in 1948, 1949, 1951, and 1958—and an NIT championship in 1946, back when that tournament out-ranked the NCAA. He also coached Kentucky to 18 Southeastern Conference titles in 42 years, from 1930–1972. His 875 victories may never be surpassed.

Rupp had his best team ever in 1947–48. They were the original Fabulous Five and their starting lineup was Alex Groza, Ralph Beard, Kenny Rollins, Wallace "Wah Wah" Jones, and Cliff Barker. That team went 36–3 while sweeping to Kentucky's first NCAA title. The starting five went on to participate as a group in the 1948 Olympic basketball competition, helping the U.S. capture a gold medal. Rupp retired their jerseys afterwards.

Rollins graduated after the 1948 season but the remaining four starters continued to dominate college ball, winning a second straight NCAA title in 1949 with a 32–2 record. Groza, from Martins Ferry, Ohio, was a 6' 7" center who was the Helms Foundation Player of the Year in 1949. Both he and Beard, a gum-chewing guard who played at Male High in Louisville, were three-time All-Americans and they were joined in their senior season by Jones, who came from Harlan County. Two years later, Bill Spivey, Kentucky's first seven-footer, became National Player of the year and combined with Cliff Hagan and Frank Ramsey to lead Kentucky to a third NCAA championship.

Kentucky might have won five straight NCAA titles during that golden era, but they were snubbed by the district selection committee in 1950 after Rupp refused to meet North Carolina State in a playoff because he felt Kentucky's better record deserved an automatic bid. Kentucky was eliminated again in 1952 after Groza, Beard, and Dale Barnstable were taken into custody and admitted sharing $2,000 in bribe money to shave points in a 1949 NIT game that Kentucky lost to Loyola. Kentucky was prohibited from playing a college schedule the following year, but the team held four public scrimmages that attracted a total of 35,000 fans.

Rupp won his final championship in 1958 with a team known as the Fiddlin' Five. Rupp had been worried about his team before that season. "They might be pretty good barnyard fiddlers,' " he said, "but we play a Carnegie Hall schedule, and it will take violinists to play that competition." When Kentucky became notorious for, as Rupp put it, "fiddlin' around and fiddlin' around, then finally pulling it out at the end," the team was tagged The Fiddlin' Five.

The Fiddlin' Five did not have the talent that characterized Rupp's other great teams, but Johnny Cox, Vern Hatton, and Adrian Smith were good enough to defeat Elgin Baylor and Seattle in the championship game at Louisville's Freedom Hall, 84–72. After that game, Rupp said, "Those boys certainly are not concert violinists, but they sure can fiddle."

Kentucky made another run at the national championship in 1966 with a team whose two biggest players, guard Tommy Kron and center Thad Jaracz, were only 6' 5". Forwards Larry Conley and Pat Riley were 6' 3" and guard Louie Dampier was 6' 0". They were known as Rupp's Runts and they had a 27–2 record, finishing one game shy of the NCAA title when they were upset by Texas Western in the finals, 72–65.

If Rupp had his way, he would have coached until he died. He felt he could win another championship with the 1972 freshman team of Kevin Grevey, Jimmy Dan Conner, Bob Guyette, and Mike Flynn who were recruited by his eventual successor, Joe B. Hall. They compiled a perfect 22–0 record. But he was approaching the mandatory retirement age of 70. Rupp supporters, led by former All-American Dan Issel, urged university officials to waive the rule and let Rupp coach at long as he wanted. But others, including many former players, felt it was time for him to step down.

Rupp apparently did not want Joe B. Hall to take over as basketball coach at Kentucky. Hall got tired of waiting and took the head coaching position at St. Louis University. Then, two or three boosters convinced him to come back to Kentucky as the heir apparent. For once, Kentucky was a state divided. In the end, the administration refused to budge. Rupp was retired, but not forgotten. He maintained an office at the Coliseum and still did his TV show, which ran directly opposite Hall's show and critiqued his coaching. Hall won 297 games in 13 years, not to mention one NCAA championship and one NIT. He won or shared eight SEC titles and made three trips to the Final Four. He kept the flame alive, but he never escaped from Rupp's shadow, even after Rupp died in 1977.

Joe B. Hall was best known for his victory over previously unbeaten Indiana in the 1975 Mideast Regionals, but his crowning achievement was an NCAA championship in 1978 in St. Louis. After Jack Givens, from Bryant Station High School in Lexington, scored 41 points as Kentucky beat Duke, 94–88 in the final, there was a sigh of relief heard throughout the state. When the team arrived home after the game, they were greeted by 10,000 fans at Blue Grass Airport and 15,000 more at Memorial Coliseum.

They had done what was expected of them. There had been enormous pressure on that Kentucky team to win it all ever since the previous March when they had lost to North Carolina in the Eastern Regional finals. Kentucky had great physical size and strength with Rick Robey, Mike Phillips, and James Lee, excellent outside shooters like Givens, Truman Claytor, and Jay Shidler, a deep bench with La Von Williams and Dwane Casey and a great point guard in Kyle Macy, who was a sophomore transfer from Purdue. They played great man-to-man defense.

Joe B. Hall likes to say the '78 team was totally focused, and claims he really enjoyed coaching it. He says he had to be tough on the players because he knew what was at stake. After Kentucky lost to LSU that February, he even suggested they might someday be immortalized as The Folding Five. He must have gotten his point across.

The day Kentucky defeated Arkansas in one national semifinal, Duke beat Notre Dame in the other. The Duke players threw their coach Bill Foster into the showers. The Kentucky locker room was silent. When the Kentucky players arrived at the hotel, Joe wanted to take the team into the country for a nice dinner, but Rick Robey told Hall the players would rather stay in their rooms and study a tape of the Duke game. It didn't take long for Givens to exploit what he saw in Duke's zone that Monday night. He shot 18 for 26 and put on one of the great individual performances in the history of the tournament. Joe B. called Kentucky's long march to the title "a season without joy" during the postgame press conference.

As soon as the game ended, some Kentucky fans began scripting an encore. As Kyle Macy walked off the floor, he was greeted by one of them.

"How many years you got left?" the fan asked.

"Two," Macy said.

"That's two more championships," he replied.

Hall left coaching in 1985 and went into banking. His only regret is that he never won a second national championship. "That sort of places you in a special category," he said.

Joe B. Hall is dead wrong. Winning one is sufficient enough to be placed in a special category. I hope someday I'm that fortunate.

With this tradition, it's easy to see why practically everyone in the state is a Kentucky fan. They all want to be part of the action—some more so than others.

Bob Wiggins, a retired engineer from Falmouth, 50 miles north of Lexington, has seen Kentucky play 476 consecutive times. He has been a season ticket holder since 1953, and comes to the games with Manual Thornton, who lives in Frankfort. Bob has been to Alaska twice and Hawaii once to keep the string alive. The last time he missed a game was back in 1977 because of a nine-inch snowfall. He left home for the game, but had to turn around in Paris, Kentucky.

The late Steve Rardon still holds the all-time record with 627 consecutive games attended. I got to meet him my first year at Kentucky. He made the trip to Syracuse and became ill. I visited him in the hospital two days before he died.

Tickets to a Kentucky home game are not easy to obtain. The official seating capacity at Rupp Arena is 24,000, and every game is a sellout. Chris Cameron, our sports information director, told me we could have sold 50,000 for last year's Senior Night game with Auburn. He got so barraged with ticket requests, he walked around with a NO sign taped to his shirt the day before the game.

We have 16,000 season ticket holders. The rest of the tickets go to students and school officials. Kentucky does not have a waiting list. Instead, a random drawing is held on the first day of the season. This year, there were 15,000 requests for the 20 pairs of tickets that weren't reclaimed.

Those who have tickets hold onto them. I have a friend in the horse racing business. He owns a horse farm. He's a wealthy man who was involved in a bitter divorce. "It bothered me when I lost four million dollars," he told me, "but what really killed me was that the eight season tickets were also split up."

One divorced couple made front page news when the Kentucky Court of Appeals overturned a ruling by a Madison County judge that allowed Dale Wagner to end a ticket-sharing agreement with his former wife Lois Leffler. The Wagners divorced in 1977 after 24 years of marriage, and agreed to split the cost of their two tickets—valued at $190—with each getting tickets for half of Kentucky's home games.

In 1989, Wagner told Leffler the agreement was off. Leffler took Wagner to court. Madison Circuit Judge James S. Chenault ruled in 1989 that Wagner and Leffler had shared the tickets long enough and declared Wagner could end the agreement at the end of this season. But a three-judge appellate court said Chenault went too far, and suggested Wagner or Leffler buy out the other. Otherwise, the judges ruled, the two must continue joint custody of the tickets. Wagner vowed to take the case to the Supreme Court.

A pair of season tickets normally costs $600, if bought through the athletic association. I've heard fans can buy a good pair of seats on the black market for $3,000. Two tickets on the lower level go for $5,000.

Kentucky basketball tickets are a gateway to power in this town. When he coached here, Joe B. Hall controlled 322 tickets. That's a lot, considering the demand. I have 20 tickets.

My first month here, I met a businessman who offered to help me out, just to make things more comfortable for my family. This is really nice, I thought. The people are so accommodating in Lexington.

But I did insist on paying for his services. About six months went by, and he said to me, "Look, I'd really like to upgrade my seats. Can you see what you can do?"

I said, "I'll see what I can do."

At that point, I was very hurt. I'd never had people use me for what they could get from me. I stopped calling him. When I related the story in my office, I was told, "Coach, that's what Kentucky basketball is all about. It's tickets."

Fans seated in the first ten rows behind the Kentucky bench had a good chance of being included in a painting by George Claxton called "Ruppscape," which sold for $185. Cross Gate Gallery's Greg Ladd produced 850 prints, which not only immortalized 400 faces in the crowd but also included such honored guests as President Bush, Richard Nixon, Adolph Rupp, Jimmy Swaggart, and, yes, Elvis. It's nice to know the King still had enough clout to get a ticket.

Our home games are always special events. At least one was to Scott Crosbie, the president of the student government association, who got down on one knee and proposed to his girl friend K. C. Watts, the 1990 Homecoming Queen, at halftime of the Alabama game. Of course, she said yes.

The lobby of the Hyatt Hotel is filled with fans before tipoff and Bill Bailey, a roving reporter for "Cat Calls" on WVLK radio makes the rounds, interviewing them and asking how many points they think Kentucky will win by. Win or lose, close to 10,000 stick around afterwards, just to listen to the postgame radio show I do with Cawood Ledford. When we played Georgia in Athens in February, I had to catch a 7 P.M. flight out of Atlanta, so I taped my postgame comments. More than 200 fans who had made the trip stayed around just to listen to the tape.

Fans will go to extremes to see a Kentucky game. The big thing last year was the Persian Gulf War. People kept calling Chris Cameron, trying to send him on a guilt trip, saying they needed tickets for someone who was going off to war. My first year, I received a letter from an elderly gentleman who stated he had inoperable cancer. His wish was to sit behind the Kentucky bench. I told Marta McMackin, our administrative aide and the backbone of our staff since 1976, to call him and offer a ticket to any game he desired.

"Coach, we can't possibly meet all those requests and we don't know the legitimacy of certain situations," she said. I couldn't picture anyone deceiving us by saying he had cancer, just to see a UK game.

Obviously, we obliged his wishes. He wrote me a week later and said he felt his life was complete. He died ten days later. Stories like this one are extremely puzzling to me—why a game can make such an impact on someone's life.

The demand for tickets is so great, there's going to be a push for a new 28,000-seat arena on campus in the near future. Even though C. M. Newton, who is 62, claims he doesn't want to get involved in another major project before he retires, I think Kentucky will have a new arena by the year 2000. It's difficult to think about that possibility during these economic times. But financially, it would be in the best interest of the university to build its own facility. UK does not share in the concessions and parking, and pays an exorbitant fee for rental. The ticket allocation would be cleaned up to some degree, as well.

This frenzy is not limited to Lexington. I had to shake my head at all the blinking lights and sirens as the deputy sheriffs in Louisville provided a police escort for our team from our hotel to Freedom Hall when we played Morehead State. I'm an honorary sheriff over there, and anytime we play in Louisville, the department insists on giving us the red carpet treatment.

Even though the loyalties are divided in that city, Jefferson County is still a stronghold for Kentucky. When we played Western Kentucky at Freedom Hall, 10,000 people showed up for a half-hour shootaround the night before the game. But there's precedent. Nineteen thousand fans had crowded into the same arena in 1988 to watch a similar practice the day Kentucky played Georgia. The fire marshal had to lock the doors to keep more people from trying to squeeze in.

Kentucky basketball has always been surrounded by that type of support. You could say it's a life or death situation. Why else would the Kentucky Association of Funeral Directors schedule their convention each year around a Kentucky game? This year, they were in town for the Alabama game. They held a tailgate party at the Hyatt, even though most of them did not have tickets to the game.

John Pelphrey grew up in Paintsville, where the feeling for Kentucky basketball has always been strong. John got our team to sign a card for a man up there who was dying of cancer but was such a Kentucky Wildcat fan he refused to take any morphine on game days because it made him too drowsy to concentrate on the action.

When the man died, they buried the card with him in his casket.

My first year, I went up to see a prospect play at Paintsville. We were in a helicopter in the mountains. It was very foggy and our pilot landed on this little airstrip in Mt. Sterling, less than halfway to Paintsville. There was a light on at a nearby house and the manager of the airstrip answered the door. Don Johnson, the person who owns the helicopter, said, "Look, we got coach Pitino in the helicopter. He's trying to get up to see this young man play."

"Okay, there's my Ford Bronco," the manager said. "Go ahead and take it and just drop it off when you're done." It was an hour and a half drive. He gave us his van and told us, "I love the Wildcats."

We offered payment for the use of his automobile. He was startled by such an offer, suggesting an autographed picture would be ample reimbursement.

I got off cheap. Dudley Webb, a longtime Kentucky booster, once shelled out $16 million to build a new hotel downtown, just to help Kentucky in its bid for the 1985 NCAA Final Four.

Some Kentucky fans help their team in other ways. A family in Pikeville made their six-year-old son sit on the dining room table with his feet crossed Indian-style during Kentucky games and remain that way until the end of the broadcasts. Any time a Kentucky player would shoot a free throw, they would all rub his head for good luck.

Closer to home, Rena Vicini, Chris Cameron's assistant who is from Lynch, up in the mountains near Corbin, used to keep a scorebook of every Kentucky game when she was growing up and says she would cry her eyes out anytime Kentucky lost. She is not above asking for divine intervention during games. She still keeps her hands folded in prayer at the scorer's table anytime we shoot a free throw. No one is allowed to speak to her. If you think that's crazy, consider Chris's graduate assistant Julie Watson, who still has a story she wrote back in sixth grade called "Big Blue Riding Hood," in which Denny Crum, coach at Louisville, is the big bad wolf and our heroine gets engaged to Kyle Macy at the end of the fairy tale.

Speaking of Kyle, when he played for Kentucky, Ralph Hacker, who owns the radio station that does our games and does color on the UK radio network with Cawood, said he knew at least ten families in Lexington who named their babies Kyle.

The passion in Kentucky can be put to good use. Every year, The Lexington Child Abuse Center holds a charity auction. One of the items auctioned this year at the Big Blue Bash was the game ball from our victory over Eastern Kentucky.

I got up at the podium in the ballroom at the Radisson Hotel, along with our four seniors, and started the bidding at $5,000. It was temporarily stalled at $18,000, but I got it going again by saying the players would autograph the ball and even come over to the winner's home for dinner after the season.

The basketball finally went for $24,000.

The coaching staff traveled to Owensboro to play a benefit for Junior Achievement. Our staff played against the townspeople. We raised $17,000. Before the game, they auctioned off dinner at my restaurant, Bravo Pitino!, with Joanne and me and it went for $1,100.

Imagine people paying $10 to see a bunch of coaches play? They had over 2,000 people there to see our over-the-hill gang—the Kentucky staff and Ralph Willard, one of my closest friends who's now the head coach at Western Kentucky. We played six-minute quarters. Billy Donovan, one of my former players at Providence who is now one of our assistants, scored 29 points in 21 minutes. He was the only one of us who was in good enough shape to play full-court basketball.

Kentucky fans are not only generous with their time and money. They are also free-handed with their advice. Marta figures she must receive about 200 pieces of mail each week. Most are from fans recommending prospects. But we also get some zanies.

Right after I announced on radio that my wife Joanne was going to have a girl, I received a letter from a woman in Cincinnati, giving me the addresses of vasectomy clinics in that town and northern Kentucky. I guess she figured six children is enough.

Then there was the letter from the professor at Ohio State who claimed he loved to see guys whip Bobby Knight. It was simply addressed to The Basketball Coach. Kentucky.

"Sir": it said. "I would congratulate you and your team on

beating Indiana if your boys were not so dumb stupid toward the end. They led by ten with three minutes left and even my dog knew they could sit on the ball and kill the clock and slide into victory. But no. Your dumb stupid boys kept firing wild shots that the Hoosiers picked off and almost won the game."

I also get my share of unsigned hate mail. Here's one from West Virginia that accused us to trying to injure the West Virginia players during the opening round of the preseason NIT.

"We were prepared to root for Kentucky all year but after watching your extremely dirty play against West Virginia we hope you lose all your games. How much did you pay the official. People all over have noticed this. . . . It wasn't enough you tried to push them, shove them, run into them, but your attempt to injure them was all too obvious."

It was signed, "Sports Fans."

Hey, I've been accused of worse. Every Monday night, Cawood and I do a radio talk show called "The Big Blue Line." The show is picked up by nearly 100 stations in the Kentucky-Indiana-Ohio area. It is also picked up by WICE in Providence, which is doing all of our games again this year.

We have our regulars. But calls come in from all over the state as well as from Indiana and southern Ohio. Most of the callers tell Cawood they'll miss him once he retires. From me, they always want to know how many points we're going to win by and why Richie Farmer doesn't play more.

Cawood's favorite call this season came from Andy Parsons, who wanted to bet his teacher $20 Kentucky would beat Indiana.

"How old are you?" I asked.

"Twelve," he said.

What expectations. I can't wait to talk to him when he's 18.

# --2--

# A BITE FROM THE BIG APPLE

There were two storms raging in different parts of the country May 19, 1989. One tornado set down in Lexington, where the NCAA wiped out Kentucky.

That same day, the Chicago Bulls blew the New York Knickerbockers out of the NBA playoffs and into Lake Michigan. I had been the head coach of the Knicks for an uneasy two years. My dream job was fast turning into a nightmare.

I'd loved the Knicks since I was a child, growing up in Queens. I used to go to the Garden all the time. I was watching on TV the night when Willis Reed dragged his bum leg out on the floor and the Knicks beat L.A. in the seventh game of the 1970 championship series. I could quote you chapter and verse on all the big games when Willis, Dave DeBusschere, Bill Bradley, Dick Barnett, and Clyde Frazier played for Red Holzman.

My friends and I used to mimic how the players would run

out after having been introduced. Earl Monroe didn't have to worry about sprinting too far. He would step twice, wave, and turn back to the bench.

I tried that, too.

It was nearly 20 years later when the Knicks finally called. In retrospect, I wish my line had been busy.

The beginning was heady. The Knicks came out of nowhere my first year to make the playoffs and won 52 games and the Atlantic Division championship the next season. I had three years left on my contract, but I was thinking about walking away.

Let me clear up one thing: Al Bianchi, the general manager at the time, didn't chase me out of New York. But his meddling with the team by constantly second-guessing our style of play didn't help matters.

It was a far cry from my experience coaching elsewhere. I always felt I had the support of the people with whom I worked at Boston University and Providence. But I never sensed this from Al Bianchi.

Al was an NBA lifer. He had been around the league, first as a player, then as an assistant coach for 30 years. He was from the old school. But he had been the Knicks' general manager for only 24 hours when he had to hire a new coach. Gulf & Western, the team's owner, was trying to decide between Larry Brown, Jim Valvano and me. Al didn't want Valvano because he had no pro experience, so it came down to Larry Brown and me. Bianchi felt Larry Brown was too temperamental. I had spent two years as a Knicks assistant under Hubie Brown in 1984 and 1985 and I knew Bianchi did not like Hubie at all, ever since their days in the old ABA. But, in Bianchi's eyes, I was the best of the lot. Even though he didn't know me or my style of play, he felt he'd have no problem working with me. The only major problem he had was that I worked under Hubie Brown.

Our ideas concerning the way the game should be played were very different. Al felt the best way to win in the playoffs was with a good half-court offense. He pointed to the Detroit Pistons, who were the defending champions in 1989, to back up his theories. I thought the Pistons' offense was slow. Pick and roll, guards crossing underneath the basket, and a great one-on-one game between Dumars and Thomas. Their field goal accuracy? 47 percent. The Pistons won because of defense, not a proficient half-court offense.

He didn't think the Knicks could win a championship with pressure basketball. Al felt running and shooting threes was fine for the regular season, but our lack of a halfcourt offense could be a liability that might come back to haunt us in the playoffs.

I thought that was total nonsense. If you look at our team stats for 1989, the Knicks averaged 117 points and were third in the league in scoring. We shot 48 percent from the field, and that was with taking the most three pointers in the history of the league. We were 36 percent from the pro three-point line, so you can imagine what we were shooting from two-point range. We were getting great shots, and Patrick Ewing, Mark Jackson, Gerald Wilkins, Charles Oakley, and Trent Tucker were all having a banner year.

My feeling was: Why hire me if that's not the style of basketball you want? It's like hiring Pete Carril of Princeton to coach Las Vegas. I had been coaching that style for seven years, and believed in it. I had seen it work often on the college level with Jack Ramsay at St. Joseph's and John Thompson of Georgetown. The Chicago Bulls won an NBA championship in 1991 with trapping defenses.

I felt we could make an impact defensively in the NBA as a pressing team. I thought we could make the opposition take six or seven seconds in the backcourt, slow them down until they could get over half-court. Then I felt they would have only 12, 13 seconds left on the 24-second clock to run their plays, and we could generate a lot of offense from our defense.

The problem was that our differences weren't kept behind closed doors. Our dirty linen was splashed across the back pages of the New York tabloids.

There had been an element of mistrust from the beginning. Al said he never stuck his nose in my business, but in the first games I coached in New York, at half time he was discussing plays that we could use with the assistant coaches. In fact, my assistants joked about it, saying he was sending plays down to them, written on a napkin. They never showed me the plays, figuring it was a joke.

When I took the job, Al told me he felt if we could compete for an NBA title in five years, we'd be ahead of the game. He apparently moved up his timetable without telling me.

At least, I kept to my timetable when the Knicks went after me the first time. The Knicks' management contacted me in early April 1987, right after I had coached Providence College to the Final Four. The idea of my coaching the Knicks was actually the brainstorm of Gary Wichard, a New York agent.

The Knicks had just fired general manager Scottie Sterling and interim coach Bob Hill, and Gary thought I would be a good candidate for the coaching job. He spoke about it with Dick Evans, the Knicks' president, and Evans liked the idea.

I spoke with the Knicks' braintrust and even though the New York papers had me penciled in as Bob Hill's successor, it didn't materialize. No offer was made.

At the same time, the Phoenix Suns became interested in me, too. Jerry Colangelo, the GM of the Suns, had called me just before the Final Four to wish me luck and to ask if we could talk about the coaching vacancy there. At the time I said, "Yes," but I didn't want to go to Phoenix after I had started negotiating with the Knicks. However, I had already made a commitment to visit with Colangelo, and it had been publicized.

I became very interested in the Suns job when Joanne and I flew to Phoenix. I knew the Suns had just gone through a drug scandal, but I felt the situation could be turned around. The one point Colangelo stressed was that, if I was hired, I would not be allowed to retain the assistant coaches. One of them was Al Bianchi. Colangelo wanted to start with fresh people. John MacLeod and Al were with the Suns for 14 years.

In the end, however, I knew we would not be moving to Phoenix. We had just gone through a major tragedy in our lives. The day the NCAA bids were announced, our six-month-old son Daniel had died, and we were still grieving. Joanne didn't want to leave her family or her friends.

When we came home from Phoenix, I told the Knicks I felt their next coach should be in total control of the basketball operations, with a GM in charge of contracts. I think the job would have been offered to me then, but the New York media began spreading rumors that Don Nelson of Milwaukee was also being considered. The writers started asking, "What's the hurry to hire Pitino?"

My entire professional life was splashed across the papers. When the Providence *Journal* printed I would sign with the Knicks, push came to shove. My kids were harassed at school that day, and I finally told the media I would make a final decision on whether to pursue the job by May 1.

A few days before the deadline, I met with Evans and Jack Diller, the Vice President of Madison Square Garden Sports Group, and they asked me if I could push back my timetable. I said no, the whole thing had gone on too long.

Subsequently, I signed a five-year contract with Providence College. Lou Lamoriello, the AD at Providence, wanted to put a buy-out clause in my contract, in case I wanted to go to the NBA someday. But I honestly believed I was going to be at Providence for the next five years.

Three months went by and I received a call from Jack Diller in mid-July. He told me he wanted to fly up to see me. The Knicks were still searching for a coach. They had just hired Al Bianchi to be their general manager, and he was part of the search committee. The Knicks were very interested in Jimmy Rodgers, the Celtics' assistant, but Red Auerbach wanted a second-round draft choice for his services and New York did not want to give that up. I didn't know why Diller wanted to see me, but I said, "Sure." He walked in and said, "Look this is confidential. My boss Dick Evans doesn't even know I'm here. From Day One, I wanted you to be our coach, but we couldn't make it happen in time. You had to know by May First, and we couldn't let you know by that date."

I didn't know if he was making it up or not. Then he said, "Look, if we could open this up again, would you be interested?"

I said I wouldn't, because I was under contract at Providence and felt the school wouldn't give me permission to leave. Besides, my summer basketball camp had just begun. So, who did Gulf & Western contact behind my back but Lou Lamoriello, who had just left Providence to take a job with the New Jersey Devils. Lou told them, "Yes, he could get permission. Father (John) Cunningham, the President of Providence, is an academician and he will not stand in Rick's way if that's what he wants."

I was at the dentist in Rhode Island having a cavity drilled when I was called to the phone. It was Jack Diller. He wanted to speak to me. He said he had received permission from Father Cunningham. I couldn't believe it. I got on the phone with Father Cunningham and said, "Father, did you give the New York Knicks permission to speak with me?" He said, "Yes, Rick, I feel they want to pursue you and you have a right, just like an English professor, to pursue your career if that's what you want. If you want to stay at Providence, we'd love to have you. If you want to leave, we will understand."

I said "Father, you don't have to do that."

He said, "No, Rick, I'm not holding anyone back."

I began negotiating with the Knicks at the Logan Airport Hilton the next day. That night, I left to speak at a rally for the Bay State Games at the Boston Garden. Ray Flynn, the mayor of Boston and a former Providence player, sought me out, just to shake my hand. When he introduced me, he said my decision to remain at Providence had made him a happy man. I felt sick to my stomach.

After the speech, I went back to the hotel to continue the

discussions with the Knicks. Mitch Dukov, a Cleveland based financial adviser, was with me. He had replaced Gary Wichard. Wichard had asked for way too much the first time around—a four-year deal that started with money that was beyond my imagination, plus a million-dollar interest-free loan, a New York apartment, and bonuses that could have led to millions. I felt uncomfortable with all those items.

The second time around, the Knicks drew the line. They said they would speak to me about the job, but that I couldn't have Gary Wichard represent me. They said they couldn't get it done with him present. We met for about ten hours. Whenever a new topic came up, Diller would get on the phone in another room and speak to somebody back at Gulf & Western.

The Knicks offered me the job at one o'clock the next morning. They wanted me to sign on the spot. But I told them I needed a few days to think it over. John Marinatto, the Providence sports information director, thought I didn't need any time to consider the proposed deal. John was like a little brother to me. He was extremely close to my family and definitely wanted me out of the Knicks interview. He insisted on traveling to Boston with me and stayed in the room next to our meeting (probably with a glass to the wall). When it was time to leave, he stated we should get back home and forget this New York nonsense. When I left Providence, he took it harder than anyone in the state. First, Lou leaves, and now me.

I got back to Providence at three in the morning and contacted Lou Lamoriello, the man who had hired me at PC. I told him I wasn't sure what to do. I felt guilty. He told me I had to do what was best for me and my family. I went to see Father Cunningham the next day. He told me the same thing. So the ball was in my court.

I spent that Saturday night agonizing over the decision. The next morning, we went to breakfast with our next door neighbors, the Duchins. I told them we were very comfortable living in Providence. But something Gloria Duchin said left a big impression on me. She said, "When you're thirty-four years old, that's not the time to feel comfortable. At thirty-four, you should go for the challenge."

I signed with the Knicks that afternoon, leaving behind two of the greatest years I've spent in coaching.

I knew I was in the NBA when, in the first meeting after accepting the job, I sat there with Al Bianchi, our assistants Stu Jackson and Jim O'Brien, our assistant GM Hal Childs, and our two scouts Dick McGuire and Fuzzy Levane. We actually had a serious discussion about whether to trade Patrick Ewing to the Houston Rockets for Ralph Sampson. Our talks got serious enough that we intended to send our team physician, Dr. Norman Scott, to examine his knees.

I wanted to know why.

When Patrick came out of Georgetown in 1985, he was one of the most celebrated players of a generation, perhaps the next Bill Russell. He was the first player selected in the NBA draft, and was given a ten-year contract worth close to $30 million. But Ewing had been a disappointment in the pros. He was having problems with his knees and had only played 113 games in his first two years. The Knicks' braintrust felt he was underachieving, and thought they might be able to pull the deal off.

To Bianchi's credit, he convinced us all to wait and see how Patrick did, thinking maybe we could get more out of him.

The Knicks were going nowhere fast, and there was constant talk of a major shakeup. But Bianchi accomplished a lot by taking his time. The Knicks wanted to trade the rights to Mark Jackson, an unsigned rookie guard from St. John's, to Detroit. In return, the Knicks would obtain forward Sidney Green. We needed help on the boards and weren't sure about how effective Mark Jackson would be in our system. Al convinced us to wait and see how the players reacted before doing anything rash. Management followed Al's advice and Mark went on to become Rookie of the Year that season. We ended up getting Green for Ron Moore and a second-round draft pick at the end of training camp, and he wound up becoming a serviceable backup.

The Knicks also wanted to send center Bill Cartwright to Chicago for Charles Oakley, a powerful young rebounding forward. I was all for it. But Al wouldn't pull the trigger because the Bulls wanted Trent Tucker, one of our shooting guards, included in the deal. Bianchi held out and we ended up with Oakley a year later in a straight swap for Cartwright. Bianchi's experience really helped in understanding trades. If you're overly anxious to deal, the opposition will have the upper hand. By showing patience, the weak become weaker. Panic and pressure make people react quicker in the NBA.

Late that summer, we decided to make Patrick Ewing the leader of this team. We felt he could be the dominant center in the league if he lost 20 pounds and became again the power player he had been in college.

At the same time, before the start of the 1989 season, Al and I made a tough decision not to sign Bernard King. Bernard King led the league in scoring back in 1985. He was a phenom and a Knickerbocker. I had seen it firsthand when I was Hubie Brown's assistant. The Knicks went to Texas on a road trip and he scored 50 points in each of three straight games. I felt he was the best competitor around, but he had missed playing the previous two years because of a serious knee injury. He alienated Gulf & Western when he came back and asked for a multiyear deal at his old salary of $875,000. They wanted to go with youth. In their minds, King was past history.

Dr. Norman Scott, the Knicks' team physician who performed successful knee surgery on King, thought it would be in Bernard's best interest for him to play elsewhere, away from our running, pressing style. He felt Bernard's knee could hold up in the NBA, but he wasn't sure it would hold up in the Knicks' style.

I liked our team during my first NBA training camp as a

head coach. I thought we had tremendous enthusiasm. The coaches had a close relationship with all the players that first year. Patrick, Oak, Mark Jackson, Johnny Newman. The players kiddingly referred to me as Rick the Ruler. I treated them like a college team.

We were playing spirited basketball and really started coming on during the second half that season. I can still remember the night we beat the Indiana Pacers in the last game of the regular season to clinch a playoff spot. We had gone through an entire season and it came down to Indiana vs. New York in Indianapolis. We both had identical records, so it was winner take all. We won the game by a point at the buzzer when Kenny Walker, an ex-Kentucky star, blocked a shot by Steve Stipanovich. The players were piling on each other, rolling on the floor.

Jack Ramsay was coaching the Pacers and Jim O'Brien was married to Jack's daughter, Sharon. I said to Jimmy, "Are you going to spend any time with Jack this evening, or would you like to go out for a few beers?"

"Rick," he said, "the last person I'd want to see tonight is my father-in-law. He's not going to be a happy man."

"Do you mean, after forty-five years of coaching, he's going to take this loss that badly?" I asked.

"Worse than ever," Jimmy said.

That showed me what I had to look forward to in later years.

At the end of my first year as a head coach in the NBA, I almost returned to Providence and coaching college basketball. Gordie Chiesa was fired, and I could have had the job again. I thought about it. There was so much second-guessing in New York from the fans who sat behind the bench and the media who sat across the way. Life was a lot simpler at Providence. I missed mingling with the students, playing racquetball with our trainer Eddie Jamiel, hanging out at the Players' Corner Pub with my close friend Jodi DiRaimo and playing three on three at midnight in Alumni Gym.

Joanne and I talked about it. A lot. We decided to stick it out.

In hindsight, it was a mistake. At that time, the most satisfying situation for me was at Providence College. I should have never left. It was a great marriage. I can't say the same for my affair with the Knicks.

By the middle of my second season, the Knicks were on their way to a twenty-six-game winning streak at the Garden. Outwardly, the team was on a roll, and had the support of the fans. But, internally, it was a different story. Al and I had stopped communicating. Neither one of us tried to talk to the other, so we both went down because of our stubbornness.

Part of the problem could be traced to the locations of the team and the management. Our offices were up at SUNY-Purchase in Westchester County, where we practiced. Al's office was in Madison Square Garden, at 4 Penn Plaza, an hour's driving distance away. Upper level management—Gulf & Western—was located uptown. So, you had certain segments of management and players who rarely saw each other except on game days.

Actually, we had only one public blowup during those two years. In January 1989, we had come back from 17 down to beat the Nets. But the big news wasn't the score. It was a brief argument I had with Rod Strickland, our rookie guard. When I felt he wasn't putting out the effort I wanted, I took him out of the game and told him I was sick of his Joe Cool act.

Several of the New York writers overheard the incident. The back page headlines in New York *Newsday* the next day read, "Wise Up Rick." And there was a picture of Al with comments from him ripping me for openly chastising a player. That really bothered me. I stormed into his office and we exchanged some harsh words. He tried to apologize, claiming his comments were taken out of context, but it was too late.

Most of our combat occurred behind the scenes. It was okay for Al to leak stories to the papers, but when Peter Vescey started taking my side in his column in the *Post*, Al did not handle it well. One of the first things Al told me when I was hired was "We don't have to worry about Peter Vescey, he's a friend of mine." Well, when the media was ganging up on me, Peter Vescey took the other side because he knew what was going on. He felt the stories in the Newark *Star-Ledger* and the New York *Daily News* had been planted by Al and felt he had tried to threaten him by saying "If you go after me, I'll feed these other guys stories."

Al thought I was feeding material to Vescey, when, in fact, that was not the case. There wasn't one time I spoke to Peter about Al. Not once. I was smart enough to know if I did try, he'd crush me in return. Vescey can say many things to blast people, but he's not for hire.

The media had a feeding frenzy at our expense. At best, the New York papers are tolerable when you're winning. They're brutal when you're losing. I was lucky I never had to suffer from the trashing that Ray Handley of the Giants or Davey Johnson of the Mets endured.

Or even Hubie Brown for that matter.

Hubie was one of those coaching gurus who made his reputation when he took a bunch of no-name players with the Atlanta Hawks and made them play like a contender. He was famous for the lectures he gave the media after games. When he was head coach of the Knicks, he gave me my first big break when he hired me in 1983, offering me a chance to jump from my coaching job at Boston University right into the NBA.

Hubie had his moments in New York. His 1984 team reached the Eastern Conference finals against Boston. But he became a victim of magnified expectations once Ewing arrived. When Camelot didn't materialize, Hubie was buried by the tabloids. They were upset about his suddenly unimaginative offense. They were critical of his decision to play Ewing and Cartwright together. And they were quick to overlook the fact that both King and Cartwright were hurt. Hubie had gone from the penthouse to the outhouse overnight in their eyes. He used to read everything and it chewed him up. At the beginning of the 1987 season, after the Knicks got off to a 4–12 start, Hubie was fired and replaced on an interim basis by his former assistant Bob Hill, who lasted less than a year.

Al Bianchi did not want to be another fired GM like Scottie Sterling, so in February 1989, he traded a 1989 first-round draft choice to Portland for forward Kiki Vandeweghe. Vandeweghe was being promoted as a proven scorer who, Al thought, could be the final piece of the puzzle, but he hadn't played in over a year because of a bad back. It took him a month to get in shape and when he did come back, he upset the delicate chemistry of our team because the lineup had been set.

Madison Square Garden network didn't help things when they ran a promotion comparing the Knicks of the early '70s to our team: Ewing to Willis, Oakley to Dave DeBusschere, Jackson to Clyde Frazier, Gerald Wilkins to Dick Barnett, and Vandeweghe, a guy who had never even started for us, to Bill Bradley. Johnny Newman, our starting forward, was so upset by the ad, he came to see me and asked, "What's the deal?" I tried to reassure him. I told him I had no intentions of changing the lineup.

We had other problems, too. The media started to criticize Mark Jackson for what they perceived as a flamboyant playing style and tried to build a case for dissension with a report that Jackson and Gerald Wilkins had gotten into a nasty argument on a plane.

I was just trying to hold down the fort.

When we swept the Sixers in a three game miniseries the media said, "They got lucky." When we lost to the Bulls the same writers knocked us because we had the home-court advantage. As it turns out, the Bulls had a pretty darn good team—they won the championship a year later.

I could see the handwriting on the wall. I should have learned a valuable lesson from Hubie Brown and Dave DeBusschere, Phil Esposito and Michael Bergeron of the

Rangers. When a coach and a general manager don't get along, they'll both be fired. I didn't want to follow in Hubie's footsteps. I was getting out before it happened to me.

And I had an option. C. M. Newton of Kentucky had been calling ever since March, shortly after Eddie Sutton tendered his resignation.

When C.M., a former Kentucky player and a highly respected coach at Vanderbilt, was hired as athletic director at his alma mater, his first responsibility was to find a coach who would comply with NCAA rules.

His original shopping list included Pat Riley of the Lakers, a UK grad; Mike Krzyzewski of Duke; Lute Olson of Arizona; and me. But that list was cut down quickly. Krzyzewski told Newton he wasn't interested. Riley said the timing wasn't right. C.M. interviewed Olson, who had previously turned the job down in 1985, at the Final Four in Seattle. He wanted Olson to fly to Lexington for a new round of discussions. But Lute canceled the visit and signed a contract extension with Arizona, disappointing Kentucky fans for the second time in four years. One local newspaper columnist angrily referred to Olson as "Loot."

C.M. first called me in March 1989 and said he would like to come up and "eyeball" me. I got on the phone with all my friends in New York and asked them if they knew anyone from the South who could tell me what "eyeball" meant. I didn't know if it meant an interview. I didn't know if it meant he was going to offer me the job.

He flew to New York in a private plane and made a special visit to my home. He offered me the job on the spot. He did not paint a rosy picture.

I told him I thought the Knicks had a shot to progress deep into the playoffs and it would be a long time before I could let him know. He said he had to know right then if I would visit. The pressure back in Kentucky was becoming immense. I totally understood, but couldn't give him a commitment. I asked him who he was going to pursue for the coaching job.

He said he was going to talk to P. J. Carlesimo of Seton Hall, who had just coached his team to the NCAA championship game. I thought that was a great choice. C.M. liked P.J. and invited him to Lexington to meet with the screening committee immediately after the season. Reporters followed his every move. In the end, P.J. felt he was more comfortable with the New Jersey scene, and wasn't sure how a bachelor would adjust to life in Lexington. Especially if he insisted on keeping his beard.

P.J. tracked me down one night on my car phone as I was driving to the Garden for a Knicks game. I don't know how he got the number. He started reading me contract figures. I thought he was talking about Kentucky, but he said they were from Seton Hall and then told me he was staying. His new contract was as good as that of any coach in the Big East, with the exception of Big John Thompson at Georgetown, who has an agreement only God knows about.

I have to give C.M. credit. We were getting ready for the Chicago series in mid-May and, out of the clear blue, he called again and asked if he could speak with me after the season was over. "Look," he said, "it didn't work out with P.J. We're willing to wait until the Knicks win the NBA championship if you'll tell us you'll take an interview."

I said I wasn't really interested, but thanked him again. I thought I should keep Al informed because I didn't want him to hear about it secondhand.

When I filled Al in at our practice court in Purchase, New York, he said, "Rick, you should never close the door. I saw what happened to John MacLeod in Phoenix. After all his years there, in the end, they didn't have any loyalty to him. You should always keep your options open." That was not the answer I was looking for. Al wasn't saying it in a mean sense but, at that point, I didn't know if he wanted me or not. That was about the lowest point I had with the Knicks.

On Sunday, May 21, two days after the 1989 season ended for the Knicks, David Roselle, who was then president of the

University of Kentucky, called and asked if there was any way he could talk me into coming down for an interview. We spent 45 minutes on the phone and I finally said I'd make a visit.

Dr. Normal Scott, one of my best friends and the godfather to our son Ryan, thought Kentucky could be a good move. He said the Knicks situation was turning into a horror show. There was only one person who wanted me to stay. That was my neighbor down the street, Stanley Jaffe.

Stanley, who produced *Black Rain* and *Fatal Attraction* for Paramount, was a diehard Knicks fan.

I was playing softball with my children on the same field where Glenn Close tried to kidnap the little girl in *Fatal Attraction* when I saw Stanley drive up. He said to me, "Joanne says you may decide to go to Kentucky and she doesn't want to go."

I told him Al and I were not getting along.

"What's your greatest fear?" he asked. "You got the years on your contract."

"The years mean nothing to me," I said. "I just don't want to get fired. I would be willing to take a substantial pay cut to guarantee the rest of my contract." I wanted to see the system improve, and it did take time and patience.

Stanley came up with the idea of renegotiating the contract so Gulf & Western would have to pay me $1 million, in addition to a buyout, should the corporation decide to fire me. I followed that advice, and approached Diller with the idea. I told him I didn't want a raise. I just wanted to see this thing through, to see if we could win a championship. But Diller refused to take the offer up to Martin Davis, the chairman of the board of Gulf & Western.

Stanley couldn't believe it. He advised me to counter with a $750,000 offer. Diller refused again. He said, "Not ten thousand. You're under contract."

I wanted some guarantees, because I felt Bianchi wanted former Phoenix Suns' coach John MacLeod. That was his guy. When I told Stanley, he was irate. He said, "I'm going to take it to Martin Davis myself." I thanked him for his offer, but I felt the situation was too far gone.

Al still thinks he's being blamed for my departure. After I left, he claimed our mutual dislike had nothing to do with my decision. He claimed I was planning to leave all along, and was just using the Knicks job as a springboard to get a big-money college position. There is no question Al and I talked about going back to college coaching someday, because my job with the Knicks was not going to last forever. But I certainly wasn't using the job as a springboard.

The day I left the Knicks, my lawyer Michael Goldberg and I had a meeting with Gulf & Western to clean up our affairs. I agreed I would not speak about the Knicks for three years and would not take another head coaching job in the NBA during that time.

As I was leaving the building after the final meeting with Gulf & Western, I overheard Al talking with some of the writers. They were asking him, "Who are you going to get?"

My body wasn't even cold and he was saying, "We're going to go after John MacLeod."

I knew then my gut feeling had been right. Well, Bianchi didn't get John MacLeod, Al's old boss in Phoenix who had since gone to Dallas. Even though MacLeod had only one year left on his contract with the Mavericks, he opted to stay with them. Bianchi was left with my assistant, Stu Jackson. I think he really hurt Stu when he told the newspapers, "I just wanted to show everyone you could have no coaching experience, take over this team and win."

It didn't take long for the camaraderie and the delicate chemistry of the Knicks team to disappear. That wasn't a tough prediction. I knew there was going to be a power struggle. Stu Jackson lasted only a year and a half before Al replaced him with John MacLeod, who was out of coaching and doing radio for the Pistons. I thought it would be great for Al to have John MacLeod, but I felt badly about the way Stu was handled by the New York Knicks organization.

Apparently, Al is still paranoid about me today. He told Harvey Araton of *The New York Times* recently that during Stu's tenure, I had been running the team from Kentucky and that Stu had been listening to everything I said.

While researching the column, Harvey checked Al's statement with Stu, and wrote that Stu and I had made a pact when I left the Knicks. As long as he was head coach of the Knicks, we agreed not to speak to each other. The only time I spoke to him while he was the Knicks' coach was when I had heard that John MacLeod would be interviewed for the job.

Obviously, the person who was hurt the most in this scenario was Stu Jackson. He should have never been hired, nor ever have been fired. I got what I deserved by not communicating properly with the general manager. Al got what he deserved for not winning enough after my departure. He finally got his man in there, but between them they could not generate enough wins.

To this day, Al thinks I fed Peter Vescey the material for his column the day he was fired by the Knicks. That is total nonsense. Al came out in a TV interview afterwards and implied he was going to get Peter Vescey and me. I had to laugh at that.

Ironically, last spring, I read that Paramount had just named a movie producer as chairman of the board of Gulf & Western. He was Stanley Jaffe. Diller was fired. Evans was fired. But, for me, the damage was already done.

Gulf & Western hired Pat Riley as the Knicks' coach in June 1991, and it looks like he has finally captured New York. I'm so grateful for that because all the negatives can be put to rest—the what-ifs of the world that feed on negative behavior. Pat had had tremendous success with the Lakers in the '80s, winning five NBA championships. He is a self-taught coach. He was a star on Rupp's Runts. He played in the NBA and went from a pro player to a radio broadcaster to a coach.

I'm just not sure how long Pat will enjoy the atmosphere in

New York. Right now, everybody's excited to have him. They're all pumped up. But in a couple of years, the media will start to complain that Riley spends too much time on his clothes and his hair. It's already starting. Riley has infuriated a lot of the writers there. They can't get to him. He puts up a wall and they can't get on the other side of it, and that bothers them. But it's great for Pat and the Knicks.

# --3--

# *COURTSHIP AND MARRIAGE*

The search for a new basket-ball coach at Kentucky had taken longer than anyone in Lexington imagined. In fact, Robert Lindsay, a local disc jockey at WVLK, announced the first week of May that he would camp out on a billboard until a new coach was named.

Lindsay was a big UK fan from Paducah. He started living 20 feet above the highway the first week of May. The station supplied him with a tent and a recliner, and they even had his TV wired for cable. His wife was pregnant, and his new life-style probably got old after about three weeks.

I visited the campus just before Memorial Day.

Kentucky put on a full-court press after I accepted Roselle's invitation. The university wanted to make sure I felt right at home. C.M. sent his associate athletic director Gene DeFilippo and wife Anne to New York on a private plane stocked with various Italian meats and cheeses to pick us up. They sent an

Italian to get me, figuring I would get excited about all the *paisanos* in Lexington. The problem was, aside from Gene and me, even Columbus would have had a difficult time rounding up any more Italians in the city.

When I arrived, reporters were everywhere. TV trucks were parked in front of every hotel—even Fred Kerber of the New York *Daily News,* who covered our team when I was with the Knicks. C.M. wanted to keep everything quiet. He arranged for Joanne and me to have dinner with him. Joining him would be his wife Evelyn, Gene DeFilippo and Anne, assistant AD Larry Ivy and his wife Lorraine, and Jerry Claiborne, the football coach, and his wife.

Just as we were about to enter the restaurant, Jerry Tipton, a reporter for the Lexington *Herald-Leader,* came up and confronted me with a story from my past.

When I graduated from Massachusetts in 1974, I had taken a job as graduate assistant at the University of Hawaii. While I was there, the school was placed on probation. My name had been linked to the investigation.

It was an old story, but in light of Kentucky's tarnished past, I had no reluctance in dropping out after C.M. visited us after dinner and told me he thought it would be best to cancel the process. C.M. felt Kentucky didn't need any more negative publicity and that the *Herald-Leader* would make it difficult for all of us. When I went to bed that night, I decided I would continue as the Knicks' coach and they could go on with their search.

C.M. was beside himself. For a brief moment, he actually considered naming himself as coach for a year and bringing in Kyle Macy as an assistant with the idea of grooming him for the job. Kyle was one of the most popular players in Kentucky history, but he had no coaching experience.

I did not have an uninterrupted night's sleep, either. C.M. hadn't wanted anyone to know where we were staying, so he put us up at a house owned by the mother of Farra Alford, one of his former players at Alabama. Some secret. We got back to the house about one o'clock in the morning, and must have triggered the alarm system. When the police arrived, the officer who came to the door said he knew me.

"We were trying to guess where you were staying in town," he said.

We had our bags packed and were ready to leave when C.M. banged on the door at 7:30 the next morning. He had spoken with David Roselle and told me the president was not concerned about the Hawaii incident. "He's totally comfortable with what you stand for and, if you agree, he wants to proceed with the interview," C.M. said.

About this time, I was having second thoughts. But I decided to go through the process, rather than leave under a cloud.

I met with the media early that morning over at the Wildcat Lodge, where the players live. I convinced them that the Hawaii story was a dead issue. I said I felt I could turn Kentucky around quickly if I became the coach.

When I met with David Roselle, he told me he had done a thorough check of my background at Boston University and Providence and discovered I had been totally compliant with NCAA rules. When we were finished, he turned to me and said, "I feel very comfortable that you're the person for the job, if you want it."

He reiterated that the Kentucky program could do all the things his alma mater, Duke, was doing, both athletically and academically. He also said he and C.M. would give me enough support to turn the program around in four or five years.

I stopped one step short of accepting the job because I wasn't sure whether Joanne wanted to make another move at this time. We spent another day in Lexington and we met with the pastor and guidance counselor at Christ the King School to discuss our three children, Michael, Chris, and Ricky. We left for New York the next morning, escaping from the media who had converged at the main terminal by flying out of the old Diamond Shamrock hangar.

When I had left Providence for the Knicks, I had no time to think over my decision. This time, I took Memorial Day weekend to weigh the pros and cons. I felt this would be a good move for the family. Joanne was less sure.

Both Joanne and I suffered an enormous personal tragedy with the death of our son in March 1987. For the six months of his life, Joanne was getting up at six in the morning, driving 90 minutes from Providence to Boston each way to the hospital, and staying until seven at night. She did this seven days a week. No days off. Finally, after six months, the baby came home with a clean bill of health. She came to New York to cheer Providence in the Big East tournament. While we were both away from home, our son died of crib death. We think of him all the time, and visit his grave in Cranston. To this day, I've seen a difference in Joanne. Without her strong faith, she never would have been able to carry on in life.

I was really worried about her for the next few months. After I accepted the Knicks job, I felt it would be a chance for her to be physically close to her family, who lived in Long Island, when she needed their support. I'm not saying that's the sole reason I left Providence, but it was a consideration.

After we moved to Westchester County, we talked her brother Billy Minardi into moving two miles away from us. Bedford also provided Joanne with her best friend in life, Lillian LaPenta, who owns a nail salon in town. They were inseparable. The two of them are like Laverne and Shirley.

I knew uprooting the family one more time would be difficult. I needed another voice to convince Joanne that Kentucky was a good opportunity. I invited P. J. Carlesimo to meet us at Bravo Gianni!, our favorite restaurant in New York. P.J. and Joanne are good friends. He said he liked Kentucky, and I asked him to repeat that to Joanne. When we weren't talking about the angel hair capellini, the tomato sauce and basil, we were talking about how great it was in Kentucky. She caught on quick to the sell job, but finally agreed to give Kentucky a try.

I knew at least one person would be happy if I took the job.

My first day as coach, I stopped by and told the disc jockey he could come down from the billboard.

I knew exactly what I was getting into the day I accepted the job. It was staring me in the face every time I looked at the cover of the May 29, 1989, issue of *Sports Illustrated;* the one with the headline KENTUCKY'S SHAME.

I was inheriting a program that had a history of problems and was no stranger to controversy. The school had been involved in a point-shaving scandal in the '50s, and the current NCAA probation was its second in 15 years.

Kentucky had the worst image of any school in America when we took over the program. Most people remember the Emery Air Freight incident. Chris Mills, a 6' 7" blue-chip prospect from Los Angeles, had signed with Kentucky and was expected to start playing the next season. An Emery envelope containing training films was sent to Mills's father in the spring of 1988. It came open in transit, and the Emery clerk found twenty $50 bills in with the videotape. The national media attention gave the NCAA a springboard to investigate the Kentucky program. Again. While the year-long investigation was being conducted, Chris Mills enrolled and played his freshman year.

A teammate of his, Eric Manuel, also came to the attention of the NCAA. A 6' 6" sophomore from Macon, Georgia, Manuel had scored below 700 in two previous attempts at the Scholastic Aptitude Test in his hometown. He needed a 15 to project. When he took the American College Test at Lafayette High in Lexington, he scored a 23 and went on to become a starter his freshman year. Manuel was Kentucky's leading returning scorer entering the 1988–89 season before sitting out the year because of questions regarding his test score.

The university's subsequent investigation showed that 211 of 219 of Manuel's answers were exactly the same as those of a student seated nearby. Manuel denied the charges of academic fraud.

Shawn Kemp, a 6' 10", 230-pound high school All-America

from Elkhart, Indiana, had signed with Kentucky in 1987 but was sitting out his freshman year as a Proposition 48. Shortly after he signed at Kentucky, Kemp began driving an $11,000 Cavalier. Both he and his mother said it was a gift from her. Less than six months later, Sean Sutton, the coach's son, made it known that $700 worth of gold jewelry had been stolen from his dorm room. Police told the Suttons that a pawnshop video camera had photographed a suspect pawning the jewelry at the Johnson Diamond Exchange on East Main Street in Lexington.

The man in the photo turned out to be Shawn Kemp. It was stated in private circles that Kemp did not take the jewelry, but that another teammate did. Apparently, he asked Shawn if he could sell it, and that's when Shawn turned up at the pawnshop. Although the Suttons didn't press charges, Kemp left Kentucky shortly thereafter and enrolled in a junior college in Texas. He was drafted that June, 19 years old, by the Seattle SuperSonics in the first round of the NBA draft.

But the worst was yet to come. When the NCAA nailed Kentucky, it did it publicly and in a big way. It was such big news in the Commonwealth that six television stations interrupted their regular programming to broadcast the university's announcement. Shortly after the sanctions hit, Mills, the team's top scorer, was declared ineligible to play at Kentucky again. He transferred to Arizona.

Manuel was declared ineligible to play at any other NCAA school and he wound up spending a year at a junior college in Tennessee before transferring to Oklahoma City, an NAIA school.

It was difficult getting people to look at positives at Kentucky. Even Indiana coach Bob Knight started making jokes about the program on the banquet circuit, claiming Kentucky had finally found a way to clean up its act: they'd switched from Emery to Federal Express.

So now, it was up to us.

Eddie Sutton had recruited a lineup of Rex Chapman, Eric

Manuel, and Sean Sutton at guard, Chris Mills and Shawn Kemp at forward, LeRon Ellis at center, and a bench that consisted of Reggie Hanson, Richie Farmer, Sean Woods, John Pelphrey, and Deron Feldhaus. Had all this talent stayed together, Kentucky might have won at least one national championship, possibly two.

But most of the marquee names were gone by the time I arrived. The NCAA had allowed all of the players except Manuel to transfer and gain immediate eligibility once the sanctions came down. So, instead of inheriting a dream team, I was left with an empty cupboard.

Rex Chapman left after his sophomore year, one of only a few Kentucky players ever to turn pro early, a year before the NCAA dropped the hammer. The loss of Chapman was a particularly crushing blow to Kentucky fans. He was a 6' 5" guard from Apollo High in Owensboro, Kentucky.

He had grown up as a big Louisville fan. Owensboro was only a couple hours away from Louisville, but he succumbed to the pressure. "If we hadn't signed him, the state might have declared a day of mourning," Sutton said.

Chapman became such a cult hero in the Bluegrass that writers renamed Lexington, "Rexington." He scored 1,073 points in just two years and could have been Kentucky's all-time leading scorer if he had stayed a full four years. There was friction between Chapman and Sutton. A lot of people told me Eddie was jealous of Rex. When Eddie tried to reshape Rex's game, Kentucky fans thought he was stifling Rex. His father Wayne thought so, too. From all indications, his dad was the swaying influence, convincing Rex to turn pro. Rex was the seventh player taken in the 1988 draft, selected by Charlotte. Given the way he has played early on in the NBA, it would have been beneficial for Rex to stay in school at least one more season. But the bitterness about the sanctions was so great, it was probably in Rex's best interest to leave.

LeRon Ellis, Kentucky's top shot-blocker and second-leading rebounder, transferred to Syracuse the summer after the sanctions hit and was eventually drafted in the first round by the L.A. Clippers.

Sean Sutton, the assist leader and third-leading scorer, spent a year at Lexington Community College, then transferred to Oklahoma State after his father Eddie took the head coaching job there. Believe it or not, Sean wanted to stay at Kentucky. I agreed to it. I was going to let him walk on, and he would pay his tuition. Then I started getting the worst hate mail. Some of the stories were unbelievable. Everybody told me Sean was a Division II player and they wanted him out of town. So, I had to rescind my offer to allow him to walk on. I told him it would be in his best interest to go elsewhere. He was very upset that I had broken a commitment. He became a very good player at Oklahoma State. It would never have worked here; he would have had to carry too much baggage. People could not accept him playing ahead of Richie Farmer any longer.

The nucleus of our first team consisted of Deron Feldhaus, John Pelphrey, Richie Farmer, Sean Woods, Jeff Brassow, Derrick Miller, Reggie Hanson, and Jonathan Davis. The first time I met with them, I kept waiting for the big guys to walk through the door, but there were no giants in this group. I felt Reggie Hanson and Derrick Miller could play on this level, but that everybody else did not belong at Kentucky. I looked at Jonathan Davis. He was a wonderful young man, but he was a 6' 6" center. I felt he should have been at Eastern Kentucky or Morehead. As for Richie Farmer, he made Billy Donovan look like Charles Atlas. John Pelphrey and Deron Feldhaus seemed like a team's 11th and 12th men.

None of our players was taller than 6' 7", and each one must have felt about two feet tall after the NCAA had embarrassed them. They were the end of the bench. Their self-esteem was at rock bottom.

And I almost dealt them another blow.

When I first got there, I considered moving the players out of the Wildcat Lodge. The Lodge is one of Kentucky's greatest legacies. It looks like an Alpine ski lodge, and has housed the basketball team since 1978. But C. M. Newton and David Roselle didn't like the way it was being run under the jurisdiction of the basketball coaches, and wanted to place the players in the regular dorms.

Joe B. Hall talked me out of it. "Rick, if you move the players out, you're making a big mistake," he said. "You can do that at Vanderbilt and some other places, but you can't do that at Kentucky. The student body will not treat a University of Kentucky basketball player like a student athlete. They'll keep them up all night. They will not have any privacy to study in a normal fashion." Joe B. Hall also told me the Lodge was one of Kentucky's greatest recruiting tools. Why take it away?

Joe B. was right, and I'm so happy now that I didn't move the players. The Lodge is currently under the jurisdiction of residential housing. It operates under the same rules as all the other dorms, and half of the residents are non-basketball players.

Housing them in the Lodge gave the players a sense of identity with past UK teams. Now, we had to convince them they were part of that tradition.

We brought in Frank Gardner, a psychologist who had worked with the Knicks, to test the team. I needed to know who was a leader, who lacked confidence, who wanted to take the big shot. I found that they were all insecure about what was ahead. I needed to ease those fears. I built them up; I told them how valuable they were. I didn't try to make them up into something they weren't. But I wanted to convince them that even average athletes, playing well together, could accomplish great deeds as a team.

I knew I had not inherited the L.A. Lakers, but I wanted to coach in the same style I used with the Knicks and Providence. I hired Ray "Rock" Oliver away from Pitt to get the players in shape for the running, pressing game I wanted them to play. The first time we took them to the track, they looked like a Tuesday-Friday barroom softball team. But, after six weeks of running, weightlifting, and sprinting, we finally started to see some results.

With Rock, the players didn't have much choice. The first time he was introduced to the team, he pulled out a picture of his petite wife and his preschool children and passed it around. "Don't make me choose," he said, pounding the table. "If I don't get you guys in shape, I'll lose my job, and my family won't eat."

Rock would have made a great drill instructor. At Kentucky, he was running his own bootcamp. The first time Sean Woods worked out, Rock had him push his favorite toy—a heavy resistance machine—across the gym and back ten times. Sean tried to be macho. He didn't want to show how much it hurt.

"You look like you're in pretty good shape," Rock said.

"Not bad," Sean said.

"Okay," said Rock, "let's go get something to eat. I have a bologna sandwich in my office."

Sean threw up on the spot.

He wasn't the only one who struggled through preseason that year. Richie Farmer showed up weighing close to 191 pounds, and was having trouble running two miles in the required 12 minutes. The day before our first Blue-White scrimmage, Richie looked like he was finally going to make his time. He crossed the finish line right after John Pelphrey.

"John, if you belong to a church, say a prayer," Rock said. "You just made it. Your time was 12:00.

"Richie: 12:01."

Richie discovered later that Rock had no idea what his time was. He had broken all the stop watches in frustration.

In addition to Rock and Billy Donovan the ex-Providence star who had led us to the Final Four, I had a staff of Ralph Willard, who had been my assistant coach with the Knicks; Herb Sendek, who had worked for me at Providence; and Tubby Smith, the current head coach at Tulsa, who had been an assistant at South Carolina and had a strong reputation as a recruiter in the Deep South.

Billy, Tubby, and Ralph all played in our scrimmages because we didn't have enough players to go five on five. Billy loved it, especially when I let him play the role of Chris Jackson before our game with LSU. There were times when I thought Ralph and Tubby were going to die.

We wanted to bring Kentucky basketball into the '90s, both in the stands and on the floor.

I feel it's important that fans are able to jump up and down and act like kids. In the past, I'm told, Kentucky fans waited for the buzzer to sound at the end of games. Then, they'd say, "Whew, we got another win." That's not how basketball should be watched. It should be fun to play and entertaining to follow.

The one thing that struck me when I arrived was that the fans at Rupp had become more of a theater crowd and less of a basketball crowd. Aside from the student section, the mood wasn't very upbeat. So we pumped up the volume on Big Bertha, the sound system at Rupp, and turned our games into a rock 'n' roll revival. "Shout" by the Isley Brothers was a particular favorite. Chris Cameron used to kid me all the time, calling me Bob Fosse because of the way I wanted to control how the music was orchestrated.

There was a lot to shout about that first year. We never lost at home, simply outworking people on the way to a 14–14 record. We even got a big 100–95 win over LSU, a team that had three future pros—Stanley Roberts, Chris Jackson, and Shaquille O'Neal. Our wide-open, fast-paced style of play brought Rupp back to life. During that year, we attracted the three largest crowds ever to watch Kentucky play at that arena.

We needed a gimmick during the first season, and the three-point offense was just what the doctor ordered. We put up 53 of them during a 116–113 overtime loss to Southwest Louisiana, and made 21 threes during a wild 121–110 loss to North Carolina. In fact, we got so good at it, we set six national records. We may have started the season as Bambinos, but by the end, the nickname "Pitino's Bombinos" really applied.

When I first introduced the three-pointer to Kentucky, some of our players were gun-shy. But we quickly convinced them the only thing worse than a bad three was passing up a good one. We shot an NCAA record 810 threes, making 281. Derrick Miller, our leading scorer, made 99 of 289. He made 8 threes in our games against Kansas, North Carolina, and Tennessee. Every time we made a three, the student section celebrated by taping a blue and white "3" card to the Rupp Arena wall near the scoreboard, beginning a new tradition.

Unfortunately, my first year at Kentucky was David Roselle's last. He left in the middle of the season and never stayed around long enough to watch the program take off. Roselle was in his first year of his presidency when the NCAA investigation took place. He felt it was time for a coaching change, but Eddie Sutton had built a lot of allies while he was here coaching. One of them was Wallace Wilkinson, the governor of Kentucky. Wilkinson wanted Sutton to stay, and was willing to fight for him.

A lot of university administrators were supportive of Roselle. They liked the fact that he had initiated an internal investigation and was cooperating with the NCAA. This was a departure for Kentucky, which had always thumbed its nose at the NCAA in the past. Roselle was convinced Kentucky was guilty of the NCAA violations. Sutton's supporters felt there was a good chance the NCAA would have given Kentucky only one year's probation had Roselle not been so anxious to cooperate. As it was, Kentucky got two.

Roselle eventually resigned, apparently because he thought Wilkinson was going to replace him. He left, claiming the governor would not authorize pay raises for the faculty. As soon as Dr. Charles Wethington was inaugurated as Roselle's successor, the pay raises came through.

In June 1990, we added Bernadette Locke, an All-America player from Georgia, to our staff. She was the first female assistant coach with on-the-floor responsibilities in a Division 1 men's program.

Bernadette had been a guidance counselor and had worked for Xerox. When I interviewed her, she was an assistant in an outstanding women's program at Georgia. She was bright, attractive, and an outstanding teacher. She also had the ability to come across well with our students, alumni, and fans. I thought she could make a great impact on our program. This was not a new idea for me. Fourteen years ago, when I was at Boston University, I thought about hiring a female coach because I thought it might help us in recruiting. But I never pursued it there.

C.M. was very big on the idea. He thought it was innovative and creative. But my staff—Herb, Billy, and Ralph—was really against it. They said we'd be the laughingstock of the men's coaching world. I didn't agree, and signed her to a contract.

When we hired Bernadette, she was featured in every sports section in America. She's been involved in all aspects of the game, including individual instruction, on campus recruiting, film analysis, academics, and career placement.

I immediately put her in charge of career placement for our players. Kentucky players had done well academically in the past, but people still saw us as a basketball factory. I wanted to send a message. In the past, a Kentucky graduate's job option might have included the NBA. I wanted our seniors to have three or four career opportunities after they graduated.

During my first two years, none of our seniors were drafted. But, our success grew. In our second season, 1991, we beat NCAA finalists Kansas and also LSU and Alabama, and lost to Indiana and North Carolina by a total of five points. We finished ninth in the final Associated Press poll. I walked away from the season wondering what we could have done in the NCAA Tournament. This time next year I would know.

On the floor, we had done better than I expected. Off the court, we were still fighting a battle to change the image of Kentucky basketball. In 1985, the Lexington *Herald-Leader* won a Pulitzer Prize for its exposé on UK basketball. In a two-part series, the paper detailed the actions of a small group of boosters who had given team members a steady stream of cash over a 13-year period. The paper interviewed 33 former Wildcats and claimed 31 knew of improper activities while they had been playing. Fifteen of them, including Kyle Macy, Sam Bowie, Dirk Minniefield, Mike Phillips, and Dwight Anderson, were involved in the interviews.

Jeff Marx and Mike York, the two reporters who worked on the story, reported players had received what they called "hundred dollar handshakes" in Rupp Arena after games. The story went on to allege the players had visited the offices and homes of boosters to receive gifts of up to $500 at a time, had sold their free season tickets for at least $1,000, and had pocketed excessive payments for public appearances and speeches. Others said they had received free meals from local restaurants.

Jay Shidler, a guard who played for Kentucky from 1976–80, made the biggest waves when he told the *Herald-Leader* he made $8,400 from allegedly selling his complimentary tickets to Cecil Dunn, who was Joe B. Hall's attorney at the time. Dunn refused to comment on the story.

Minniefield told the *Herald-Leader* he shook the hand of booster Elmer Prewitt, a Corbin physician, in the locker room a couple of times and found himself holding a $50 bill. Prewitt denied the charge.

Bowie told the *Herald-Leader* he had spoken at events where "you can get two hundred fifty to five hundred dollars. . . . I've received that kind of money." He was quoted as saying there had been players who had been through the Kentucky program who had made a living off of speaking engagements. "If I was to speak at a place and a guy gives me an envelope with five hundred dollars in it, do you take that and give it back to him, saying the NCAA says we can only accept one hundred dollars?" he reportedly said.

Otis Singletary, the Kentucky president at the time, and Cliff Hagan, the AD, said in separate interviews that they were unaware of any cash handouts to players or other rules violations. When NCAA investigators tried to look into the charges, they came up empty.

I had heard all these rumors about $100 dollar handshakes in the past, and I wasn't about to put up with them. Apparently, there had been people here in the past who took care of players. As soon as I took the job, I immediately drew the line. I met with the players and told them I didn't want them to socialize with any adults. Period.

That included the media.

The players in past regimes were more than happy to accommodate reporters. Before I got here, some of the stars were holding individual press conferences once a week, like they were Michael Jordan. It was crazy. I decided to limit access. I closed practice to the media and limited press conferences to the day before a game. I was trying to get these kids off their pedestals, so when they graduated, they would understand what life was all about after basketball.

We had to build a new perception around the community, around the commonwealth and the country. Everything was positive at Kentucky now. We had to promote all the good things that our players were doing on and off the court, so the Kentucky fans knew they were supporting a total person and not just a basketball player. Before this, the perception of some Kentucky athletes was of a spoiled individual whom everybody adored; a person so self-absorbed, he didn't realize he had to give back to his community.

I think our Committee of 101 Club is one of the best role models for our players. They are the real boosters of Kentucky. The 101 Club, led by Van Florence, got its name in 1966 when 101 IBM employees began sending a telegram to Rupp before each road game. The group has grown into a service organization with more than 300 members, and does everything from sell programs to help people find their seats at all Kentucky athletic events. These are the people who really come through when you need them. They do the work nobody else wants to do, all on a volunteer basis. They couldn't afford to give a player a $50 handshake, nor would they want to lower themselves to do that.

I had Rock go around to restaurants, movie theaters, and clothing stores and explain the NCAA rules on recruiting. I don't know if Eddie Sutton was aware of certain rules or not, but I am. I have to be, or it would spell death for our program. We must call our compliance office five times a day for interpretations. Sometimes, there are things you take for granted, but you always check them out. An innocent mistake could be blown up on the front page. It's reached a point where everyone at Kentucky is paranoid, including me.

I picked up Jared Prickett, one of our recruits, for his visit in October and we drove by Keeneland Race Track. I asked if he wanted to go in and look around. He said, "Yes." We drove up to the gate, but I had to get out of my car, go to a public phone and call the office to make sure it was legal. It was.

Herb told the players they were not allowed to play in any nonsanctioned summer leagues. John Bostick, our associate AD in charge of compliance, told him that wasn't good enough. He had to write a memo. We have to submit memos on everything. When Junior Braddy stayed with a relative in town over the summer, we had to write a memo justifying it. We're allowed to talk to recruits only once a week.

The rules can cause you to lose sleep. Herb and Billy went down to see one of our recruits, Tony Delk, in Memphis in September. NCAA rules allow only two coaches out of the office at the same time during recruiting periods. Because they couldn't get a plane back late that night, they had to drive 13 hours so I could catch a noon flight to Newark the next day.

The NCAA is like an urban police force. They can't be everywhere, so the program must monitor itself. Cheating in college basketball does go on, and it goes on like this:

Coaches will state, "I never bought a player in my life." And, for the most part, that's true. The coach doesn't offer prospects anything up front. It's an unwritten rule that the players are taken care of once they have enrolled and are part of the family. So, in essence, the school is buying athletes. On their official visits, recruits can find out details by asking players how they like the school.

Once a coach gives a player something not covered in his scholarship, or once he knows a player is receiving illegal inducements from a booster, the coach is no longer in control. The player is. So, while a coach may be able to trust that player to keep silent while he's part of the program, all bets are off after he leaves. It happens.

As we've seen from Dominique Wilkins of the Atlanta Hawks and others, pro players have said outlandish things about their university days once they leave school. It's a macho thing. They boast about it: "Hey, I was taken care of, even if my teammates weren't." A coach can risk his and the school's reputation on that kind of behavior.

I had done a lot of research about Kentucky before I arrived, but there was a lot more I needed to know. I wanted to find out the positives and negatives of the program. I met with several prominent local businessmen to find out what they thought of former Kentucky coaches.

The biggest complaint many had was that Kentucky had a reputation for being a white-bread university, even when the South was integrating rapidly. Many blamed Rupp for not recruiting black players earlier. A man of his reputation could have made a difference. But he was typical of his time and place.

In the '60s, there were freedom marches, boycotts, and sit-ins in the Deep South. But, in Kentucky, where the population was over 90 percent Caucasian, the status quo still held. There were no black Wildcats. But even Rupp's Runts, one of the most beloved teams Kentucky ever put on the floor, had to bow to the inevitable. That was vividly pointed out when five black starters for Texas Western were just too talented for this team in the 1966 NCAA championship game.

It was time for Kentucky to become progressive, but Rupp was reluctant. Rupp was under constant pressure from John

Oswald, the Kentucky president at the time, to recruit a black player. He waited until two years after Vanderbilt integrated the SEC with Perry Wallace and Godfrey Dillard in 1967 before taking the plunge and signing Tom Payne, a seven-footer from Louisville, in 1969. Payne played only one year.

Kentucky's biggest need during the '60s was for a dominant center. The state produced two during that decade—Wes Unseld and Jim McDaniels. Both black players went on to become All-America selections at Louisville and Western Kentucky. Neither was recruited seriously by UK. McDaniels came back to haunt Kentucky in the opening round of the Mideast Regionals in the 1971 tournament, the year the Hilltoppers went to the Final Four. All five of Western's starters were Kentuckians. All five were black.

When I arrived on campus, four of our eight scholarship players were black. In the 1991–92 season, we had nine minority players on a team roster of 15. The times have changed at Kentucky. For the better, that is.

# -- 4 --

# *LIFE IN THE FISH BOWL*

The first game I ever coached at Rupp Arena, I came out of the tunnel and I thought I was looking at myself in a funhouse mirror. There were 10,000 Rick Pitinos staring back at me. Gene DeFilippo had ordered the lookalike face masks because he wanted me to know the fans were behind me.

I knew then it was going to be difficult to be just another face in the crowd. I even told our public address announcer not to roll my name during the introductions. I didn't want to be "Rrrrrrrick" Pitino. Rick Pitino was just fine. At least he knew who I was.

When I coached the Knicks, I had trouble getting into the Garden. I really mean that. Nobody cared who you were, and that was enjoyable. When I made my way to the bench on game nights, I always felt like I was running an obstacle course, even though it was a short walk from the locker room to the court. People would bump me. Guards, cronies. Fans. Excuse me, excuse me. Then, I'd finally get to the floor.

At Rupp Arena, it's a hike to the bench. Originally, the plan had been for me to receive a personal escort. I didn't want to have anything to do with that nonsense. Then, Van Florence came up to me and said, "Coach, do you mind if I walk you out?"

I asked him how long it would take and said I wanted to get out there with two minutes to go, so I could shake the opposing coach's hand and meet the officials.

"Fine," he said, "we'll leave in three minutes."

All of a sudden, I heard Van crackling into the walkie-talkie, "Forty-five seconds."

So, I said to him, "Van, what the hell are you doing? Shut that damn thing off."

"I'm telling security you're coming down, to make room," he said.

"Thirty seconds . . . fifteen seconds . . ."

In New York, I used to sneak by people to get to the Garden floor. I'd duck because I was afraid of the things people might throw at me for a loss the previous night. Here, they have a roped-off area and I walk out on the carpet and go right over to the bench. And, are you ready for this, the fans actually cheer.

It's hard to be inconspicuous in this job.

One of the first celebrities I ever met was Peter Falk. He loves pro basketball and he was a good friend of Hubie Brown. He acted just like Columbo. One time, he was in our locker room, speaking to Mike Saunders, our trainer. He had some sauerkraut and mustard on his tie from the hot dog he was eating. Finally, after ten minutes, I couldn't stand it anymore. I wanted to tell him, "Get a butter knife." Mike finally told him, "Peter, you got a little mustard." Falk took his napkin and rubbed the mustard in. I told you Columbo was his alter ego.

Peter Falk was a star, but even out in public, he was just a normal guy. Being in the public eye can be trying. The minute I took the Kentucky job, my life became an open book. Literally. The Sunday after I was hired, the *Herald–Leader* began running installments of my first book, *Born to Coach*. Billy Reynolds and I had written this after my first year with the Knicks. The phone in the basketball office rang off the hook with speaking requests for "Coach Patina."

Even if the fans couldn't pronounce my name in the beginning, they recognized it. I had been the Knicks' coach, and I had the endorsement of Kenny Walker, a former Kentucky star who played for me in New York. Closer to Lexington, in 1987 I had coached Providence to a big victory over SEC champion Alabama in the Southeast Regionals at Louisville. The fans there thought Alabama had a great shot at the national championship. The team was loaded with great players—guys like Derrick McKey, Jim Farmer, and Terry Coner. We beat them by 21. When it comes to wins over SEC teams, Kentucky fans have long memories.

When Billy Minardi flew in to wish me luck my first day on the job, he asked a secretary for directions to my office in Memorial Coliseum. She asked if we were related. When he said, "Yes," she said, "Oh, you must be Eye-talian, too."

I'm sure I was a curiosity that first month. I took a drive to check on the construction of our new house one Sunday and I was greeted by a line of cars about 100 yards long. The next day, I discovered a disc jockey had snuck into the yard, grabbed a handful of dirt and tried to reward it to some lucky caller as a souvenir.

In New York, I could always go over to the Carnegie Deli for a sandwich after the game and just blend into the crowd. Here, I can't go anywhere without people approaching me. I was shopping in the mall in December when some fans stopped me and asked if I would sign their Christmas presents. I turned them down in a nice way, telling them to keep it special. "It'll look much better with Santa Claus's name on it," I said.

I admit I'm a people person. In this job, it's a requirement. Even though I'm more accessible than Eddie Sutton or Joe B. Hall, the attention isn't because I'm Coach Pitino. It's because I'm the Kentucky basketball coach, and what that represents to the public. Sometimes the constant attention is tiring. It's difficult to even finish a meal without interruption. Dining out is special, and constant for a New Yorker.

But these people are the lifeline of Kentucky basketball, so I feel it's my obligation to always be gracious. If I can't enjoy the contact with the fans, I shouldn't be the Kentucky coach.

But I am the Kentucky coach, and I've made necessary adjustments to our lifestyle to make it work. I'm not sure if I can ask that of my family. My wife Joanne prefers her privacy. Her number one priority is being a wife and the mother of our four children—14-year-old Michael, 12-year-old Chrissy, 10-year-old Ricky, and 3-year-old Ryan. She doesn't give interviews, and that can be dangerous in a town of this size.

Some of the rumors about us are unbelievable. None of them are true, but they run rampant. My first year at Kentucky, Joanne was pregnant with Ryan. The fans hadn't seen her for a while, and they thought she had left me and Lexington. In fact, she was in the hospital in New York with complications from the pregnancy.

I finally had to call a press conference and tried to make light of the whole thing. "Yes," I joked, "the rumors are true. My wife has left me for Donald Trump."

No one laughed.

Joanne and I have been married for 16 years. We met when I was in high school on Long Island. She was a cheerleader, and she liked sports. I was a senior at St. Dominic's. It was summertime, and I was playing basketball in Hicksville with some friends. We decided to take a break and go to the deli for sandwiches. We were walking up a side street. We had lacrosse sticks with us—lacrosse is very big on the Island—and we were playing catch, throwing the ball back and forth. It rolled up onto the frontyard of a row house. There was a young girl sitting on the doorstep. She looked like she had just come back from the beach. I said, "Hello." She said, "Hello." Later, I asked the guys if they knew her name. That night, we were having a party and I said, "Well, why don't you call her up and invite her and some of her friends over?"

Joanne's mother comes from a family of 11. She's a strong Irish Catholic. If Joanne ever got out of line, her mother would take off her slipper and throw it at her, all the way across the room. Sometimes, when I would open the front door to pick her up, the shoe would be flying. She had to be home by a certain time, or else. Her mother never had to worry about me, because I always brought her home early for fear of that shoe hitting me.

On our dates we would usually go to a movie. Sometimes, she'd come with me to watch me practice. In the summers, I would always go over to C.W. Post college to shoot around for an hour and she'd rebound for me. She'd always want to go to the beach, and I told her if I made so many shots, we'd go in the afternoon. I would start off ahead of my goal, and she'd get excited, thinking today we'd go to the ocean. Then I'd get on a cold streak. In our three-year courtship in high school, we never once made it to the beach.

We got married after college. On our wedding night, I interviewed for an assistant's job at Syracuse. While on our honeymoon trip, I flew to Cincinnati to recruit Louis Orr, a skinny 6' 8" forward who went on to become a star with that program.

The move to Lexington was our fifth in ten years. Moving has never been traumatic for me. It was tougher on Joanne, who has her roots firmly planted in the asphalt of Hicksville, Long Island. As for the kids, they didn't care where they lived. All they wanted to know was whether they'd have nice friends to play with in our new neighborhood.

I provided them with one. When Big Brothers approached me about being a spokesman for their charity, I told them I would do it only if I could have a little brother. His name is Tim

Thompson. He's 13, and is one of the ball boys, along with my sons. I spent most of my time with him during the season, but we also took Tim with us to Disney World last spring. He's a great kid.

Because there's so little free time in my job, I value the moments I share with our family. C. M. Newton is very much involved in the Olympic movement, and wanted me to get involved. But I don't want to spend my summers taking this team to England or that team to Australia. I'm going to be selfish for our family's sake.

If it doesn't interfere with their schoolwork, I take Michael, Chris, and Ricky on the road with me. Our kids are big pro-basketball fans. We have a satellite dish in the office, and they come over all the time to watch the Knicks. One of the reasons they're so tuned in is because Barbara Kobak is an NBA junkie. Barbara has been my personal secretary since my coaching days at Boston University. For the last 13 years, she has helped me with my business responsibilities. She is invaluable. More than that, she's like a member of our family. She gets a package of newspaper clippings from the NBA office every day. The kids read them, and so do I.

I don't know if any of our sons will turn out to be players, and I've never pushed it. It's up to them. I just hope they can grow up like normal teenagers. I have great concerns about sending my children to school here in Kentucky. They aren't great athletes, and I don't want them subjected to all the pressure they're likely to get as the sons of the Kentucky coach.

The one thing that's startling to me in observing my children play on youth basketball teams is that each team is represented by a group of cheerleaders. Cheerleading is very big down here. Just as many boys someday hope to make the Kentucky basketball team, many of the girls hope to someday cheer for the Kentucky Wildcats. Our cheerleading team has won the national championship in four of the last seven years.

Probably the only person in my family who had been oblivious to all this attention is catching up quick. Ryan made his first public appearance at Rupp Arena on Senior Day. As he toddled onto the court at halftime, the PA announcer acknowledged him: "Now, making his Rupp Arena debut, Ryan Pitino." He looked right at home as the crowd applauded.

Maybe it's my Italian heritage. Maybe it's because I come from New York where great restaurants abound. But whatever the reason, I think one of life's great pleasures is eating—and talking—with family and friends. In Lexington, I'm lucky enough to have such a place, my restaurant Bravo Pitino! It is somewhere I can go to relax. And so can Kentucky fans.

We just celebrated our first anniversary in December. The idea originated after our first SEC win at Kentucky. We had just beaten Mississippi State, and one of the writers asked me if I was happy here. I said, "Yes, I'm happy. Now, if I can only find some good Italian food."

The next week I received three gift certificates to Italian restaurants.

Later that spring, I received a long letter from a young man named Kevin Daley, who is now one of our managers. He had a business proposition for me. He and his two partners wanted to open an Italian restaurant under my name. It seemed this was an idea whose time had come. Earlier I had been offered a chance to go into business with Vincenzo, who runs the top Italian restaurant in Louisville. He wanted both our names on the marquee. At that time, I didn't think I could afford to get into the restaurant business on a full-time basis.

But the idea wouldn't die. We were on our annual golf outing at Pebble Beach in the summer of 1990. During the trip, Steve Graves, one of my Lexington friends, suggested I talk to Jodi DiRaimo, who was with us, about managing a restaurant. Jodi had lived in Providence most of his life and owned the Players' Corner Pub. He had so many friends in that city, I didn't think he'd leave. But I asked him, anyway. He came down and decided to give it a try. He is co-owner and manager.

When Jodi's name is mentioned on the New York, New England, sports bar circuit, it brings instant recognition. Big East teams eat their pregame meals at the Players' Corner Pub, and celebrate there afterwards. Jodi is the perfect restaurateur. He's never met a party he didn't like.

I wanted to open a mid-scale restaurant, nothing elaborate. We decided to put the restaurant in Victorian Square, in downtown Lexington. I brought in Dave Dibble, a former lacrosse star at UMass and one of my old fraternity brothers, to be our bar manager. I hired Barbara Kobak to work in the business office.

Our small mom and pop operation has become a restaurant with all the elegance of a New York establishment. On game days, there's a three-hour wait for dinner. On Friday nights, we have violinists from the Lexington Philharmonic playing the University of Kentucky fight song. People usually get up from the table and start clapping along.

It's been nice having old friends like Jodi, Dave, and Barbara. They've made the transition to Lexington easier. Occasionally, I have some of our other East Coast friends down for a long weekend during the season. I've even introduced Lexington to some Damon Runyon characters like Jersey Red Ford, Larry the Scout, and John Parisella.

I met John when I was at Providence College. Joe Taub, the minority stockholder of the Nets, threw a Final Four party for me and John was there. John was a New Yorker, one of the leading horse trainers on the East Coast. He had a reputation of being a trainer to the stars. James Caan, Don Rickles, Don Adams, and Jack Klugman all had horses trained by John. John and his friends in the barn became big Providence fans during our tournament run. He also loved the Knicks and was a regular at most of our games. He even gave some of his younger horses basketball names like Knick Press, Pitino Ball, Stolen Pass, Friar Magic, and Backcourt Pass.

Jersey Red Ford teaches culinary arts at Durfee High in Massachusetts. Jersey had been the cook in our fraternity at UMass. I hired him. He had an impressive résumé. He had been a chef in Miami, or so his phony references stated. His first week on the job, he was cooking Beef Wellington. We thought we were at the Waldorf. Then one night I came back to the house and asked, "What's for dinner?" and he told me to go get a pizza. I did. The next night it was the same thing. Soon Jersey was telling us not to bother him. He was watching *Jeopardy* on TV, running a fraternity betting pool, and had become a campus character. So long Beef Wellington. Instead of firing him, we inducted him into the fraternity. I made him my little brother.

Jersey is the consummate sports fan. He grew up in Jersey City. He loves all the New York teams and is very vocal about his feelings. He's been known to call George Steinbrenner "a great living American." He calls radio talk shows all the time, just to needle the New England sports fans. When I became the Knicks' coach, he was in his glory. When I went to Kentucky, he started wearing a Kentucky jacket and sticking the antenna of his radio out the window of his apartment, just so he could pick up our games.

I call Jersey all the time, just to listen to the crazy messages he leaves on his telephone answering machine. He makes up a new one daily and an average of 70 to 80 people call, just to hear him bury the Celtics, Patriots, and Red Sox. I will never admit it to him, but the Red Sox are my second favorite baseball team.

I've known Larry the Scout for about 25 to 30 years. His real name is Larry Pearlstein. But everybody refers to him as "Scout" because he's usually the guy who has the scoop on everything in basketball in New York City. He saw his first game in the Garden back in 1938, when he was 13. His roster of all time greats includes Ralph Beard of Kentucky. Scout considers Beard a better college player than Bob Cousy, and isn't shy about telling people. Scout is unique, to say the least.

I also have a few friends in Lexington and the state of Kentucky—Brent Rice, a local attorney who handles some of our business affairs; Craig Turner, a real estate developer; Steve Graves, a real estate developer and architect who designed our home; Greg Williamson and Stan Kerrick; Seth Hancock, and L. D. Gorman.

They're golfing buddies. But my close friends are the members of my staff. They're the people who go into battle each day.

L.D. and Seth represent the two economic halves of Kentucky—coal and horses. L.D. owns four coal mines and two banks in Hazard, up in the mountains of eastern Kentucky. Although he's one of the richest men in the state, he prefers the simple lifestyle of his hometown.

Seth and his family have run Claiborne Farm for the past 14 years and his operation is home to 650 horses. Seth has helped develop Claiborne into a national landmark. The farm used to get upwards of 10,000 visitors a year when Secretariat, the greatest race horse of all time, lived there. Secretariat died in 1985. He is buried right beside the office, and there are always floral arrangements at his grave.

I had never really thought about owning a horse until we moved here, although I suspect that everybody in Kentucky has owned a horse at one time. Seth invited me to the Derby my first year. He had a horse he really liked a lot, a yearling named Rail. Seth, Larry Ivy, our business manager at UK, Billy Minardi, and I each contributed 25 percent. L.D. came to see Rail run his maiden race. When the horse lost, he was so upset he offered to give me 20 percent of his own horse. I've since made a trip to the winner's circle when Rail won a race at Churchill Downs. The horse made $60,000 last year, so it more than paid for the investment.

I also own 20 percent of a brood mare named Wall Street Girl. Her co-owners are Governor Brereton Jones, L. D. Gorman, and singer Glen Campbell. I just bought a piece of another horse, Tourney, with Seth. She's a two-year-old now, and Seth thinks she has the most potential.

The thoroughbred horse farms in Kentucky are feeling the effects of the current recession. The tax laws are stacked against the owners, who can't deduct their losses. Millionaires are losing $50 to $60 million and declaring bankruptcy. Calumet was $80 million in debt before the sheriff padlocked the gates in July 1991. Unless the horse farms get some federal help, they may disappear from Kentucky. That would not only alter the landscape of the Bluegrass, it would also take away from its heritage.

I feel like I'm a Kentuckian now, but I'm still adjusting to the lifestyle. I still haven't gotten into country western music. I only know one country western group—the Gatlin Brothers. I've heard of Randy Travis, but I like Tony Bennett, Frank Sinatra.

When Reba McEntire was in town for a concert at Rupp last spring, I received a call in the office. It was Marta. "Coach, Reba McEntire and Ronnie Milsap would like to meet you."

I said, "Marta, I can't. I've got to be somewhere for an appointment."

When I got back, I got this picture with the inscription, "Love ya, Reba." I was reading *USA Today* this fall, see her picture and didn't believe how big she was in the country music industry. I've since followed country music more closely, and hope I'll have the honor of meeting Reba McEntire and Ronnie Milsap at some point.

The way I figure it, the folks here are still getting used to my New York accent. I know our receptionist Suzetta Yates had problems understanding me or any other New Yorker. My first month at Kentucky, she received a phone call and the party on the other end identified himself as Gary Brokaw, Iona College. She came back to my office and gave me the message.

"Coach," she said, "there's this guy named Gary Brokaw on the line and he says he owns a college."

# --5--

# *AND I SAW IT ALL ON MY RADIO*

$T$he banners hanging from the rafters in Rupp Arena commemorate all the great moments in Kentucky basketball and all the people who made them possible.

There are the blue and white NCAA Championship banners from 1948, 1949, 1951, 1958 and 1978 and one for the 1976 NIT. There are the banners from 37 SEC Conference championships. There are retired jerseys of such all-time greats as Adolph Rupp, Dan Issel, Frank Ramsey, and Cliff Hagan.

And then, there is the banner with the microphone on it.

That could represent only one person—Cawood Ledford.

In many ways, Cawood Ledford *was* Kentucky basketball. An entire generation of Kentuckians grew up listening to him on their old Zenith radios. A station once promoted him this way: "When you listen to Kentucky basketball, you don't just hear it, you see it through the eyes of Cawood Ledford."

Cawood was not only the voice and eyes of Kentucky basketball, he was also the soul. The fans in this state considered him to be *their* announcer. They believed every word he said. He was the Walter Cronkite of Kentucky.

Cawood was entering his 39th and final year of broadcasting the Wildcats' games. When he announced in June 1991 that he was going to retire at the end of the 1992 season, it sent shock waves throughout the state. The next week, I must have received 50 letters from fans, urging us to win it all for Cawood.

That doesn't surprise me. If I can't imagine Kentucky basketball without him, think how the rest of the commonwealth feels about his retirement. Cawood received more than 500 farewell letters, but his favorite came from a woman who was celebrating her 39th wedding anniversary. She wrote that on her first date with her husband, they went out to eat and then took a drive up into the mountains. She thought, "How romantic." But he had other ideas, it seemed. He took her up there just so he could pick up WHAS. He wanted to listen to Cawood do the game.

The man is a legend—and not only in Kentucky. When I was 23 years old and just starting out in the business, I used to sit around with the old-timers at P. J. Clarke's in New York and we'd discuss the top five pro players of all time, top five college players of all time. Inevitably, we'd get around to the best announcers ever and it would always come down to two guys—Marty Glickman and Cawood Ledford.

So I knew the name Cawood Ledford long before I came to Kentucky. He lived up to all my expectations, not only as an announcer but as a person.

Cawood came to the University of Kentucky as an unknown, untested voice from Harlan County, deep in the mountains of eastern Kentucky. He helped give Kentucky basketball a bigger-than-life quality. When he broadcast the games on WHAS, a 50,000-watt station in Louisville, from 1956 to 1979, his play-by-play was beamed to 40 different states. The station received mail from UK fans in all of them. He's gone on to work for the Kentucky Sports Network, whose 100 stations now carry our games.

Cawood had an informative, no-nonsense style. He was so popular that in many households, when the games were on TV, the fans would turn down the volume on their sets and tune in Cawood. He made some of his phrases legendary in Kentucky, especially his traditional, "The Wildcats are moving to the right hand side of your radio dial." He extended the life of radio, at least in this state. In some mountain communities, I was told, "the porch lights don't go off until Cawood signs off."

And that's another thing. He's always been Cawood, never Mr. Ledford. To the farmer on his tractor with the radio strapped on his arm . . . to the coal miner returning from his shift . . . to the factory worker discussing the game the next morning. When he signs on with "Hello everybody, this is Cawood Ledford," he means everybody.

He's the ticket for the fans who can't afford the prices at Rupp.

When Cawood broadcast his first Kentucky game on WLEX in 1953, I was just a baby in New York, and Adolph Rupp was the coach at Kentucky. That night, Cliff Hagan scored 51 points against Temple. Cawood remembers that game, and many others. Cawood was one of the last links between the Rupp era and our staff.

Rupp was the most powerful man in Kentucky when Cawood first started out. He could make or break the members of the media. And Cawood knew this. They still tell the famous story that once upon a time, early in his career, Cawood criticized a less than perfect performance by a Kentucky team during one road game. When the game ended and Cawood was getting onto the team bus, Rupp called him over and asked him what he had said in his broadcast.

After Cawood repeated his comments, Rupp nodded his head and said, "Good. When one of my teams plays badly, by god, burn 'em."

Cawood's reaction: "I felt he had given me some freedom."

The two went on to become good friends. In later years, their postgame shows had elements of a comedy routine.

Cawood has seen it all. He has celebrated the championships and suffered through the scandals. To him, the longest year will always be 1988, the year of the NCAA investigation. To him and the rest of the fans, the unimaginable had happened.

"I was so miserable," he said. "It was no fun. I really dreaded the preparation work, dreaded everything. I thought I'd been here a long time, this might be a good time to quit. Then I thought that would really be a coward's way out."

But Cawood didn't leave them. He couldn't. Kentucky had to stage a comeback, and Cawood had to describe it to the fans.

During our first year at Kentucky, he would sit there, puff on his Benson and Hedges cigarettes and paint wonderful word pictures of former stars like Johnny Cox, Dan Issel, Kyle Macy, and 7' 0" center Sam Bowie, who Cawood felt could have been the best player ever at Kentucky had he stayed healthy.

Bowie was the star of the last Kentucky team to make it to the Final Four in 1984. He was drafted by Portland, just ahead of Michael Jordan. Five other players from that team—Mel Turpin, Jim Master, Dickey Beal, Kenny Walker, and Roger Harden—were also eventually drafted by the pros. I say that because Cawood felt we inherited the worst talent in the history of the program. I think that's why he had such a soft spot for our 14–14 team.

Cawood taught me more about the tradition of Kentucky basketball than anyone. I know he was happy when C. M. Newton came up with the idea of inviting all the Kentucky lettermen back to campus for a reunion luncheon. We've also honored former stars Cotton Nash, members of Rupp's Runts, and the 1974–75 Final Four team at home games. We've also started retiring jerseys of our former All-America players.

But nobody gets to the fans and the team like Cawood. When he appeared at courtside for a home game recently, the

Kentucky pep band saluted him in unison with a loud, "Hello Cawood!"

Nobody wanted to say goodbye.

When Jim Host, the Lexington businessman who put together the Sports Communications conglomerate, said Ralph Hacker would be the lead announcer on the new broadcast team after Cawood retires, I knew it would ruffle some feathers.

Ralph is the president of Lexington radio station WVLK. He is the vice president of the Kentucky Lottery Commission, the chairman of the Lexington Convention and Tourism Bureau. He was Cawood's right-hand man on radio, and at times television commentator on UK football and basketball for 20 years. He had done spot duty calling games on CBS, ESPN, and the SEC network.

I like Ralph, but I think he'll have to fight an uphill battle with the fans because he is replacing a legend. His relationship with Wallace Wilkinson and Eddie Sutton has not helped him. I admire Ralph for his loyalty to his friends, no matter in how unpopular a light it is viewed.

Kentucky basketball is big business. It goes out over the air to ten TV stations and 100 radio stations. The rights fees have brought in an incredible amount of money. In January 1992, Jim Host's Sports Communications submitted the lone bid to retain the rights—$1,525,000 a year to broadcast Kentucky football and basketball games over the next four years. Host offered $925,000 a year for the radio rights for both sports; $75,000 per game for live basketball telecasts; $21,500 per game for delayed basketball telecasts; and $12,500 per game for delayed football telecasts. In addition, Host agreed to pay the football and basketball coaches for our radio and TV shows.

I tape my TV show every Sunday morning with Rob Bromley, the sports anchor at TV 27, and Ralph Hacker. Originally, I had suggested to Jim Host that Phyllis George be my co-host.

But instead of Phyllis replacing Rob, we added Ralph Hacker. Now, there's something wrong with that thinking. Instead of Miss America, I get Ralph Hacker. Next season, I'd like to make some more realistic changes. I'd like to be more analytical and talk about our system. Maybe I'll get the chance.

There never seems to be a time when Kentucky basketball is out of season. Billy Donovan and his wife Christine moved to Lexington in April 1989. One day while he was working on his house and listening to the radio, he heard Cawood call: "Minniefield with the ball, crosses halfcourt against the Hoosiers . . ."

For a moment, he thought he was lost in the twilight zone. As it turned out, the local station was just replaying a broadcast of a Kentucky-Indiana game in the early '80s.

It's no different with television. This year Kentucky appeared on network TV three times, ESPN five times, and SEC TV nine times. Local TV picked up the rest, with the exception of our game at South Carolina, January 4.

I used to have the Lexington *Herald–Leader* delivered to our house every morning, but I've canceled my subscription.

I feel that the *Herald–Leader* sees itself as the watchdog of Kentucky basketball. The paper won a Pulitzer prize for its 1985 exposé on illegal activities of boosters within the program.

Kentucky got its wrists slapped. The paper received bomb threats and even had a bullet fired through its window. The day the story broke, the two reporters involved received anonymous death threats. One of the writers claimed he was tipped off by someone close to the program. He was told he shouldn't be surprised if, on leaving his office one day, he saw a state trooper taking cocaine out of the tires of his car. Businesses began pulling their ads, and there were bumper stickers advocating, "Send the *Herald–Leader* to Knoxville." One local club even held an Anti–*Herald Leader* rally, where they sold subscriptions to the rival Louisville *Courier–Journal.*

The paper claimed it had tapes from former players to back up its allegations. Kentucky fans wanted the paper to release them after all but two of the players interviewed claimed they were misquoted or quoted out of context. The paper cited first amendment rights and refused to do so.

Then came 1988 and the latest investigation. The paper felt the university had been involved in several coverups. Eddie Sutton had been taking heat ever since the Chris Mills story broke nationally. Sutton had said his name had never been associated with any of this, but there were so many conflicting accounts.

When the NCAA issued a report charging UK with permitting Eric Manuel to compete in regular season play when he was inelligible because his test score was not legitimate, Sutton began to issue a series of statements, seeking to protect his son Sean, who was in the same room with Eric at Lafayette High School that day, and who had given inconsistent testimony about whether he and the coach of Lafayette High School had gone to the test in a car together.

What really hurt Sutton's credibility with the media was the Shawn Kemp affair. Again, it involved Sean Sutton. Eddie filed a police report after Sean had reported the gold chains stolen from his room. When Eddie realized a video camera in a local pawnshop had recorded Shawn Kemp pawning the jewelry, he issued a statement claiming the whole thing was a misunderstanding. But every TV station and newspaper already had a copy of the police report because everything in Kentucky is subject to an Open Records Law—including Kentucky's 1989 response to the NCAA allegations.

On April 9, 1992, the state Supreme Court ruled the document was not exempt under Kentucky's Open Records Law. The Louisville *Courier–Journal* had filed a lawsuit seeking the records. It was later joined by the Lexington *Herald–Leader* and the *Kentucky Post.*

The University of Kentucky had to comply, and so released

more than 4,000 pages of material to the public. The media paid $400 for each copy, and one is available for public inspection in the Margaret I. King Library at UK's Lexington campus.

The university did not disclose an additional 25 documents dealing with the allegations against Manuel in order to comply with a federal judge's 1989 ruling keeping his academic record private. What emerged was a portrait of a program scrambling to put the best face on a bad situation. The scars haven't healed and, as a result, today, the Kentucky basketball coach must be beyond reproach. My every move is scrutinized.

Anytime I receive something I feel is taxable, I report it ... like the free telephone service I have because I do commercials for TMC Long Distance. Dawahare's department store gives me ten suits a year. Last spring, the IRS came in and audited Dawahare's. The first question they asked was, "We understand you give ten suits to Rick Pitino. Does he pay taxes on them?" You've got to dot every I, cross every T. You never know if the IRS agent is a Louisville fan.

In addition to the federal government, the *Herald-Leader*, the Louisville *Courier*, and the local TV stations are also checking into my personal business.

In September we sent out 800 letters to the Chamber of Commerce promoting a one-man motivational seminar I did that year. Anytime I use university stationery for personal business, I reimburse the school. That's standard procedure. Less than a month after the seminar, I had not yet received an invoice from the university. The Louisville *Courier-Journal* was already inquiring about this. Our assistant AD, Gene DeFilippo, knocked at my door at four o'clock one afternoon. I could see he was panicking. I told him to relax; we hadn't done anything wrong.

During the recent governor's race, my restaurant catered a Democratic fundraiser at Brereton Jones's farm in Versailles. I went over to make sure everything was in working order. He asked if I would stick around and say hello to the people. I told him I would be glad to accommodate.

I said a few words, wished him luck, but told people I did not get involved in politics. I said I could not endorse anyone as a candidate but, as a friend, I could endorse Brereton Jones as a person because I liked his stance on education and health care for the elderly. In the next few days, I received some fascinating letters, protesting my support for him.

There are times when I feel like Big Brother is watching. Jerry Tipton of the *Herald–Leader* covers us 365 days a year. His baby was due the same time as ours and the joke making the rounds in the basketball office was that he planned it that way so he could get into the maternity ward.

The media got their first chance to watch us play at our annual Blue-White scrimmage in October. At a press conference afterwards, Jerry Tipton's first question, after having not seen the team play for a year, was whether I was disappointed that Memorial Coliseum wasn't sold out. I was amazed that was all he could think about after watching an entire basketball game for the first time this year.

Everybody knows Kentucky basketball sells out every game, and has the second largest attendance in the country. My response was: "Jerry, I don't care. When are you going to stop looking for negative things? Sooner or later, you're going to stop trying to find a cloud in every silver lining."

The next day, he thought I had something against him. He came in to meet with me and brought along his sports editor Gene Abel. In a two-hour discussion, the only mutual agreement we had was that newspaper people are not negative, they're cynical. They claimed reporters must be cynical to do their jobs. I disagreed. They said they were suspicious of the University of Kentucky and had been so for a long time.

The *Herald–Leader* is always talking about keeping athletics in perspective, but I'm constantly amused at what it views as front-page news. When we played at Georgia last year, I banged my fist so hard on the scorer's table, the plywood surface flew up and accidentally ripped the dress of the school's scorekeeper. The next morning, it was a full-length, front-page story.

When workmen poured the subconcrete for the floor at Rupp, the *Herald-Leader* sent a photographer out, and *that* was front-page news. When the cheerleaders changed uniforms, *that* was front-page news. When they found out North Carolina had five more victories than Kentucky, that was BIG front-page news.

I don't see the *Herald-Leader* scrutinizing Louisville basketball or even Kentucky football the same way. The tolerance for Kentucky basketball seems to be much lower, and it shows in its reporting. But New York has taught me well about the newspaper industry, so I know the way the game is played.

Two of our players were asked to leave a fraternity party in October. Jerry Tipton was on the phone the next day, trying to get details from the president of the chapter. Later, the paper wanted to turn it into a racial issue because the players were black and the fraternity was predominantly white. After finding out that the incident had nothing to do with race, I did some research into the *Herald-Leader*'s minority hiring policy. I found out from P. J. Peeples of the Urban League that the *Herald-Leader* does not have a very good track record in that area. At the time of this writing, there are no black writers in the sports department who cover UK basketball. I find that odd.

For the *Herald-Leader* to be investigating fraternity parties is ridiculous. But there is precedent. I once went to speak at a fraternity meeting, and one of the members asked if we had any recruits coming in. I told him we did, then I asked Chris Cameron if I was allowed to speak about that.

"Yes sir," he said, "no media here."

Somebody contacted the paper within a half hour.

We had the best recruiting class in the country this year, but the *Herald-Leader* insisted on running a big story in

December, pointing out that only three of our four recruits had met the Proposition 48 guidelines, which currently require a student to achieve a 2.0 in 12 core courses and a minimum score of either a 700 in the SAT or a 17 on the ACT. They went on to say that Jared Prickett, one of our signees, did not score 700 on his SAT. *USA Today* picked it up the next day.

When I spoke with Gene Abel and Jerry Tipton earlier this fall, I told them I didn't like their printing a player's test scores while he was still in high school. "You have no right to print their standardized test scores in the paper," I said. They agreed, but only for a minute. I felt they were projecting an image to their readers that was false.

When sensitive material like that reaches print, these young men are branded. It's an embarrassment to their families. High school guidance counselors and coaches are not supposed to release test scores because it violates the right-of-privacy act. But it always leaks out, usually through a teacher who's a friend of a friend. At its recent convention, the NCAA took steps to alleviate part of the problem when it passed legislation prohibiting a student athlete from making an official visit to a campus until he meets his SAT or ACT requirement.

The *Herald-Leader* chose to ignore our wishes, and the right-of-privacy act, as well. I'll give an example of how dangerous this practice can be. On the day after the story appeared, Jared received his ACT score. He got a higher ACT score, and was eligible. But, all over the country, the perception was that he had failed. I guarantee *USA Today* won't retract and run a story saying he made his grades. The *Herald-Leader* probably wouldn't, either.

I feel that the end of a prospect's senior year in high school, when the last exam is over, is the proper time for the media to declare whether he is eligible to play as a freshman or is a Proposition 48. But for the *Herald-Leader* to mention a recruit's particular test score is not responsible journalism. I can just hear all these guys sitting around in a bar and say-ing, "Hey, you get four hundred just for signing your name." How many times have you heard that nonsense? I would like to take some of them recruiting with me.

The interest in Kentucky basketball lasts 12 months a year. Fans want to devour everything about our team and the media obliges them.

Oscar Combs has been following Kentucky basketball ever since he can remember. After he graduated from college, he bought a local weekly newspaper in Hazard. Then another. He was set for life, and could have retired before he was 40.

But his main interest, beside his vast trading-card collec-tion, was always Kentucky basketball. At the 1976 National Invitation Tournament in New York, he kept bumping into Kentucky fans from all over the country. They came from Texas, Iowa, New York, and each had an intense interest in the program. Oscar was more than happy to fill their needs. Oscar moved to Lexington and started a new publication called, *The Cats' Pause*, which catered to Kentucky's subway alumni. Oscar knew the magazine would sell because the typical Kentucky fan is not a UK graduate, but someone who has become addicted to our program.

*The Cats' Pause* is 17 years old, and has more than 10,000 subscribers from all over the world—including the former Soviet Union. *Cawood on Kentucky,* another specialty publi-cation edited by Tom Wallace, fills a similar role.

# --6--

# *KENTUCKY BORN AND BRED*

$F$or some, playing at Kentucky has always been a calling.

Adolph Rupp once said, "When a Kentucky baby is born, his mother naturally wants him to be president, like another Kentuckian, Abraham Lincoln. If not president, she wants him to play basketball for the University of Kentucky."

They could hear the siren's song in Paintsville, Manchester, Tollesboro, Hopkinsville, Maysville, and other small towns throughout the distant corners of the Commonwealth, where Kentucky basketball has become a religious experience and Kentucky players are the high priests.

I got a strong taste of that again in July 1991 when L. D. Gorman, who is on the state's Economics Jobs and Development Board, asked me to speak to a group of disadvantaged students who were in a summer jobs program at Hindman.

I flew to Hazard—a town with a population of 6,000—on a

private plane with L.D.'s son Dewey. We landed at a tiny airstrip, with a runway tucked into the mountains. We were greeted by a state trooper, who gave us a police escort, even though the four-lane highway was almost empty. On the way up the Mountain Highway, we could see the trucks carrying coal down from the mines.

The summers in Hazard are humid. There are times when the temperature and humidity combine to make conditions unbearable. But the gym at Knott Central High School was packed when we arrived. L.D. originally told me there would be about 300 kids. There were more like 3,000.

John Pelphrey, Richie Farmer, and Deron Feldhaus had driven up from Lexington to appear with me. A local rock group was performing as a warmup act, but the noise paled in comparison to the squeals from teenage girls when our three in-state seniors were introduced. Some of the girls were hyperventilating, screaming as if the Beatles had just arrived. I mean, John Pelphrey's a good-looking kid, but he's not Don Johnson.

When I took the microphone, I asked if there were any Louisville fans in the audience.

There was dead silence. "They hate the Big Red up here," Dewey assured me.

Any Eastern Kentucky fans?

Morehead State?

As soon as I mentioned Kentucky, the place erupted.

The people up there live and die for Kentucky basketball. In many ways, it's all they've got. This is Appalachia. But Kentucky basketball has always been there for them. And they've always been there for Kentucky basketball. The coal barons from eastern Kentucky helped build the Wildcat Lodge. Rupp said whenever he was in trouble, he always looked to the mountains for help. Rupp signed some great ones from eastern Kentucky—stars like "Wah Wah" Jones, Dicky Parsons, Larry Pursiful, and Johnny Cox.

Richie Farmer, John Pelphrey, and Deron Feldhaus did not

always produce that kind of reaction. They came to Kentucky unwanted and unappreciated by the coaches, the fans, their teammates, and even their fellow students. But those three combined with our other senior guard, Sean Woods of Indianapolis, to become the heart of the team that resuscitated Kentucky basketball.

It means so much to Kentucky kids to play at the University of Kentucky. When Jamal Mashburn puts on a Kentucky uniform, he's proud of it and he wants to win. When John, Richie, or Deron puts it on, it's like a priest putting on his garment or a judge putting on his robe. It's a very powerful thing to them, because they've been on a mountainside, sitting on a porch, listening to Cawood all their lives. They know all the stories about Rupp's Runts and the Fiddlin' Five. They've heard them their whole lives. You can't minimize the effect that has on their motivation.

These three dreamed of playing for Kentucky. And they were willing to do whatever it took to achieve those goals.

Their roots run that deep.


Richie Farmer's parents live on Richie Farmer Boulevard in Manchester, up in Clay County.

You'll have to take my word for it.

The street sign on his block has been stolen three different times. The police suspect teenage girls, who probably just wanted a piece of history. Richie was selected MVP in the Kentucky state high school tournament two years in a row in 1986 and 1987. He led Clay County to the state championship his junior year. He was named Mr. Basketball after having led Clay County back to the finals his senior year. He scored 51 on Allan Houston, a 6′ 7″ high school All-America who now plays for Tennessee, and on the rest of his teammates during a four-point loss to Louisville Ballard at Freedom Hall.

In appreciation, his hometown named a street after him. Richie grew up in a rural town located on the Little Goose

River in the mountains of eastern Kentucky, off the Daniel Boone Parkway about 20 miles from London. The town's main employer is the Shamrock Coal Company. When times get tough, some of the farmers grow marijuana, just to make ends meet.

This is Hatfield-McCoy country. If you're not kin or a member of the Kentucky basketball team, you'd better be careful. Deron Feldhaus, who's from Maysville, is always advising anyone who goes home with Richie to pack a gun. Billy Donovan said a bazooka might be more like it.

Richie's just a country boy at heart. He chews tobacco and loves to go hunting and fishing. He got a shotgun for Christmas, and his New Year's resolution was to learn how to turkey shoot.

He once told me, "Coach, you always know where you stand with these people. If they like you, they'll give you the shirt off their backs. If they hate you—they'll kill you."

Richie's parents and his hunting dog Boo still live on the outskirts of town, in the same one-story brick house where he was raised. It's up the hill from a barn that used to house Tennessee walking horses. His bedroom is still filled with his high school trophies—including the two big ones he received for winning the MVP at the state tournament and the net he helped cut down when his team won the title.

There is a stuffed deer mounted on the wall, along with a walleye pike. There is a stuffed wildcat sitting on the floor, near his water bed. There is a quilt on the bed that was made by his grandmother. She has stitched the details of all his high school accomplishments into it.

When Richie wants to relive his high school career, all he has to do is pop a videotape into the VCR. His mother has hundreds of them, including the one of the day he signed at Kentucky in front of a crowd of 1,600 at the old high school gymnasium. The principal let the entire student body out for the press conference. When Richie announced what everyone had suspected all along, he had to hold back the tears. He received a standing ovation from the students and the local fans who filled up the balcony seats.

Richie had fulfilled a childhood dream. He had idolized Kyle Macy, the starting guard on Kentucky's 1978 NCAA championship team. Richie was nine when Kentucky won its last NCAA title, but he snuck a radio into his bedroom just to listen to the game.

In first grade, he already knew what he wanted to be when he grew up. When Richie's teacher asked the class that question, he wrote down he wanted to play for UK. The teacher still has the note, along with Richie's first-grade uniform. She told Clay County Coach Bobby Keith back then that his team would win a state championship by the time Richie graduated. She was truly a prophet.

There were only 12 boys in Richie's graduating class in grade school. There were only 200 students in his graduating class in high school. There are only 20,000 people living in Clay County. But Richie put it on the map. He started for the varsity in ninth grade. By then, he already had his signature mustache and five o'clock shadow.

Richie made all-state three times. As a senior, he averaged 27.1 points, 6.4 rebounds and 8.7 assists. He beat out Kenny Anderson to win the MVP at the Beach Boy Classic in Myrtle Beach in 1987. He broke Wah Wah Jones's high school state tournament scoring record by over 100 points, with 317 points in 14 games.

But, most importantly, he led Clay County to its only state championship. The year his team won it all was the same year the movie *Hoosiers* came out. Bobby Keith took the team to see it the night before the Sweet Sixteen. There were so many similarities. Clay County was an all-white team from the mountains. Its biggest player was only 6' 2". Richie used to jump center—he claims he lost the tap only twice in his career—then moved to point guard to run Keith's double-stack offense. His brother Russ, who was 13 months younger, played the other guard. Boxhead Rollins, who played center, had gone to the same grade school.

After Clay County won the championship, a caravan of cars followed the school bus carrying the team on the two-hour trip back to the school. About eight miles outside town, they were met by other fans, standing on the side of the road, waving and holding signs. It was one of those storybook endings.

Richie dominated the state tournament his senior year. Eventually, the Kentucky staff walked into Richie's house and made a recruiting pitch. He was thrilled.

Like Richie, Deron Feldhaus had always dreamed about playing for Kentucky. When he was just ten years old, he accompanied his father to a coaching clinic in Lexington and got a tour of the Wildcat Lodge, which had just opened. "I never knew I'd be living there one day," he said.

Deron had never received star treatment in his own house. His father Allen, Sr., who is 6' 5", played for Rupp in the early '60s. Allen's nickname was "Horse," and he's still remembered for breaking Jerry West's nose when the Cats played West Virginia in the 1961 Kentucky Invitational Tournament.

His father coached at Mason County, where all three of his sons played for him in a 6,500-seat arena. Allen Jr. went on to play at Eastern Kentucky. Willie played at Morehead. Deron was the baby of the family, and his brothers used to gang up on him when he was younger during roughhouse pickup basketball games. Once Deron began to grow, he found that he could hold his own.

When Deron was in ninth grade, his parents were divorced, but his mother Dottie stayed in Maysville, so Deron could play for his father. It wasn't always easy. "When we would go on the road, the opposing fans would ride me," he said. "They'd call me 'Daddy's boy' and 'water boy.' It just toughened me up."

Deron made all-state twice in 1986 and 1987, and led Mason County to the quarterfinals of the Sweet Sixteen as a senior. Sutton saw Deron as a hard-nosed kid he could bring off the bench, so he signed Deron early.

You might say John Pelphrey was born to play basketball. When Jack and Jennie Pelphrey sent out the birth announcements for their firstborn son, it had a picture of a baby shooting a basketball. Although John Leslie is a family name on his mother's side, his father says his son was named after ex-Celtics great John Havlicek.

The Pelphreys took John to see his first game when he was eight months old. Jack was coaching at Piketon, Ohio, at the time, and the Pelphreys took their firstborn to watch the Ohio state tournament in Columbus. It is hard to know whether he was crying because he was teething, or pulling a Bobby Knight.

John and his younger brother Jerry, who plays for Eastern Tennessee, took to basketball early, playing countless games in the driveway in Paintsville. Their big fear was that loose balls would be crushed if they rolled into the path of oncoming cars. Because John's parents were both teachers, he never had a problem getting a key to the gym. Like Richie and Deron, John too had dreamed of playing for Kentucky since sixth grade when he started grabbing his socks before shooting free throws—just like Kyle Macy.

The small town in eastern Kentucky where John grew up is better known as the home of Loretta Lynn, Crystal Gayle, and the Kentucky Apple Festival. Before he arrived, Paintsville High had little basketball tradition. But from 1985 through 1987 John and Joey Couch, the 1991 captain of Kentucky's football team, led their team to three straight appearances in the Sweet Sixteen. John was selected Mr. Basketball his senior year in 1987, and later signed with UK. John's parents bought a new Cadillac so they could make the two-hour drive to Lexington, just to watch him play.

It could have been a fairytale come true for all three. But John and Deron were redshirted their first year in 1987, the same season Kentucky went to the NCAA Sweet Sixteen. In 1988, Richie played as a freshman and even had a big moment, making a three-pointer at the buzzer to give Kentucky a one-point victory over Ole Miss at Rupp Arena.

Richie played in 27 games that year, averaging 3.1 points and thirteen minutes of playing time. But he went from being a star to a scrub on Kentucky's first losing team in 62 years. Deron got his first taste of playing time the same year, averaging 3.7 points as a sub. As for John, he was on the roster, too, that year but averaged only 1.7 points and missed eight games with a stress fracture.

Richie was upset because he wanted more playing time. Deron and John did, too. Then Eddie Sutton resigned that March. He was followed out the door by most of the better players. For those remaining, it was a brandnew game, but it was the only game in town because no other major college was recruiting them.

They had no idea what to expect after the NCAA sanctions hit. They only knew it wasn't going to be the same. The immediate result was no scholarships, no television, a big *P* on their chests. They didn't want to be remembered as part of the team that brought the Roman Empire down. They wanted to build Rome back up, and they stayed to do it.

Their lives have changed in the last three years. They were central to what we accomplished. John became a great leader. Richie became our most dependable outside shooter. And Deron became the ultimate sixth man, in the grand tradition of John Havlicek and Frank Ramsay of the Boston Celtics.

For Deron, the team always came first. When I thought we might need a scholarship for another big man last year, Deron offered to give up his student aid and walk on if we signed Chris Webber, a 6' 9" high school All-America center from Detroit. It didn't happen, but it doesn't lessen his selflessness.

They are three of the biggest reasons why this will be one of the most beloved Kentucky programs in history. And it's easy to see why.

Even though 1992 the last hurrah for Richie, Deron, and John, we still have two more Kentucky-born players on our roster. The tradition continues with Travis Ford, a 5' 8" junior guard; and Chris Harrison, a 6' 3" sophomore guard.

Travis Ford, who the players call "Doogie" because he reminds them of Doogie Howser on TV, is from Madisonville. He averaged 31.7 points and 8 assists as a senior at North Hopkins High and was selected the MVP at the McDonald's Capitol Classic. He really wanted to come to Kentucky, but Eddie Sutton never recruited him because he already had his son Sean and Richie Farmer on the roster. Travis signed at Missouri and played there for a season. But he still followed Kentucky all the time. When the NCAA put Missouri on probation after his freshman year in 1990, he made known his intentions to transfer.

I was spending the summer in New York when his father Eddie, who coaches the Kentucky Junior AAU All Stars, called me. "Listen," he said, "I guess you're not interested in my son because you would have called."

I told him that wasn't the case. The reason we hadn't called was because we thought Travis didn't have an official release from Missouri. When Eddie told me the paperwork was in order and that Travis would like to consider Kentucky, I told him we were interested. Then he said Travis was going to visit North Carolina. Then LSU was going to send a private plane to pick him up.

I got upset.

"Okay. Then he's not interested in Kentucky."

"No, he is."

"Well let me say this, Eddie. If he takes one step on Carolina's campus, he will not be given a scholarship to the University of Kentucky."

"Why?"

"Because, from what I understand, it's been a childhood dream of his to play for the University of Kentucky. Now, I'm giving him a scholarship, passing on some high school All-Americans like Travis Best and Cory Alexander. If your son visits other places, I take it he wants to be recruited again, just like he was in high school. I don't believe transfers should ever leave a program unless they have a program to go to. So, if you're not sure what you're looking for, Kentucky's not the place for him."

Eddie called the next day and said Travis was coming to Kentucky. Then, Eddie said he wanted to hold two press conferences—one in Madisonville and one in Lexington. I had to put my foot down again. I told him there would be only one press conference and it would be short and to the point.

I can appreciate how Eddie felt. He's Travis's father. But he's also a coach, so he appreciated how I felt.

Chris Harrison was the leading scorer in the Commonwealth his senior year. He averaraged 39.4 points and 4.8 three-pointers for Tollesboro, a Class A school whose enrollment was just 150 students. The mountain town was tiny, and his uncle was his high school coach. Chris had a high game of 73 and a green light to do whatever he wanted. He also had his own fan club, 300 strong, who wore T-shirts with his name on them and followed his every game.

Chris committed to us before the start of his senior year. There were some questions about whether he could play at this level, but I took him because I liked what I saw when he attended our basketball camp. I was playing him in a game of one-on-one and I liked his moves. That, combined with the fact he was a Kentucky kid, convinced me to take a chance.

Just like we had with his roommate Richie.

I've learned never to underestimate Richie's popularity among the fans in Kentucky. Richie told me he has been receiving letters lately from Karen Brown, a woman who's in prison for a contract murder. She even named one of her pet fish Richie.

"Coach," he said, "she's been upset about the way you yell at me."

"I hope you told her it's for your own good, Richie," I said, fearing she may get out of prison in the near future.

# --7--

# *THE CURTAIN GOES UP*

$\mathbf{T}$he anticipation started to mount at six o'clock the morning of Friday, October 18, when the Vallandingham family from New Albany, Indiana, just across the river from Louisville, arrived to begin a 34-hour vigil outside Memorial Coliseum.

Robert Vallandingham, a fireman in his early 60s, and his wife Laura drove down to Lexington with their 29-year-old twin sons, Donald and Ronald. They brought along lawn chairs, a radio, a cooler, newspapers, and a book of puzzles.

They had been first in line for Big Blue Madness—the official celebration honoring the start of another basketball season at Kentucky—last fall, and had become celebrities for a day when several fans snapped pictures of them. This year, when someone sent them a letter, threatening to beat them out, the Vallandinghams got up at four in the morning just to ensure their position.

I invited them in to watch our practice that afternoon, but they were concerned about losing their place in line. I told them, "If you do, I'll ask the people in front of you to move." They didn't budge.

That night, it turned cold. The temperatures got down in the 40s. The staff at Memorial Coliseum gave the family unique wristbands that bore the words, "1st in Line," and told them they could spend the night in a hotel and reclaim their spot in the morning. They still didn't budge, huddling in the corner by the ticket window. I wasn't surprised. I had seen the intensity that surrounds our version of Midnight Madness.

Chris Cameron, our sports information director, had worked since June to choreograph this event, which was part Broadway, part Vegas revue, complete with bells, whistles, and flashing lights. In addition, we had the school pep band, formal introductions of the players and staff, a highlight film, and a half-hour intrasquad scrimmage. Something for everybody.

When I was coaching at Boston University, I tried to stage something like that once at the Case Center gymnasium. I even arranged for champagne. Only 14 people showed up, and most of them were my relatives.

Memorial Coliseum has 10,000 seats, and every one of them was filled. The NBC affiliate in Louisville planned to televise the entire spectacle live, from eight to ten P.M. WKYT-TV, the CBS affiliate in Lexington, which carries our games, had to televise it on a delayed basis. The reason? They were committed to the World Series, although at one point I heard they were toying with the idea of running the Series on a delayed basis.

We could have held Big Blue Madness at Rupp Arena, the cavernous coliseum in the heart of downtown where we play our home games. But Chris and Gene DeFilippo liked the idea of people waiting in line. They liked the idea of a frenzied atmosphere. Chris Cameron said it best: "We won't move it, not until we have to turn 13,000 people away."

Memorial Coliseum opened in 1950. It cost $3.9 million by the time it was completed, and was considered one of the showplaces of the South. From the beginning, tickets were at a premium. The situation got to the point where only the season ticket holders, student body, and faculty were admitted. The rest of the fans had to settle for information from the radio and newspapers.

The building served Kentucky well. The team won every game played there until January 8, 1955, when Georgia Tech won in an upset, 59–58. The loss broke a 129-game home-court winning streak, dating back to the old Alumni Gym days in 1943. "When the game was over, nobody moved," Cawood recalled. "Everyone sat in absolute stunned silence."

Kentucky was 308–38 from 1950–1976, when Rupp Arena opened.

When I arrived, I discovered the team was still using the same locker rooms that C. M. Newton had used when he played for Adolph Rupp in 1951. We had no proper weight room, only a row of Nautilus machines tucked away under a section of bleachers. And our offices were cramped.

C.M., Gene DeFilippo, and Larry Ivy hired local architects. They devised a plan to remove 2,000 seats in the north end-zone and replace them with a two-story complex that would provide modern facilities for the team and coaches, as well as office space for the administration. The cost of the renovation would be $1.2 million. The Kentucky Athletic Association raised the money in seven weeks. Now, if I can only get them to replace that old scoreboard timer we have to reset by hand anytime we run a drill. I don't think Adolph Rupp would mind.

The official start of practice was actually 12:01 A.M., October 15, but we moved the celebration back to the weekend so we could accommodate four of our biggest recruits—forward Rodrick Rhodes of St. Anthony's High in Jersey City, center Walter McCarty of Harrison High in Evansville, forward Jared Prickett of West Fairmont High in Fairmont, West Virginia, and guard Tony Delk of Haywood High in Brownsville, Tennessee—who were all in for their official visits.

We knew we were tampering with the traditional Midnight Madness Kentuckians had come to expect, but we hoped the fans would forgive us once they understood what was at stake.

We had our recruits over to our house Friday night for a get-together with the team. We gave rings to the players and coaches for achieving the best record in the SEC in 1991. They tailgated with us at our football game the next afternoon. Then we took them over to the gym.

It's a good thing we arrived early. It was a mob scene. The fans lined up four and five deep in both directions on Euclid Street. The lines snaked completely around the block. The doors opened at 6:30 P.M. By 7:10, the fire marshal ordered them shut, leaving several members of the Board of Trustees outside looking in. We finally squeezed them in through a back entrance. Chris Cameron came out and said, "We turned away four thousand people."

The lights went out at eight. The music to "Eye in the Sky" by The Alan Parsons Project came on, and the season blasted off. I knew this would be a moment to remember as I stood at half-court with a microphone, surrounded by a wild-eyed crowd dressed in blue and white.

One of the highlights of the night was Chris Harrison making 16 straight free throws. Most of the fans who watched our scrimmage that night must have thought they were looking at a Top 10 team. We were no longer the underdog or, as John Pelphrey said, the little engine that could.

But looking at our team, I had more questions than answers. This was the deepest team and the best group of shooters I had coached in my three years at Kentucky, but I still had reservations. I didn't know who was going to replace our departed senior captain Reggie Hanson at center. I didn't know who would become our shooting guard. I didn't know whether we could play good enough defense to survive a dangerous schedule.

Our league was so much stronger. Alabama, LSU, and Arkansas were all ranked nationally. Florida, Georgia, Tennessee, and Vanderbilt were all talking NCAA tournament.

We had to play Indiana, which was ranked second in the nation and was the Big Ten favorite, at the Hoosier Dome in Indianapolis. We had to play Ohio University, which was picked to win the MAC. We had to play Massachusetts, the preseason favorite in the Atlantic 10. We had to play state rivals Louisville, Eastern Kentucky, Morehead, and Western Kentucky. Notre Dame, West Virginia, Georgia Tech, and Arizona State were also on the schedule.

And we were walking a thin line every game. I felt we could win the SEC championship, or lose to anyone on our schedule.

The Associated Press ranked us in the Top 10 in the 1991 final poll, but I had serious doubts about whether we could have advanced very far into the NCAA tournament, had we been eligible to play. We treated every game like it was the end of the world. This intensity took its toll on the team. The players were exhausted by March. This season, I decided to prepare a little differently because I was concerned about burnout. Instead of trying to be ready by the end of November, I was pointing to the end of February.

I felt we had gained a distinct advantage last year because we averaged 30 hours a week on the practice floor. This year, a new NCAA rule restricted practice time to 20 hours a week, with one day off. We had to make every second count. The 20-hour rule really slowed our progress because we couldn't do any film work. Instead of an hour of individual instruction in the morning, we did 40 minutes. Our practices went for almost two and a half hours. We did 15 minutes of film work, when formerly we had done an hour a day. It cut down on our learning and made team development a slower process.

I was hoping Jamal Mashburn, our 6′ 8″ power forward, could inspire the others to quicken their paces. He had gone from a rookie to an impact player in just one year. When I looked at our senior class, I didn't see any NBA players. Jamal was our only potential pro, and he was a 19-year-old sophomore. Mash had been his team's go-to guy ever since his sophomore season at Cardinal Hayes in the Bronx. He had not been rated that high by the so-called gurus, nor had he been selected to play in any of the big national all-star games, but we considered him the best player in New York. He later proved us right when he led his team to the state championship and was named Mr. Basketball. And he did this in a year when the New York City Catholic League produced such high school All-America players as Klahid Reeves and Derrick Phelps at Christ the King and Adrian Autry and Brian Reese at Tolentine.

Mash played for the New York Gauchos, one of New York City's two AAU powerhouses. I've always had a strong relationship with Lew D'Almeida and Dave McCullough there, and with Ernie Lorch of the Riverside Church Hawks. They feel their players will get a lot of discipline and love if they come with us.

Everybody recognized Jamal's ability, they just questioned whether he would work hard. I remember recruiting him. I was in the Gaucho gym, talking with Jamal and his mother. It was noisy because there was a game going on downstairs. Neither of us could hear the other very well.

Finally, I said, "Jamal, everybody says this is a bad marriage. Why do you want to go to Kentucky? You will have to do all this work. We have a style of play that demands hard work."

He said to me, "Everybody says I have the ability to play at the next level and, in order to do that, I need to be forced to work hard."

I felt he'd been misunderstood so I invited him to make an official visit. When he showed up at our office, he was wearing a Syracuse cap. That gave me a bad moment.

But he sat there and told me, "Coach, I want to come."

I told him to go home and think about it.

"No," he said. "I want to play for the Knicks' coach."

So much for the glorious Kentucky tradition. When you're recruiting in the East, sell the Knicks, at least until we were off probation. When you recruit in the South and Midwest, sell Kentucky.

Sometimes if a player is quiet and shy, he gets labeled as lazy or not intense. Jamal left a big impression with us long before he played his first game at Kentucky. After Mash dominated a preseason scrimmage, John Pelphrey described him as having a "monster body." Soon afterwards, Jamal Mashburn became known as "Monster Mash."

Mash set a Kentucky freshman scoring record with 31 points against Georgia. He led us in rebounding 12 times. But he often deferred to Reggie and the upperclassmen. Mash never liked the spotlight.

He has the potential to be one of the greatest players ever at the University of Kentucky. He's a combination of Karl Malone and Jeff Malone, a 240-pound power player with the ability to shoot the ball from the perimeter. But I knew he had to step forward, much like Danny Manning did his senior year at Kansas in 1988. I also knew he couldn't do it alone if we wanted to reach our potential. He needed help inside from one of our centers.

We had to choose among 6' 8" sophomore Gimel Martinez and 6' 9" freshmen Aminu Timberlake and Andre Riddick. I figured anything Andre and Aminu gave us was a plus. Both came in weighing less than 200 pounds. You can get away with being physically immature at the one, two, or three spots; but when you are a four or five man, you have to be physically mature. Jamal was, last year. Gimel wasn't, but Rock got him to bulk up 25 pounds over the summer so we had hope.

Gimel, whose parents fled from Communist Cuba, was a high school All-America player at Miami Senior High. He suffers from scoliosis, and overcame a 37 percent curvature of his spine to became a high-profile recruit. As a senior, he averaged 24.2 points, 12.1 rebounds, and 4 blocked shots while leading his team to a third consecutive Florida state championship.

Gimel was being courted by Duke and Villanova. He received close to 150 pieces of correspondence from Iowa. He committed to Kentucky after watching one of our games at Rupp.

Once we signed Gimel, a lot of fans thought we had solved our problem in the middle. But Gimel had some major adjustments to make, both on and off the court. He struggled with the cold weather. Kentucky is a lot closer to the Midwest than the tropics. The first time the temperature dipped toward freezing, he bundled up in a jacket and gloves with a hat and ski mask. He had no idea how to take care of his car in the winter, either. When he failed to install antifreeze, the engine block cracked.

Gimel averaged just under two points as a freshman and took his share of criticism. Patience is not a virtue of the Kentucky basketball fan.

Aminu came from De La Salle High in Chicago. He was voted one of the Top 10 recruits in the city by the Windy City Roundball Review. We thought he was leaning toward Indiana or DePaul, but he visited during Big Blue Madness and committed to us when he saw an opportunity to play immediately. He averaged a modest 13.8 points and 6.8 rebounds during his senior year. His statistics might not have looked impressive, but his high school played a conservative, half-court offense and averaged less than 60 points a game. During the season, Aminu's grandfather died and he shuttled between his mother's house on the north side and his grandmother's house on the south side, helping his grandmother with the chores.

Andre grew up in the Linden projects in one of the toughest sections of the city. His father was fatally struck by a cab two blocks from his East New York tenement in 1980, when Andre was five. His older brother was murdered on the No. 2 subway train for his gold chain, when Andre was 13.

Andre was a near victim of drug violence himself last summer. A week before he was supposed to leave for school, Andre and his friends were heading home from a pickup game in a nearby park when eight cars suddenly pulled up and the occupants began firing in the direction of the projects. Some of the residents returned the fire. Andre hit the pavement, hoping to survive.

Andre was lucky. Basketball proved a way out, even though his friends had to beg him to play at Bishop Loughlin High in Brooklyn. Andre was a second team all-city pick. He was an unskilled offensive player, but he averaged 7.6 blocks his final two years in the New York City Catholic League. He was just a big, awkward kid when he started. But I felt he was the biggest sleeper in the country. As soon as he arrived, I started calling him "MacAdoo" in an effort to make him more offensive minded. My greatest concern was how to get Andre to like basketball. It was our greatest hurdle with him, getting to work at his sport.

And then there was Sean Woods.

Sean was our starting senior lead guard. He was very popular, but he wasn't from Kentucky. Our fans embraced John, Deron, and Richie because they're from the Commonwealth. Sean understood this. He grew up in Indiana, another big basketball state where Hoosier hysteria has been known to take over. The fans there feel the same way about home-grown players who play for Bob Knight.

Originally from Gary, Indiana, Sean learned the game on the asphalt courts of an inner city. He developed a slashing, driving game. "There was no such thing as a jump shot," he said. But he didn't need one. When he was 12, Sean led his team to the national Biddy Basketball title.

He moved to Indianapolis two years later where he became a two-time all-state player at Cathedral High School. He chose Kentucky over Indiana, Purdue, Iowa, and Georgia for two reasons. First, his mother grew up in Lexington and his grandmother still lived there. Second, Sean had a good relationship with Dwane Casey, the Kentucky assistant who had also recruited his AAU teammate Shawn Kemp.

But Woods's world fell apart the following year. Sean not only had to sit out his freshman season in 1988 because of his Proposition 48 status, but he also had to live through the NCAA investigation. When Casey was implicated in the Emery Freight incident and Kentucky went on probation, Sean thought about transferring elsewhere. His mother convinced him to stay at Kentucky. I'm glad she did.

Sean dedicated himself to developing a jump shot over the summer. Monty Dupree, a friend of his from high school who plays for Xavier of New Orleans, came down to visit Sean for a month and a half and made sure he stayed in the gym.

I had originally penciled Dale Brown, a 6' 4" junior college All-America from Gulfport, Mississippi, into the other guard spot. Dale came to Kentucky with the reputation for being a great shooter. He averaged 21 points at Gulf Coast Community College. The night Herb saw him, he made seven straight three-pointers to get his team to the junior college nationals in Hutchinson, Kansas.

But Dale struggled with our system. When he was in junior college, his team didn't run many plays, and their offense consisted of clearing out a side for Dale. The largest crowd he ever played before at Gulf Coast was 2,000. Most of the time, there were less than 100 fans in the stands. It was a major adjustment for him. And for Rock. Dale had never gone through any strenuous conditioning. The first time he stepped on a treadmill, he almost ran into a wall. He wanted to quit that day. As a matter of fact, he actually came into my office with his bags packed four times before October 15.

He was homesick all fall. Richard Williams of Mississippi State called me to tell me Dale made a call to him about transferring there. I was disappointed in Dale, because he never came to me to talk about this homesick business. I could have saved him the price of the phone call because in order to transfer from one SEC school to another, he'd have to sit out two years. Richard told me Mississippi kids were a lot different.

Being a part-time psychologist is one thing, but handling Dale's moods was another. When adversity set in, often Dale would get down. If he had a bad grade or found a math course too difficult, he wanted to leave. If he was in a shooting slump, he wanted to leave. Dale spent much of his time in down cycles. I was hoping to change that with a constant barrage of positive reinforcement.

Another option I had at shooting guard was 6' 5" junior Jeff Brassow. Eddie Sutton recruited Brassow. Brass was an All-District player at Alief Eisik High in Houston, averaged 17 points his senior year, and made a statewide name for himself when he was selected MVP of the Fort Worth Lions' tournament.

Jeff played for us right away because he could shoot the three. During the fourth game of his freshman year, he scored 20 points against Middle Tennessee and made four threes in just 21 minutes. He got 25 against LSU later that year, making seven threes in the second half. Jeff continued to improve last year, starting 22 games and averaging 8.1 points.

The rest of our roster consisted of 6' 3" junior guard Junior Braddy, 6' 4" sophomore guard Carlos Toomer, and Henry Thomas, a 6' 5" junior from Clarksville, Tennessee.

Junior was the only one of five walkons from my first year still with the team. He came to Kentucky from Middleburg High in Jacksonville, Florida where he averaged 25.8 points and 8.6 rebounds his senior year. He had a chance to play baseball and basketball at the University of Tampa, but he came to Kentucky and tried out for the team. The day after he made the team, his career almost ended. He was late for practice and I wanted to throw him off the team. But Herb convinced me to keep him because we had only seven scholarship players. We gave him a one-year scholarship his sophomore year and renewed it this season.

Carlos was our most controversial recruit my first year. We discovered him when we went to Corinth, Mississippi, to recruit Stephen Davis, who eventually signed with Ole Mississippi. Carlos averaged only 13 points in high school, but I was impressed with his athleticism and thought he could help us defensively on the press. Carlos didn't get much playing time as a freshman and I was afraid he might get caught in a crunch. We had six guards on the team and Carlos didn't have the benefit of the off-season to make himself better. When he went home in August, he broke a bone in his right hand during a pickup game. He was in a cast for the next month.

Henry Thomas had a limited role on the team as a backup to John Pelphrey and Jeff Brassow last year. His career at Kentucky never got started. In a routine physical exam before the start of practice his freshman year, doctors discovered Henry had a torn anterior cruciate ligament in his left knee. Henry redshirted that year. He played in 14 games as a sophomore but he visibly favored the knee. Doctors told him he risked permanent damage if he had attempted to continue playing, and we gave him a medical scholarship.

In the past, during preseason, we took our team on the road, holding scrimmages at various high schools around the state. The gyms were always packed. When we went up to Clay County, for example, the townspeople hung signs on telephone poles and street signs reading WELCOME HOME, RICHIE and WE LOVE YOU RICHIE. When we went to Mason County High School, Deron had his jersey retired at halftime before almost 3,900 fans. I wanted to go to Manchester, Paintsville, and Maysville this year, but the NCAA ruled we couldn't leave campus.

We still wanted the fans to see their team, so we put 1,500 tickets on sale in those three towns for our October 29 scrimmage in Memorial Coliseum. The fans who showed up got to see Deron score 27, John get 25, and Richie get 21. But they also saw Travis Ford go down midway through the second half with an injury to his left knee. He iced it the rest of the game, then had it x-rayed the next day. The news wasn't good. The doctor told us he had fractured his knee and could miss up to six weeks in rehab.

Jamal Mashburn started to come into his own during our first exhibition game, November 10. He scored 29 points and grabbed 8 rebounds as we beat Athletes in Action—a team that had three former pros—Lorenzo Romar, Ray Tolbert, and David Woods—at Rupp Arena. Jamal scored 10 of his points in the last 11:18 when we came back from a 68–59 deficit to win, 82–77. After the game, Romar said Jamal played "like an adult."

Four days later, in a game against the Soviet touring team, Mash scored 24 points and grabbed 8 rebounds as we won, 112–92. That victory brought back memories of the exhibition game we had played against the Soviet national team the previous year. They buried us. The Soviets were notorious for their physical style of basketball in the past when they had one national team.

Gimel Martinez scored 8 points and grabbed 5 rebounds in 17 minutes against the Soviets. That was certainly an improvement since he hadn't scored against Athletes in Action. That game, I saw a side of the Kentucky fan I had never seen before. They started getting on him and were booing him.

Heading into our season opener against West Virginia in the preseason NIT, I still wasn't sure who would be our starting center. I also had questions about our shooting guard spot after Dale missed all eight three-pointers he attempted in our two exhibitions.

No wonder Herb, Billy, and the rest of our staff weren't getting any sleep. We would get up at 5:30 every morning in September, show up at the gym, and play full-court pickup games before our staff meetings at 7 A.M.

Billy and Herb are like two altar boys—*organized* altar boys. They don't swear; they don't smoke; they are unique; they are workaholics.

Billy played for me at Providence. He barely got off the bench his first two years. He averaged just 2.4 points as a sophomore, and actually thought about transferring to a Division II school. But, once we got him to lose 25 pounds, and put him through some intense individual instruction, he blossomed. I started calling him "Billy the Kid," and we posed him in a cowboy outfit before his senior year to boost his image. Five months later, he was a star when we won the NCAA Southeast Regional and earned a trip to the Final Four. I hired Billy to develop the players' skills the same way we had developed his.

Herb had straight As in high school. He played Division III basketball and graduated summa cum laude from the business school at Carnegie Mellon. He is the classic overachiever. He is the most organized, dedicated young man I have ever come across. Herb got engaged to Melanie Scheuer last fall and planned his wedding for May 9, so it wouldn't interfere with recruiting. Melanie, a former basketball player in high school, understood. She had been around Herb long enough.

Herb always wanted to be a coach. His father had been one, and he was a true student of the game. I never thought Billy would get into coaching. I thought he was too meek. When he played in the Final Four, he was on stage quite a bit. He played in the NBA. He worked on Wall Street, where I'm sure you have to make your presence known. He developed his personality and became more aggressive and outgoing, but he still remained humble.

Billy is the eternal optimist. Herb is more conservative. The two like to needle each other. Billy, who went out and bought an Armani suit, likes to tease Herb about his wardrobe. Last summer Herb called him up in a panic. He had to go on the road the next morning and asked Billy to pick up his clothes at the dry cleaners.

"Everything I own is there," he said.

Billy figured he better bring along at least $25 to pay the bill. When he went to pick up the order, the girl at the desk handed him a blue blazer and a pair of gray slacks. "I do a lot of mixing and matching," Herb said later.

Herb constantly kids Billy about his appetite. Billy just inhales those Blimpie sandwiches we take on our road trips. I tease him, too, asking him if he wants to take some spaghetti back to his room after our team meals.

I've had nine assistants go on to become head coaches. When they were ready, I supported them. But Billy and Herb are both under 30, and I'd like to keep them at Kentucky. I want them to enjoy this scene a little longer. Billy was offered the Brown University job last year and I didn't think that was a good move for him. Nothing against Brown—it's an outstanding academic institution. But why come to Kentucky to go back to Brown? He would have taken a pay cut and given up an opportunity to recruit some of the finest high school basketball players in America.

This is Bernadette Locke's second year with us, and she has fit in well. She was married last summer to Vince Mattox, a former Virginia football star who is a teacher at Athens Academy. We went to the wedding, and I was honored to present the toast. "Everybody realizes how big basketball is in Kentucky," I said. "You're now looking at the first lady of Kentucky." At the moment, they're having a commuter marriage, but Vince plans to move to Lexington.

Everyone on our staff appreciates the job Bernadette has done—teaching, on the phone with parents, and handling career placement. If the rest of the country found out what we already know, there would be more female coaches hired in Division I men's basketball.

I knew Mike Atkinson, our volunteer assistant, from basketball camps at Providence College. He is a chemistry teacher at Sachem High on Long Island. He coached at Suffolk Junior College last year, but was trying to hook on at a four-year school. The best I could offer him was a six-month job. He made a big sacrifice to come here. He took a leave of absence from his school and his family. His wife Peggy and three children—six-year-old Derrick, four-year-old Mimi, and two-year-old Neil—were back in Long Island. I hope it turns out to be a good deal for him. NCAA rules changed this season and this was the last year for volunteer coaches and graduate assistants. It's a shame. That's the way a lot of others started in the business.

Rock Oliver is a former defensive back at Ohio State. I think he has some Woody Hayes in him. He loves aggressive behavior. He's hooked on those ESPN shows like *Shark World* and *Wilderness.* He loves to demonstrate how a lion attacks a water buffalo, complete with sound effects. Rock was the most physical player in our pickup games. Even his friends aren't immune. With a well-placed elbow, he cracked the ribs of his good friend Tubby Smith while the two were jockeying for position on a rebound.

In addition to the coaches, our staff included long-time equipment manager Bill Keightley and trainer JoAnn Hauser. Bill's staff of student managers were Jeff Morrow, Spence and Vin Tatum, Ken Gayhert, and John Farris. Ashley Mitros was JoAnn's student assistant trainer and our video man was Joe Matthews.

Bill had been around Kentucky for 31 years, almost as long as Cawood. He was a full-time mail carrier, part-time equipment manager until 1987 when he took the job full-time at the university. His nickname is Mr. Wildcat. A visit to his cage in the back of the coliseum is like taking a walk through history. This is the closest thing the place has to a Kentucky basketball museum. I find it strange that a university so rich in basketball history has no place for its basketball trophies. If North Carolina has one, so should we.

As soon as you enter the cage, you can see a banner hanging up that reads KENTUCKY SEC CHAMPS 1991. Bill keeps that around just to remind him that we were still the best last year, even though the conference didn't officially recognize us as such.

There are a number of NCAA Final Four trophies, just sitting there on a table, collecting dust. There is also an imposing picture of Rick Robey and Mike Phillips setting a pick on George Hooker of Mississippi State during the 1978 championship season. Hooker was 6' 6", but he looked dwarfed by comparison.

But the most interesting item is the back end of a stuffed deer hanging on the wall. It arrived in 1978 and Bill hangs good-luck charms around it—a lion's-head from Hong Kong, a bunch of hat pins, and a pair of fuzzy red dice.

JoAnn just joined us. She had been the baseball trainer. She was the subject of a blossoming romance when the season started. She was dating Willie Feldhaus, Deron's older brother. I couldn't resist teasing her about it when I found out. I called her into my office and told her we didn't allow our staff to date relatives of the players. She was really upset. I tried to keep a straight face, but I finally cracked up.

Our managers are all Kentucky kids, high school athletes who want to be part of the greatest program in the world in their minds—Kentucky basketball. They've met a lot of basketball legends. After listening to some of my friends from the East when they picked them up from the airport, they've received an education they could not have gotten in 20 years in Kentucky. They've learned about the streets of New York in a very short period of time.

# --8--

# *ALL RHODES LEAD TO KENTUCKY*

**R**odrick Rhodes had to hear the cheers.

They started midway through our intrasquad scrimmage at Big Blue Madness when a group of Kentucky students sitting across from our bench began chanting: "We want Rhodes. We want Rhodes."

They weren't the only ones.

When I first took this job, my goal was to bring in one great player a year from the greater metropolitan area of New York. It still is. We signed Jamal Mashburn my first year. Then we signed Andre Riddick. But we felt Rhodes was the key. He was a big name. He was generally considered one of the two best prospects in the country, having started for Bob Hurley, Sr., at St. Anthony's of Jersey City as a freshman.

I felt Rodrick had a good visit but I didn't realize how good it was until he told Rock he was going to commit when he got home. I spent the next two nights waiting by the phone. The call finally came Monday night. Rodrick told me he was ready to commit, but he wanted me to do him one favor. I had told him Joanne was pregnant with our sixth child and he wanted me to name the baby Rodrick Jabbar Pitino, Jr.

I said to him, "Even if it's a girl, I'll name the baby Rodrick.' " That was 11:10 P.M.

At 11:20, the sports news came on TV. Alan Cutler of WLEX-TV had called Rodrick at home earlier that evening, learned of his decision and announced it on the air. "Shock of the year," he said. "Joanne Pitino is pregnant. But here's an even bigger surprise. Rodrick Rhodes has committed to Kentucky." Then he repeated the story.

Joanne was two and a half months pregnant and she still hadn't told her mother. So we ended up calling her folks that midnight.

I was ecstatic about both announcements.

When a college gets a Bob Hurley kid, you know he's going to be fundamentally sound and worth fighting for in recruiting.

Two days before Rodrick's official visit, Bob Hurley told me Rhodes wanted to cancel, that he was going to Seton Hall. But Hurley and Rodrick's sister, Gail, made him honor his decision to visit our campus.

"With all the time Kentucky has spent recruiting you, you owe it to them to check it out," Hurley told Rhodes. "If you come back and Seton Hall is the school for you, then choose Seton Hall."

Rodrick was very impressed by the atmosphere on his visit. He wanted to go to a school where he could concentrate on basketball and not be concerned about the hassles of the East Coast. Two more pluses in Kentucky's favor: He liked Rock and Bernadette.

He had a choice of whether to go to Seton Hall and blend with other St. Anthony's players who were already there, or try something new.

The New York papers were always speculating about me

going back to the NBA someday. If other schools were going to knock something about Kentucky, that's the most obvious thing.

On the way to the airport after his visit, Rodrick asked me, "Coach, will you see me graduate?"

I said, "Rod, unless it takes you nine years to finish I'll see you graduate. I have five years remaining on my contract."

It wasn't finished, yet, though. Rodrick was supposed to sign the second day of early signing period, November 14, at five o'clock. He never did. Then, I got a call at one A.M. from his sister and her husband asking me about a story in the *Village Voice*, claiming I had a gentlemen's agreement to coach the New Jersey Nets.

My response was "This has been in a lot of newspapers and I've already told you once before I'm not going anywhere."

His sister's husband asked if I would say that publicly at a press conference. I said, "Sure, I would." So I did and I said it was my intention to see all the recruits graduate. Not that I would go elsewhere, but it's very difficult for a coach to promise anything like this.

That was at noon. Four hours later, I received a call from Rodrick Rhodes saying he was going to decide during the April signing period.

I said, "For what purpose?"

"For Prop. forty-eight," he said. "To see if I can make it."

"Wait a minute," I told him. "We'd already told Walter McCarty you're the guy to get the scholarship. So why would you not sign the scholarship? If you're a Proposition forty-eight, the national letter of intent you sign is not binding, anyway."

I started to think there were other problems. He asked me to call at 5:00. I did, and I could hear arguing in the background. Then Rodrick asked me to call back at 5:15. I did and Gail said, "Look, he needs more time." I could hear arguing in the background again and a voice saying, "You're not going to sign any papers."

I called back at 5:30 and his brother Reggie asked me if I

could call back yet again. I said, "No, I'm not going to call back. You have my number in the office. When everything is discussed, please call me back."

We finally got a call at 6:15 saying "It's done. The letter is signed and we're going to mail it out tomorrow."

We asked Gail to send the letter by Federal Express (yes, we switched to Federal Express) to make sure it didn't get lost in the mail. She did. When we called and told her she was going to have to pay for the package, she told us she could have sent it through the regular mail and saved $12.

Rhodes's signing did so much for our image. Rodrick saw how happy Mash and Riddick were here. He came from a similar background, so he knew he would have friends. With John Pelphrey and Richie Farmer leaving, he felt he would have an opportunity to play right away.

I felt Rodrick would be a pied piper. He was such a good kid. Everybody on the team and the other prospects got along well with him. Eventually, we received commitments from Walter McCarty, Tony Delk, and Jared Prickett, giving us a clean sweep of the prospects who had visited during Big Blue Madness.

McCarty was generally regarded as the best big man in the Midwest. Delk was a scoring machine who averaged 37 points per game as a junior and had NBA range. Prickett was a hard-nosed kid who had the potential to be a bigger version of Deron Feldhaus. We had the No. 1 recruiting class in the early signing period, according to the gurus.

Delk wanted to come, choosing us over Arkansas. I didn't like his game when I first saw him at the Nike camp. Later in the July observation period, I became impressed when we watched him work out with his AAU team. Coaches jumped out of their seats when he scored 41 points—21 in the fourth quarter alone—in the semifinals of the 17-and-under national tournament at Jonesboro, Arkansas. His only request of me was to wear the same uniform number he and his brother Ricky wore in high school—double zero.

McCarty chose us over Purdue and Evansville. He was a late bloomer in high school who did not play varsity as a ninth grader and averaged only six points as a sophomore. But he could do so many things. He was quick, had good hands, could put the ball on the floor, block shots. I felt he was one of the three or four best prospects in the country. I thought he had the same potential as Mash, and that was unlimited. He was 20 pounds away from being a dominant player in college.

We offered McCarty a spot on Kentucky's roster, even though we knew he did not have enough core courses to qualify for freshman eligibility. We originally had backed off, as did several other schools, but then we discovered he had received bad advice from a guidance counselor. What are you going to do? He comes from a good family and we didn't feel it was a gamble.

Prickett comes from a coal mining family. His father, who played on the 1967–68 Fairmont State team in West Virginia that finished runnerup in the NAIA Tournament, still likes to challenge Jared one-on-one.

With Prickett, it came down to Notre Dame and Kentucky. Notre Dame was telling him he could start for four years. We were telling him he could be in the Top 20 for four years, with a chance of going to the NCAA tournament each year. The question was playing time over winning. Not that Notre Dame won't win eventually, but they lost their three best players and will have to build from scratch.

Herb did the most incredible in-house recruitment I've seen in quite some time. We were leading in most areas over Notre Dame in Jared Prickett's mind. He thought we were a better team. He felt we had more potential. He knew we could play in the tournament. He saw an opportunity to play. The big point Notre Dame was pushing was what a Notre Dame education could do for him someday. Herb used his own education as a parallel to what Jared would go through. He talked about the bell curve.

"Right now," he told Jared, "you are just an average student. All of your test scores are average, and it looks like you are showing an average intellect for grasping high school and, down the road, college work. I'm not knocking that. You can certainly overachieve. I'm not here to tell you that Kentucky is better than Notre Dame academically. Certainly we have our programs, but Notre Dame is probably regarded as the better school academically.

"Still, if you take an accounting course, we will use the same book as Notre Dame. You will be taught the same way at Notre Dame, with the exception of two things: One, your competition at Notre Dame will have the average ACT scores of twenty-eight to thirty. Here at Kentucky, it's twenty-three. It would be like competing against professional athletes on the basketball court. When people grade you on the bell curve, you're going to be graded, not by what you get on a given exam, but by what your competitors, who are coming in with a much higher intellect than you are showing, score on that test. At Kentucky, courses will be taught at a slower pace because your competition will be in the same boat as you. So, you will be able to get the same knowledge, but you also will be able to compete more effectively."

Herb mapped out the whole thing. He even brought in the names of the textbooks Jared would use in accounting and history if he came to Kentucky and showed him they would be the same books that are used at Notre Dame. I think that really hit home.

Prickett also knew there might not be a scholarship available if he waited. Mark Atkins, a 6' 5" junior college prospect from Kankakee, Illinois, told us he was going to commit when he came back from his visit to Nebraska, where two of his high school teammates had gone. At Kentucky, the first recruit who says yes is the one we take. Atkins gambled and Prickett got the scholarship.

That should put an end to all the whispers that we couldn't recruit. I used to hear that all the time my first two years here.

I guess some people do forget about probation.

Recruiting news is almost a sport at Kentucky. The fans here are so name conscious, they still want players from the *Parade* All-America team. Each fall, all they talk about is recruiting. They want to know who we're involved with early on in the process. If I'm recruiting one particular prospect, there might be seven or eight writers calling him once, twice a week to find out where Kentucky stands. I know these people are just doing their jobs, but it doesn't help us. It can hurt us. The parents say, "I don't want my kid going into that. It's too much."

We are trying to get our fans to understand that times have changed. In the past, Kentucky recruited players solely on name recognition. But our team's success last year was based more on chemistry than on individual reputation.

I believe a good recruiter rates a player not only on his athletic ability, but also on how he fits into the system. So many of these recruiting services the fans devour just look at a prospect's physical attributes. Running and jumping are important, but what I look for in a prospect is how he runs a motion offense, how he fits into a pressing system, and whether he can face up from 18 feet to shoot a jump shot.

I remember listening to Oscar Combs on the radio in November. He claimed the people of Kentucky were ready to lynch me last year because of what they perceived as a poor recruiting year. We had been involved with all the big names—Chris Webber, Cherokee Parks, and Tom Kleinschmidt. They were three of the Top 10 prospects in the country. Parks signed with Duke, Webber signed with Michigan, and Kleinschmidt went to DePaul.

In reality, there was no reason for us to get a player like Parks. We weren't on TV, we weren't in the tournament, and we carried the stigma of breaking the rules. The last time people saw Kentucky on TV, they were not winning, and were suffering through an internal investigation. We couldn't catch a cold, and we still went down to the wire with Parks.

I'm convinced we could have gotten Lawrence Funderburke. Funderburke was a high school All-America forward
from Columbus, Ohio, who started his career at Indiana but
left after just nine games when he had a falling-out with
Bobby Knight. He wanted to come here. He began attending
classes at St. Catherine Junior College in Springfield, Kentucky, in the fall of 1990. He was even hanging out at the
Lodge all the time because he and Travis Ford were good
friends from their AAU days.

When Funderburke attended one of our games, the Lexington *Herald* ran a picture. That set C. M. Newton off. He said
Funderburke would never wear a Kentucky uniform. Part of
the reason stemmed from C.M.'s relationship with Knight.
C.M. had been one of Knight's assistants on the 1984 Olympic
team.

C.M. was also put off by past history. When Funderburke
was in high school, Bill Chupil, an alumnus of Kentucky,
drove him down here to some of the games. When the NCAA
began investigating Kentucky in 1988, they labeled Chupil a
friend of the university and Kentucky backed off. C.M. felt if
we took Funderburke, it would be sending a message to the
NCAA Kentucky was still willing to take shortcuts. Funderburke eventually signed with Ohio State.

We were among the leaders for Cory Alexander and Travis
Best—two of the hottest high school guards in the country—
but we decided to take Travis Ford, instead. We signed Chris
Harrison, who was the best player in Kentucky. We beat out
Indiana and DePaul for Aminu Timberlake. Andre Riddick
chose us over Massachusetts. But the so-called recruiting
gurus didn't even bother to rate our recruiting class in the
Top 50. The backlash was inevitable. One local sportscaster
even suggested that everybody cheated to some extent and if
Kentucky wanted to compete on a bigtime level for the best
recruits, we were going to have to play the game.

We're not going to do that, even if it means losing a great
player. Cliff Rozier, a 6' 9" forward from Bradenton, Florida,

had decided to leave the University of North Carolina after his freshman year and was looking to transfer. Rozier made his official visit to Kentucky on Derby weekend last spring and verbally committed to us that Saturday. But, that night, Sean Woods drove Rozier to Louisville, 70 miles way, to attend a Derby party. NCAA rules do not allow a recruit to travel more than 30 miles from campus.

The last thing I said to Sean was "Don't buy any souvenirs. Don't talk to any boosters and don't go to any Derby parties in town." So, what does he do, he takes Rozier to a party at the home of the son of the Louisville team physician. Kids! When I found out, we immediately reported the violation to the NCAA and announced we were dropping out of the running. Rozier eventually signed at Louisville.

Sean's a good kid. He had been our best recruiter for three years. He just made a mistake, and we all ended up paying for it. "Don't worry," I told Sean. "There's nothing you can do about it. Don't try to justify it, because you can't. What you can do is make up for it on the basketball court." Then, I had him perform 30 hours of community service, had him stay in his room 30 hours and held him out the first 30 hours of practice.

We could have appealed the Rozier decision. But, because I thought we were totally knowledgeable of the rules, we were wrong. We lost not only a great player, but we lost him to our archrival.

Right now, there's tremendous tension between Kentucky and Louisville, and a lot of it stems from the recruiting of Dwayne Morton. Morton is a 6' 7" forward from Louisville Central who was the best player in Kentucky two years ago and one of the top prospects in the country. He committed to us on his visit. He said to me, "Coach, I want to play ball for the University of Kentucky." He told everybody on the team he was coming, too. Everyone was elated and excited. We had outrecruited Louisville for Morton.

I said, "Great. Go home, talk to your mother, take a couple

days and call us." Most young people are impressionable and make impulsive decisions on the spot. His mother didn't want her son to come to Kentucky. She admits now she interceded, reminding her son of his lifelong desire to attend Louisville.

Kentucky has traditionally had problems recruiting great black players from Louisville. To my knowledge, they've signed only one—Winston Bennett. Past history works against us. Louisville still uses Rupp's reluctance to recruit blacks. When we were recruiting Morton, one of the first things his mother brought up was Tom Payne. That was 25 years ago, and a lot has changed since then. Kentucky is not a white-bread university anymore. These are the '90s, not the '50s.

The night before the early signing period began, Denny Crum had dinner with Morton's mother and his high school coach, Ralph Johnson. Morton announced for Louisville the next day. During an interview, his mother let it slip that she had met with Crum during the 48-hour dead period, when no live contact is allowed.

Crum was suspended by the NCAA from September recruiting for the following year, but Louisville still ended up with Morton. I find it hard to believe their coaching staff did not know that any contact during the dead period is against the rules. Denny Crum stated that the high school coach picked up the tab for dinner! I was really happy to hear about that. High school coaches, because of their exorbitant salaries, always pick up the tab for college coaches. I would have liked the opportunity to make a final pitch for Morton. And I would have liked the opportunity to get a free meal.

What bothered me the most about the situation was the fact that we turned down another prospect, forward Stephen Davis of Cornith, Mississippi, because coach Johnson told us we still had a chance for Morton. The coach wanted to turn the recruitment of this player into a in-state competition between Kentucky and Louisville. He felt if Morton eliminated Kentucky early, it would affect Morton's chances of being selected Mr. Basketball. Well, that didn't happen. But we didn't find out where he was going until we heard it on a radio station.

I'd love to recruit the state more, especially Louisville. But we didn't feel there were any prospects from Kentucky who could play for us this year. Carlos Turner, a 6′ 4″ guard who played for Fairdale High in Louisville, was regarded as the leading candidate for Mr. Basketball in preseason. We were thinking about recruiting him but, in attending the Final Four last spring, Herb and I ran into Irv Stewart, a ticket broker from Lexington who was very familiar with the Kentucky high school basketball scene. He told us that recruiting Carlos Turner would cause trouble. I told him he shouldn't say that.

"Look," he said, "you don't know me. You're from New York City. I know you've dealt with city kids all your life. I'm telling you right now not to recruit the kid and if you don't listen, you're going to get burned. If you want a young man who's going to leave the Lodge and go out and find crap games, if you want a young man who's going to get into trouble, then you recruit him."

Herb and I had second thoughts so we called Stan Hardin, his high school coach, to check out all these rumors. He told us, "He's definitely not interested in studying. He misses a lot of classes."

At that point, we decided not to recruit him. We never sent him a letter. It turned out Irv Stewart was on the money. Turner eventually signed at South Carolina, where Stan Hardin had taken an assistant's job. Two days after he committed, he allegedly stabbed his former girlfriend several times and then stabbed himself. Turner and Nicole Shivers had two children together. People who knew Turner said he was distraught because she had broken up with him and was seeing someone else. Turner has since pleaded guilty to assault and burglary in juvenile court and was sentenced to one year in a state psychiatric facility instead of prison. He was only 17.

I made a special trip to Louisville in July just to watch Tick Rogers, a 6' 4" guard from Hart County. He was the number one recruit on Ralph Willard's list at Western Kentucky, and I thought he could have been a star there. He signed at Louisville after Denny Crum allegedly said he would be a starter by his sophomore year.

Kentucky has a great tradition, but only a few high school players are talented enough to play for us. However, if one state legislator had his way, we might be forced to take the best player in the state, whether he's good enough or not. Representative Roger Noe, a Democrat from Harlan County, filed a bill in the Kentucky legislature in February. If passed, this legislation would give the state's top three high school sports stars—Mr. Basketball, Miss Basketball, and Mr. Football—their pick of athletic scholarships from the state's universities. The universities, it appears, would have no choice in the matter.

Among Noe's constituents is Scott Russell, Kentucky's Mr. Football in 1991. Russell rushed for a state record 7,090 yards during his career at Evarts High. He wanted to go to Kentucky, but was not offered a scholarship. Noe's legislation would have allowed Russell or others to write themselves onto the roster. That's a joke. It's one of the most ludicrous things I've ever heard. Russell is attending Lees-McRae College in North Carolina.

Ideally, I believe 30 to 40 percent of our team should be from Kentucky. If it's a close decision between taking an in-state player and one from out of state, I'd always take the Kentucky player. But I'm not about to be pressured into putting a player on the roster just because he's from Kentucky. The NCAA is going to cut the amount of scholarships a school can offer from 15 to 13 by 1993.

The only person who's really mentioned it is Tom Wallace. Two years ago, he told me we should recruit Bryan Milburn, a 6' 6" forward from Russell Springs, Kentucky. We went to see him play, but we felt he wasn't a good enough shooter for our system. He eventually went to Vanderbilt.

I got my first taste of what recruiting is all about right after I graduated from eighth grade. My family had moved out to Long Island and I was to attend the public school there. During that summer, I was playing ball at Theodore Roosevelt Park in Oyster Bay with Gary Ellison, a teammate of Ralph Willard at St. Dominic's. He asked me where I was going to school and I said, "Locust Valley, or I'm going to commute to Archbishop Molloy in Queens."

He said, "Well, why don't you go to St. Dominic's? They have a great basketball tradition." I told him I hadn't taken the entrance exams to get into Catholic school and he said, "If you can shoot the way you're shooting today, that won't matter."

Then, he said, "Wait here. I'll be back in ten minutes."

He drove back in his car and had someone with him in the front seat. I couldn't make out who it was. We started playing again. After about ten minutes, the passenger, Father Suave, who was the athletic moderator at St. Dominic's, called me over and asked me if I'd like to go to school there.

"Tell your parents we'd like to have you at St. Dominic's," he said. "Look, if it ever comes up, just tell people because you moved, you didn't have the opportunity to take the exams. Given the circumstances and because you have one of the best jump shots for a kid I've ever seen, we can probably do something."

I had a good high school career and I visited 13 campuses, including Navy, Canisius, Niagara, William and Mary, Davidson, Southern Cal., South Carolina, Louisiana Tech, UConn, and Massachusetts. I actually wanted to go to Connecticut, but Dee Rowe, the coach at the time, couldn't make up his mind. I ended up going to Massachusetts. I signed at the press table on the floor of Madison Square Garden in 1970, right after UMass lost to Marquette in the NIT.

I thought about playing ball in Europe after I graduated from college, but when a graduate assistant's job opened at Hawaii, I jumped at the chance.

Little did I know how much jet lag I would accumulate. Bruce O'Neal, the coach there, wanted to recruit the East

Coast. I made weekly trips from Honolulu to Long Island to see Reggie Carter, a local high school All-America guard. I saw him play 20 times at Long Island Lutheran. I would leave for New York on a Sunday, see Reggie play on a Tuesday, return to Hawaii on Wednesday and fly back to the mainland on Saturday or Sunday. If they had given out frequent flyer miles then, I would have held the record.

Carter shocked everyone when he chose Hawaii over North Carolina. I was actually regarded as more of a recruiter than a coach after we signed Carter, George Lett and Edward Torres, a pair of all-city players in New York, and Henry Hollingsworth, who was first team all–Long Island.

I took a job at Syracuse two years later. My first year we recruited Rick Harmon, a highly touted prospect from Cape May, New Jersey. Harmon's final four schools were Indiana, Villanova, Syracuse, and Michigan State. I saw him play every game. I would leave about three o'clock from practice and make a five-hour trip to the Jersey shore. I would arrive about five minutes before tipoff, see him play, get a bite to eat, and drive through the night back to Syracuse. I traveled with Harry Tzivanis, a Syracuse usher at basketball and football games. We got back at five in the morning, had breakfast, and I went to work.

That was real recruiting, and it was relentless. The winner was who could see the kid the most times, who could get to know the girlfriend. That's when you had guys like Dave "Pitstop" Pritchard, Eddie Beidenbach, George Raveling, Leonard Hamilton, and Lefty Driesell. They were the traveling legends of the recruiting world.

Herb Sendek brought back the golden age of recruiting. Even though he had never been out of the country before, he flew to Tapei in July to watch the Jones Cup competition because the U.S. team had three junior college players—Darrin Hancock of Garden City, Kansas; Mark Hutton of Barton County, Kansas; and Mark Atkins of Kankakee, Illinois—we wanted to see.

I loved Hutton's talents. I thought he was a Stacy Augmon with a jump shot. We originally felt we had a better shot with him than with Rhodes. But he ended up at Auburn because he had a girlfriend who attended school there.

That was the exception. I don't think there are great recruiters anymore. Take Michigan's Fab Five. Steve Fisher is a very good coach, but he's a quiet, reserved individual. The school itself had a lot to do with Chris Webber, Jalen Rose, Juwann Howard, Ray Jackson, and Jimmy King signing there last year. It also didn't hurt when Steve Fisher hired Perry Watson as an assistant coach. Watson had been Rose's high school coach at Detroit Southwestern, and was very close to the Webber family.

With the limited-contact restrictions imposed by the NCAA, TV basically does 50 percent of college recruiting today. It helps you sell your product. Look at our program. Not being on TV hurt us my first year. Kentucky was like the plague, imagewise.

But we must be doing something right.

I coached at Boston University for five years and we had five NBA draft picks. Gary Plummer went in the second round to Golden State; Thomas Channel was selected in the second round by Seattle; Wally West was a fifth-round pick by the Bulls. Steve Wright went in the sixth round to the Celtics and Tony Sims was selected by the Knicks. None of those guys except Plummer were highly recruited.

I was at Providence for two years. Take a look at the people we recruited. Eric Murdock was selected in the first round by Utah. Abdul Shamid-Deen—who is currently the highest paid player in France—went in the second round to Seattle, and Marty Conlon made the roster in Seattle.

During the Joe B. Hall era, Kentucky signed 36 high school All-Americas. But players like Derrick Hord, Bret Bearup, Dickey Beal, Jim Master, James Blackmon, Ed Davender, and Roger Harden never played a minute in the pros. As of this season, Rex Chapman, Winston Bennett, and Sam Bowie are the only former Kentucky players on NBA rosters. Today, a high school All-America's chances of making it to the pros depends on his work ethic. An inflated ego spells disaster for these young men. Too much publicity makes them believe they've arrived, when the hard work should just be starting.

Years ago, when I first started coaching, it was easier to recruit great players. There was no Proposition 48 to worry about. Now, the SEC has adopted a rule that will eventually forbid any conference school from offering a scholarship to any Proposition 48 students. At the moment, we're limited to one a year. This is surprising, given the state of secondary education in the Deep South.

The NCAA has upgraded its academic requirements across the board. To be eligible to play as a freshman, a recruit must score at least a 700 on the SAT or a 17 on the ACT. In addition, he must earn a 2.0 in 13 high school core courses. Within the next three years, the minimum will be raised to 2.5, and 750 on the SAT with a sliding scale. It might not sound like a big deal, but to many inner-city youngsters, it could be an unattainable goal.

I think many college administrators would benefit by joining their coaches and visiting the inner-city schools where many of our players live. Maybe then they would see firsthand what's keeping the young black athletes from achieving academically early on. It's their environment and their early education. Fifth, sixth, and seventh grades are the formative years of education, not eleventh and twelfth grades. That's when they perform, because they understand what's at stake.

I've always felt that raising the standards discriminates against minorities because current standardized tests are culturally biased. If the presidents want to show real concern about education, they should make all freshman ineligible in the revenue sports of football and basketball, then give them four years of playing time. Most freshmen aren't mentally ready for college, even though some are physically mature.

# --9--

# *HUMBLE BEGINNINGS*

Dick Vitale was in town to broadcast our first two games in the preseason NIT in November.

Couldn't you hear him?

Dick went to Three Chimneys Farm to interview Triple Crown winner Seattle Slew for ESPN, and he was talking about his All-Thoroughbred teams. Whoops. Seattle Slew tried to bite him. By the end of the film clip, there was Dick mugging for the cameras and hugging the Kentucky Derby winner.

Dick told me he had us already penciled into the semifinals in New York. Prime time in the Garden, baby, along with Texas, Georgia Tech, and Oklahoma State.

We had already defeated West Virginia, 106–80, in a first-round game. A victory over Pitt and I would have been coaching against Eddie Sutton. The Kentucky fans would have loved it. More than 1,000 planned to make the trip. Back in September, when I spoke to a local alumni group, the door prize was a trip to New York.

I'm sure it would have been a promoter's dream, too, with three New Yorkers—Tommy Penders of Texas, Bobby Cremins of Georgia Tech, and me—coming home for Thanksgiving. I was excited about showing our players New York City, especially guys like Deron, John, and Richie, who come from small towns. I had been to Maysville, Paintsville, and Manchester. I was all set to tell the bus driver to drive right to Times Square. I couldn't wait to see the look in their eyes when they got out, walked around and met some of the people there.

But it never happened. Instead of touring the Big Apple, going to see *Miss Saigon* on Broadway, visiting the Stock Exchange and watching the Knicks play Miami, we got to spend the holidays at home after losing to Pitt, 85–67, at Rupp Arena.

Pitt played out of its mind. Their players hurt us badly in the low post, taking advantage of our decision to play them straight up instead of doubling down. Darren Morningstar, Pitt's big 6' 10", 250-pound center, ripped us for 27 points and 10 rebounds, getting most of his field goals inside against Aminu Timberlake, whom I started at center. We had a great deal of difficulty with their size. Pitt was a typical Big East team. Their starting frontline averaged 240 pounds. Our freshman centers were only about 200. It showed.

We didn't help ourselves, either, making just 7 of 36 three-point attempts and shooting just 27 percent. In the end, we panicked. We tried to make up the deficit in a hurry. Our players have the freedom to take open three-pointers, but our shot selection was terrible.

It was an ugly way to end a 22-game home-court winning streak. For the first time in my career, I could honestly say another team had outhustled us. Some of our fans had a hard time believing it, too. Most of them sat there in silence. The students behind our bench tried to wake them up by chanting, "Sell Your Seats" when they started to leave early.

Larry the Scout, who was visiting for the weekend, and Ralph Willard were both standing in the hallway near our locker room afterwards.

"I wouldn't go in there if I were you," Ralph told Scout.

"What do you mean?" Larry said. "Of course, I'm going in there. I've known Rick for years."

Ralph just shrugged. When Scout went in, I was so upset, I told him I would drive him to the airport the next morning. "It's going to be a long weekend," I said. Ralph told me later Scout was stunned. He just kept shaking his head.

This was Kentucky's first loss at home in three years, and I didn't know what to expect when I went out to do my radio show. But about three or four thousand fans stayed around and gave me a standing ovation. That made me feel great. To borrow an expression from George Bush, I think we're seeing "a kinder, gentler" Kentucky fan. But it also made me feel down, because I thought I had disappointed them. I left immediately after the show and went home to look at game films until three in the morning.

The next day, I felt bad about Scout. I told him he could stay.

I ended up giving our Broadway tickets to the Pitt team and prepared for a long week and a half. I really felt bad for Joanne. We had planned to attend the christening of her sister's baby boy. Joanne and Michael, who was the godfather, flew up there together Saturday without the rest of us. Coaches rarely make weddings, christenings, or birthday parties. But you learn to take the good with the bad.

It was a tough lesson for the players. They thought they were pretty good after our victory over West Virginia. Who's Pitt? It almost looked like they had been listening to Dick Vitale, which was a bad idea at the time.

I had lunch with Dick the day before the Pitt game. He was at Bravo's, with Joe B. Hall and two other senior vice presidents who work with Joe at Central Bank. Vitale was in rare form, telling anyone within earshot how Kentucky was going to blow Pitt away by 30 points. I hope everyone realized I was arguing with him about his predictions.

That afternoon at practice, he told Jerry Tipton that Pitt coach Paul Evans would have to do a miracle coaching job in 24 hours for Pitt to have a chance. The next morning, it was headlines in the *Herald–Leader.* "Don't worry, baby: Pitt may be no match for UK."

I know Dick didn't cost us the game. But he certainly lighted Pitt's fire. Dick Vitale is no Danny Sheridan. He should have promoted the game for his network, not knocked the game as a mismatch. I hope this teaches him a valuable lesson about college basketball. If he wanted to go out on a limb, why not pick Northeast Louisiana to beat LSU? He had nothing to gain by picking Kentucky to win. All he did was create enemies. He doesn't need that in his profession. I hear Paul Evans grabbed him after Pitt's shootaround and started yelling at him. They had bad words, and Paul used that to motivate his players.

If nothing else, I felt a blowout like this would do our players some good. We were ranked fourth in the AP preseason poll. The best thing for us may have been a dose of humility. It made us realize we had to work hard to achieve our goals.

I'm not sure if I conveyed that idea to the Kentucky media. Two games into the season and they were already getting edgy. Ralph Hacker was talking to John Pelphrey, and the first question out of the box was "Do you still think you're a Final Four team?"

Maybe things had come too easily for us against West Virginia. Our starting lineup for opening night was John, Jamal, Sean, Jeff Brassow, and Aminu. We played a near-perfect game for this early in the year, making 16 of 32 three-point attempts and holding Gale Catlett's team to just 8 three-point attempts. I thought West Virginia would be pretty good by the end of the season, but we put on a clinic. Herb did an out-standing job scouting them. John Pelphrey scored 26 points. Jeff Brassow scored 23. We shot 63 percent, winning convincingly, even though Jamal had only 15 points.

West Virginia must have scouted our game against Athletes in Action when Jamal had a big game. Judging from the way the Mountaineers constantly fronted him in the post, Mash was going to be a marked man all season. But we felt if we played that well, it might not matter. The other thing that pleased me that night was our rebounding. Apparently, the word on us was that we were soft on the boards, and I mentioned that when I spoke to the team during our pregame meeting. We outrebounded West Virginia, 44–29.

We had gone through six or seven great practices before our first game, and we were going into the season on an uptick. We were playing very well together. And the shots went down. When the shots go down, you get into your press easier. You feel better about yourself.

I felt better just watching Travis Ford, who made the most spectacular play of the game. Early in the second half, after West Virginia had cut our lead to 9, Travis was caught between two West Virginia players. He made a no-look, over-the-head pass to Deron for a layup to stop the rally and spark a 14–0 run. My heart almost stopped. I had never seen that before.

When Travis suffered a serious knee injury during our first exhibition, I thought he would be out at least six weeks. But he was back practicing the Friday before our opener, about a month ahead of schedule. He was still only about 70 percent healthy and probably shouldn't have played. But Travis got 13 minutes because Richie Farmer had come down with his second case of the flu this season and never got off the bench. I joke a lot about Richie's fragile health, but he was really sick.

I also began my personal campaign to bring Cawood back for another year. Van Florence gave me a T-shirt to wear to my postgame show. It had a picture of Cawood on it with the words, THANKS FOR 39 YEARS. Only the 39 had been scratched out and replaced by 40. "Forty" sounds like a nice round number to me. I think I'm going to get our crowd to start chanting, "One More Year" some night. If I can get him to stay through next year, I'll definitely try to get him to break Rupp's record.

It still bothered me the night before Thanksgiving when Dick Vitale came on during the introductions for the NIT and said, "Wait a minute, that isn't Kentucky. That's Pittsburgh. That's not Rick Pitino. That's Paul Evans." I had to sit there and watch all that. Maybe it was a blessing in disguise. The way we played against Pitt, we couldn't have beaten Oklahoma State anyway.

Sometimes, you just can't win. One writer even blamed me for poor attendance at the NIT. He wrote, "If Rick Pitino had done his job and gotten his team here, the crowd would have been 90 percent better." So, now, I was responsible for attendance. I probably would have been held responsible for crowd control, too.

We needed practice time. During the holidays there's no restriction on practice. I told the players there would be cots in the gym because I didn't want them to waste time walking across the street to Wildcat Lodge. I was just kidding. I thought. Actually, I enjoyed the week and I didn't make it a boot camp. We spent about three to four hours a day on basketball—executing, getting ready, starting to talk about who we are, understanding our roles. We must have spent about 30 hours in the gym. The practice limitations were off because we were on holiday.

Practice is a course outline for a coach. You can tell how your team is playing. The last two years the practices had been strenuous and energized. This year I noticed a different air about our players. It was like "Hey, we're good. It's okay. We'll get it done." That's not the case. Once you think you have it made and embrace success, you'll never get it done. Pittsburgh woke us up.

This is one of my greatest concerns coaching at the University of Kentucky. The fans adore our players, almost to a point where it's not normal. I can see where it would be very easy to fall into a comfort zone. This is dangerous because it impedes progress, stifles future growth, and prevents players from reaching their potential. They never get better. They just stay the same.

We had Thanksgiving dinner at the Hyatt. It was an "all you could eat" buffet, but for the players it was like going to McDonald's. They did not sit down more than twenty minutes because they knew they had practice. They had practice from 11:30 to 12:30, then they left at 1:00 and got to the Hyatt at 1:05. Then they had a practice at 4:00.

The reason they didn't eat a lot stems from last year. I had Mash, Sean, and about four other guys over to my house for a seven-course meal. We had soup, a little eggplant parmesan, ravioli, turkey. I told them, "Go ahead back for seconds."

"Coach, what about practice?" they asked.

I told them not to worry about it. "You got plenty of time to digest," I said.

Well, all of them threw up and never got through practice. So they said this year they were going to eat light.

Anytime you motivate a team after a loss, you have to visually show them what they did wrong, let them watch the film without commenting. Let them see themselves, what bad shots they took. Let them hear what the announcers had to say about them.

Everybody tends to make excuses if something goes wrong. Oh, it's not my fault we lost, it was the other guy. I told them, "This is the problem. We can't do anything about the Pitt game. What we're interested in is creating the solution. Going back to basics, what got us here in the first place. And that's an incredible work ethic. Treat the Pitt loss as fertilizer to help future things grow."

The team seemed to be in pretty good spirits. We even had four players modeling new haircuts. Aminu Timberlake was the barber, shaving off his own flattop and those of Jamal, Sean, and Junior Braddy—a move Mashburn told TV reporters was symbolic of our new attitude. I guess that's what's known as bonding. Even though the flu bug hit the team and knocked Sean out of practice for a couple of days, we finished the holidays more upbeat than we had been at the start of the week.

I originally planned to redshirt Chris Harrison. He had put on 15 pounds, but he still needed another ten before he could be effective. Those plans fell through Tuesday December 3, the day before our game with Massachusetts. We were scrimmaging at Rupp when Jeff Brassow, who had been averaging 15 points, went to make a backdoor cut, jumped to catch a pass, and heard his right knee pop as his foot touched the floor. The players gathered around him as JoAnn Hauser examined him.

I knew it was serious as soon as I saw him writhing on the floor, screaming from the pain. So did the team. You know how they knew? Jeff is the toughest guy on the team. Ankle injury, four stitches in his arm, four stitches in his head, and he comes back and plays. But this time, he had torn the anterior cruciate and the lateral miniscus. I've seen this happen five times. Bernard King, Eddie Lee Wilkins, Henry Thomas, Herb Sendek, and now Jeff Brassow. He was done for the year. I felt we should be able to get him a medical redshirt, which would give him two more years of eligibility if he's 100 percent. If not, he'll graduate.

Jeff flew to New York the next day where he underwent reconstructive surgery performed by Dr. Norman Scott at Beth Israel Hospital. When I spoke to the parents immediately after the diagnosis, I advised them of the options. He could have the operation here, at home in Houston, or go to New York. I knew this could be politically touchy, so I stayed neutral. In the end, it came down to expertise. Dr. Scott had operated on Bernard King, and King came back two years later as an All-Star. Norm had operated on more severe cases than anyone else.

I knew we'd miss him. Jeff was our Doug Collins. He was perpetual motion out there, moving without the ball. He ran backdoors, shot the threes. He led the team in deflections. When he comes back, he and his girlfriend, Mia Daniel, who plays for the women's basketball team and also underwent the same kind of operation, will have matching scars.

I was very concerned about our game with Massachusetts. I knew their coach John Calipari very well, and believe me, they weren't just taking the game for a big guarantee. John would not have invited himself to Rupp Arena unless he felt he had a good chance to win.

I met John when I was a counselor at Five Star camp and he was a camper. He wasn't that talented then, but he got the most out of what he had at Moon Township High near Pittsburgh and later at Clarion State. He was a good floor general, which is what you call point guards who can't play at the next level. John went on to become an assistant at Kansas and Pitt. He became interested in the UMass job four years ago. I was on the selection committee and I told the school I would stay involved to make sure the right candidates became finalists.

Originally, they had offered the job to Stu Jackson, my former assistant with the Knicks. He turned it down. Then, the committee turned to Calipari and another candidate. The votes were split evenly between the two. Hurting John's chances were the rumors concerning his relationships with Lou Carnesecca of St. John's and Rollie Massimino of Villanova. Massimino was upset because he felt Calipari had continued to recruit Bobby Martin for Pitt after Martin had given Villanova a verbal commitment in December.

Lou was upset about a wild rumor that Calipari had told a St. John's recruit not to sign there because Carnesecca was dying of cancer. To this day, Lou believes that story is true. I can't imagine John would ever stoop that low, although I wouldn't put it past him to say Looie would not see a prospect graduate because he would retire from coaching. But saying he's dying from cancer is pushing the limits of wanting a player a little too far.

"Stop it right there," I told the committee. "A lot of people are upset with John Calipari because he's hurting them in re-cruiting. I'm telling you people right now, because of all the criticism, I recommend you hire John. It's all jealousy and fear. If you want to get this thing going, you have to hire a guy everybody respects in the recruiting world." And they did.

I was really proud of what John had accomplished at UMass. He took over a program that had gone through ten straight losing seasons. In just four years, he had turned Massachusetts into a Top 25 team. Massachusetts was picked to win the Atlantic 10 Conference. They had just won the Great Alaskan Shootout with a 68–56 victory over New Orleans. Massachusetts was a veteran team. They did not have a starter taller than 6′ 7″, but I thought they had a stronger first-eight players than Pitt or West Virginia.

We caught UMass at a good time for us when we played them, December 3. They had played a midnight game Monday in Anchorage, then traveled 22 hours to get to Kentucky. We eventually wore them down with our full-court pressure, 90–69. We had much better shot selection than we had against Pitt. We shot 50 percent, taking the ball inside when they tried to pressure the perimeter.

Jamal had 28 points and 10 rebounds and Richie, who played a lot in the second half because Sean was still having problems catching his breath from the flu, had 22. Massachusetts looked like they just ran out of gas in the second half, when they shot just 34 percent and scored only 28 points.

I told Jamal I wanted him on the perimeter in our motion offense once every five times. The rest of the time, I wanted him inside. As for Richie, he took the wind out of Massachusetts' sails by backing in to the lane for pull-up jumpers whenever Massachusetts attempted to make a run in the second half. Then he helped put the game away by making ten straight free throws.

I started Dale Brown in Brassow's spot. Dale had only two field goals and was still struggling with the mechanics of his shot. The best part of his game was his defense. He did a pretty good job on Massachusetts' leading scorer, Jim McCoy, who makes more off-balance shots than anybody in college basketball. McCoy finished with 22 points, but had to earn them.

I decided to bench Travis Ford, whose knee still was bothering him. He didn't realize it, but after about two minutes, he still had a noticeable limp. I knew he was discouraged, but I wanted him to be 100 percent. I had not seen him play well since he transferred from Missouri.

We weren't there yet, either, but we were showing improvement. Last year, we constantly passed the ball until we got the shot we wanted. We had some games where we had 25 assists. We had only 13 against Massachusetts.

This was the first time I was disappointed in our fans since I'd been here. I didn't like their attitude. When I sent Gimel in, I heard them say, "Oh no, don't put him in." The fun was gone. They didn't want a close game. They wanted a blowout.

I didn't want John Calipari to be discouraged by the final score. I made a special visit to the Massachusetts locker room afterwards to speak to his team. I invited John and his staff back to Bravo's after the game. I was talking to Frank Mac-Inerney, the Massachusetts AD. We were talking about old times since he had been there when I played. All of a sudden, John Parisella, who was staying with me for the week, walked up and started in: "You taught that young whippersnapper a big lesson."

"No, no," I said, trying to be diplomatic.

John didn't get the hint. "Big lesson," he bellowed. Finally, I had to tell him Frank was John's boss.

"We're just kidding," John said, picking up his shoe and inserting it in his mouth as soon as MacInerney left.

If John Calipari stays at Massachusetts, he'll eventually have his name retired in the rafters at the Curry Hicks Cage, along with two of my former college teammates, Julius Erving and Al Skinner. The only way they'll ever retire my uniform is if Jersey Red steals it.

I just hope UMass can hold on to John. Even though the state is economically devastated, the university should have money for basketball as long as they earn a bid to the tournament. John has a clause in his contract guaranteeing him 10 percent of any revenue the school gets from tournament participation. UMass is already planning to build a new 9,600-seat arena.

As a Massachusetts alumnus and a contributor to the program, I want the coach to be happy.

# --10--

# *THE COACHING MERRY-GO-ROUND*

**I**f I've heard it once, I've heard it a thousand times: Are you going to stay at Kentucky?

I know why I'm asked. I've had three jobs in the last six years. But I promised Jamal Mashburn I would stay until he leaves. I said the same thing to Rodrick Rhodes. I plan to stay the length of my contract, which runs through 1996. Besides, if I left before then, it would be professional suicide.

On the other hand, it would be presumptuous of me to say I'll stay longer than that because no one can predict the future. Look at Mike Krzyzewski, the pillar of Duke. He could have been the coach of the Boston Celtics today if it hadn't been for an 11th-hour lobbying effort by Red Auerbach on behalf of his former player Chris Ford.

I enjoy building a basketball program—or rebuilding one. Both the highs and the lows. I like implementing systems that work. Boston University may not be a Who's Who in basketball today, but we helped create a strong foundation for that program. The same with Providence College and the Knicks.

Kentucky is on the way back, too. It's happened much more quickly than anyone here—including me—expected. This led to speculation among members of the New York media that I might be getting itchy to come home.

The season had barely started when the first volleys sounded. All I wanted to do was practice, practice, practice after our loss to Pitt in the preseason NIT. That was how I planned to spend my Thanksgiving vacation. But on Monday, November 25, 1991, the New York *Post* ran a story, claiming that I had a gentleman's agreement with Joe Taub, the minority stockholder, to coach the Nets. I didn't know the writer, Frank Isola. I had never spoken to anyone from the *Post*. And the only agreement Joe and I had was his investing $20,000 to become a limited partner in Bravo's. It didn't matter. I spent the next three weeks defending my integrity and defusing rumors about my future.

I wasn't the only one confused by this sudden onslaught. My children were really upset. "Wait a minute, Daddy," they said, "we're Knicks fans."

As I told them, I had no interest in the Nets job for many reasons. For one, I was happy where I was. For another, there were too many cooks in the front office spoiling the Nets' broth. Third, the Nets already had a coach, Bill Fitch, who had a year and a half left on his contract.

I started to track down the story. I discovered the writer, Frank Isola, was new in the business. He called me later that afternoon and said to me, "Look, I understand you're upset with something I wrote in the *Post.*"

I said, "I'm not upset, but I just want to let you know none of your facts are accurate. In the story, you say you're quoting sources close to me. I know the people close to me. One is Billy Minardi. I know you're not speaking with him. And I know you're not speaking with Jersey Red. And my mother does not speak to reporters."

He said, "Well, my sources say they know you pretty well."

"They couldn't know me very well," I told him, "because none of what you printed is accurate. If you want the truth, here it is: I have no interest in the Nets."

The next day, I called my second press conference in three weeks. I said I'd bet the *Post* $20,000 I wouldn't be coming to New Jersey. That the money would go to charity. I also said, right after that, it was only a joke. The local media had taken it literally.

*The New York Times,* which is supposed to be the ultimate in journalism, printed a similar story Thanksgiving. In the *Times*'s version, Bob Hurley said Rhodes had probably believed me when I said I was going to stay. Hurley had problems swallowing it, however.

The papers quoted Hurley: "It's a horror story and we go through it again and again. These guys will tell you they're staying and any one of them will leave. I've known Rick since he was at Five Star camp. But I know how close he is with Joe Taub. Like the rest of these guys, his agenda is about wealth."

I had Julie Watson from Sports Information call Bob Hurley about those quotes. He told her they were "absolutely" taken out of context. I thought so. Hurley claimed that when he talked with Harvey Araton, who wrote the story, he was talking about college coaching in general, not me specifically.

He told Julie: "Today, when a coach switches jobs, there is usually a great deal of money involved. But that is the college game in general. As far as questions regarding whether Rick Pitino will stay at Kentucky, I didn't address it at all. I simply said that, as a coach myself, I never even ask a college coach if he plans to coach for four years.

"Now, as Bobby Hurley's father, I do hope that Mike Kryzewski plans to stay at Duke for four years for my Bobby. But, as a coach, I don't ask. I do think a large part of the attraction for Rodrick is Rick Pitino. And I know his family is concerned about it.

"Coaches play such a large part in the decision-making

process for recruits. If a coach leaves, the NCAA should then allow the young man to make one more visit. I think Rick is a great guy, and I didn't say anything specifically about him to Harvey."

I believed Hurley, but I should have known rumors don't die easily in New York. Two weeks later, I was a major topic of discussion on ESPN's "Sports Reporters." Can you believe it? The NFL was winding down; the NBA was starting up; but Mitch Albom, Tony Kornheiser, and Mike Lupica were discussing whether I'd stay at Kentucky for the length of my contract. It must have been a slow news day.

Channel 27, which does my TV show, ran some footage from that "Sports Reporters" broadcast. This renewed local interest in the story. I decided to air my views to Cawood after our December 10 game with Southwest Texas.

I said, "I tell everybody I'm staying, then they come out with all this garbage. What they're saying is they don't believe me. If the station that does my TV show doesn't believe me, I should probably take it elsewhere." The crowd roared its approval. "The local media should stop checking outside sources when the primary source is right in their backyard," I added.

I had a feeling my comments would set off some sparks.

I didn't have long to wait.

The next morning, I received at least three calls from Ralph Gabbard, the station manager at Channel 27. I didn't return any of them. By lunchtime, I received a letter from him.

I spoke with the sports staff at Channel 27 for about ten minutes before practice that afternoon. On the 6 o'clock news, Rob Bromley, their sports anchor, made an on-the-air apology. He said he had known me for two and a half years, admired me and would take me at my word. He added that station management felt the same way.

It was a busy day. That same morning, in a story that appeared in the *Herald-Leader*, Jim Host claimed I had overstepped my bounds. He said I was out of line, trying to intimidate station management. When I learned Host had neither seen the tape nor heard my comments to Cawood, I was further incensed.

Jim Host has since apologized privately. I thought he should have done so publicly.

But, that's not all. Jerry Tipton put in three calls to Joe Taub.

"Should I call him back?" Joe asked me.

I told him there was no reason.

I finally got out of the loop December 16 when Joe Taub spoke with Tom Leach of WVLK radio and said I was never in the picture with the Nets.


How did all this happen?

The summer before, I was having lunch one day with Joe Taub. Joe said to me, "Look, I'm considering buying a large piece of the Nets. If I'm the majority owner, I'd like you to come in and be the coach."

He told me he could put together a package that would have made me the highest paid coach in the history of the NBA. It also would have given me a small piece of the team. I told Joe I was committed to Kentucky. In fact, the reason I was in North Jersey that day was to watch Rodrick Rhodes play in a summer league game.

"It's not about money," I stated. "Right now, I want to see what I'm building at Kentucky through. And, it's going to take longer than I thought."

He understood, and it was never brought up again.

I hadn't heard from Joe Taub for a while. He called me out of the blue just before Christmas. Joe said he was going to let Bill Fitch go. I asked him if he had told Fitch. He said, "I'm going to tell him tomorrow."

Then, I asked him what I could do.

"Well," he said, "I'm considering three people for the job—Mike Fratello, Stu Jackson, your ex-assistant, and Jim Valvano."

I told him they were all outstanding candidates and he couldn't go wrong with any one of them. He asked me who I liked the best and I told him they were all strong in different areas. Mike Fratello was a veteran NBA coach and had coached the Atlanta Hawks to some 50-win seasons. He knew the league better than the others, and had much more experience dealing with the professional athlete. Stu Jackson had never received the credit he deserved for his work with the Knicks. I thought he had a bright future ahead of him.

Then he asked about Valvano.

Jim Valvano had something the other two guys didn't have. He was a outstanding coach in college. More importantly, he could put people in the seats, which was a major problem for the New Jersey Nets. Jim Valvano is a P. T. Barnum, a promoter.

Joe called the next day and said the Nets were going with Valvano. Then, Joe and Jerry Cohen, the Nets' president, offered Valvano the job just before New Year's.

Rudy Martzke of USA Today reported this. That was the downfall of Jim Valvano as the Nets' coach. When Martzke mentioned it in his column, the majority owner, Alan Aufzien, was angry. He said Joe Taub could not make such a decision because he was only a minority stock owner of the Nets. Joe's rebuttal was that Cohen had been present when the deal took place.

The next day, Bill Fitch received a vote of confidence. Valvano would have had grounds for a lawsuit if he decided to pursue it. I was glad I was out of it.

And away from the NBA.

When David Stern became the NBA Commissioner, he did a tremendous job marketing the sport. But I think pro basketball has reached its zenith and is on the way down somewhat. Julius Erving and Magic Johnson have retired. Larry Bird is approaching retirement. Michael Jordan says he wants to play only three or four more years. I don't see any young superstars with great charisma on the horizon. I think there's too much parity and not enough excellence. With the excep-

The support we receive from our student body is phenomenal. All 7,500 students stand the entire game—every game—at Rupp Arena. Credit: David Coyle

Our fans show their feelings for Cawood at one of our postgame shows. No matter where we go, there are always several hundred fans who stick around after the game. Credit: David Coyle

The home of the Cats—our 24,000-seat Rupp Arena. Credit: David Coyle

John Pelphrey (center) was our spiritual leader. Here, he makes a point to Deron Feldhaus (left) and Richie Farmer. Credit: David Coyle

Our family picture—Ryan steals the show again. That's Christopher, me, Ryan, Richard and Joanne, and Michael in back. Credit: David Coyle

Our seniors know how to spell "Cats"—isn't education wonderful? Credit: David Coyle

Our cheerleaders have won three national championships, and do a great job with our crowd. Here they welcome John Pelphrey into the starting lineup. Credit: David Coyle

Air Farmer—this is the highest Richie ever jumped in his career. Credit: Amy Boyanowski

Bob Knight and I discuss how I can get one of his sweaters. Credit: David Coyle

I can't believe we got that call. Credit: Gary Landers

Mash was a monster in our first NIT game, against West Virginia. Credit: Amy Boyanowski

I knew Pel wasn't the quiet, reserved one. Here he is, mugging for the cameras after our SEC championship victory. Credit: Charles Bertram—Lexington *Herald-Leader*

Mash and Pel did everything but Duke it out with Christian Laettner in the NCAA Eastern Regional Finals. Credit: David Coyle

Sean be-deviled Duke
with shots like these.
Credit: David Coyle

Mash was all smiles as
he helped cut down the
nets after the SEC
tournament. Credit:
David Coyle

Our trainer Rock Oliver
gave Pel a lift after our
first-round win over Old
Dominion. Credit: David
Coyle

My son Ricky thought he could toughen up Mash before our first game in the SEC tournament. Credit: David Coyle

This is what our seniors had been waiting for—an SEC championship. Credit: David Coyle

We're back and the fans knew it—over 3,000 showed up at Bluegrass Airport to greet our team after the Duke loss. Credit: David Coyle

tion of the Chicago Bulls, I don't think there'll be another 60-win team in the near future.

It's not a coach's game in the NBA. Because of the salary cap, management has limited choices in making personnel changes. Trading players is difficult and complicated. It's easier to fire the coach, especially after a losing season. NBA coaches are treated like excess baggage, at times. It's an insult to our profession. The irony is the new coach usually doesn't do any better. It's just cosmetic.

There are exceptions, of course. Pat Riley, who allegedly makes $2 million a year coaching the Knicks, comes to mind. As does Don Nelson, who owns a part of the Golden State Warriors. But unless a coach is single or is independently wealthy and can afford to be fired, the NBA is not the place to look for job security. The NBA will have to come up with some new promotional ideas to maintain this level of excellence. I put nothing past David Stern. He is the best commissioner in all of sports. In all likelihood, the NBA will have two to four teams from Italy and Spain by the year 2000.

To be honest, the college game has changed a lot, too. I can still remember sitting with fellow coaches, moving salt and pepper shakers around, in an effort to bring the x's and o's of the game to life.

It doesn't seem like it was that long ago.

Today, the NCAA is cutting our hearts out by restricting the number of coaches on staff. As of this year, the max allowed are two full-timers and one part-timer, who can earn only $16,000. No volunteer assistant, no graduate assistant. I think there should be three full-time assistants and no part-time assistant.

At the same time, the pressures on college coaches to win are increasing. There was a time when 18 victories was considered a good year. Now, coaches are judged on whether their teams make the NCAA Tournament or not. And only 64 of 300 Division I schools can.

Maybe my philosophy on winning differs from that of other

coaches. I have no problem with coaches getting fired for consistent losing seasons. I don't care if they have 100 percent graduation rates. I know a lot of coaches have said there's a double standard. But I believe we are not paid to graduate players. We are paid to win, and to win without cheating. Graduating players really has very little to do with the coach. It starts and ends with the student athlete. A coach can make sure the student attends class and receives the proper tutorial help, but the young man has to want an education.

I hope the '90s will bring us closer to ending cheating in college sports. Back when coaches were making $30–$40,000, guys were willing to take more gambles. Today, when some coaches' contracts rival those of CEOs, most are not willing to risk either their salary or their prestige.

And, with the NCAA on a morality kick, why would anyone take the chance?

If the NCAA slaps a school with a violation, the administration fires the coach or forces him to resign. Jerry Tarkanian is a classic example. He was Las Vegas basketball for almost 20 years. Now, he's just a mirage in the desert.

Kentucky is fortunate that our president Dr. Charles Wethington knows the game of basketball and loves it. He even goes to high school tournaments. This does not surprise anyone who knows him. He's a native Kentuckian from Casey County. But he's also an administrator and he's told me that, under no circumstances, would he tolerate any cheating in this program.

I agree with him. When you get to Kentucky, you don't have to cheat to be great, because you're Kentucky. It would be as if IBM was wiretapping computer companies to find out what they're doing. They don't need to do that—they're IBM.

Most players come to school to learn, both on and off the court. For a coach, there is so much more teaching to do on the college level than in the pros. I think there's much more learning to do as well.

I think it would be exciting to take a year off, go around to various campuses and watch other coaches in action. I've never had that opportunity. If I ever get the chance, the first stops I would make would be Duke, Princeton, and Xavier.

There are some coaches in college basketball I really admire. One of them is Mike Krzyzewski of Duke. I think he epitomizes what a college coach should be. I don't know Mike well, but I think he does a great job. He's been to the Final Four five of the last six years and has won one national championship. He cares about his players. He gives them discipline. He makes life fun for them. He teaches them how to cope with both success and adversity.

Pete Carril of Princeton has really impressed me because of his willingness to adjust. He dominates the Ivy League every year. He makes nationally ranked teams tremble when he's seeded against them in the NCAA Tournament. He achieves this just about every year, even though he does not have scholarship talent. There are certain stubborn coaches who refuse to change with the times. Because of their reluctance to do so, the game is passing them by. But Pete, who is the ultimate in disciplined half-court offense, is still growing as a coach. He has incorporated the three-point shot into his slow-down game.

I'll always have a special feeling for Pete Gillen of Xavier. He's a friend and really has it together. We worked together for two years at Hawaii. Xavier is a small Catholic school in Cincinnati, but Pete has given it a national profile by taking his team to the NCAA tournament six of the past seven years. He has been approached by Providence, Virginia, Notre Dame, and Villanova. But he's happy where he is, and with what he is. But Pete Gillen would be just as happy teaching religion in high school again.

Not every college coach can be Mike Krzyzewski or Pete Gillen. There will always be room for Jerry Tarkanian and Billy Tubbs. The game needs certain rebel coaches because basketball is a microcosm of life.

I spoke at Jerry Tarkanian's testimonial in April because I

think he's done a lot for the game as a coach. Tark may not be everyone's idea of a college coach, but it's hard to argue with his results. He won a national championship in 1990 and reached the NCAA Final Four in 1991. He's been able to take kids from tough backgrounds, motivate them, teach them how to play hard, and give them a sense of teamwork.

Tark was a slowdown coach at Long Beach State. He's adjusted every step of the way. He has come to terms with the fast break, full-court pressure and then the three-point shot. Tark's players really seem to like him, too. Larry Johnson and Stacy Augmon turned down millions of dollars to turn pro after their junior year. Instead, they came back and played a final season for him, even after the NCAA put Vegas on probation.

Some people make fun of Tark's image as a Father Flanagan. But I think Lloyd Daniels was better off going to Vegas than staying on the streets of Brooklyn taking a bullet in an argument over drugs. I don't think it's right for his fellow coaches to judge Tark for anything other than what he accomplishes on the court. We're not God. It's up to the NCAA to decide whether he's innocent or guilty in basketball matters.

I don't know what went on at Vegas or the reasons why. Tark likes to tell the story about the time when he was coaching Long Beach State and his players got off the plane in T-shirts and torn jeans. At the same time, UCLA was getting on the plane in their leather and fur jackets.

"Now, who were the crooks?" he asked.

Maybe neither team.

# --11--

# *YOU'RE IN MY ARMY, NOW*

$\mathbf{B}$obby Knight could never run for public office in the commonwealth of Kentucky. He coaches Indiana. That's bad enough, but a lot of the fans here still remember back to 1975, when he smacked Joe B. Hall in the back of the head during one Indiana-Kentucky game in Bloomington.

Knight had always been openly critical of the way he felt the Kentucky program was being run. Once, while being interviewed by Cawood Ledford, Knight was invited to talk about the long-standing rivalry between the two great basketball schools. Knight refused.

"Not with all the crap that's going on here, Cawood," he said.

Our fans never forgave him for it. They never forgave him for the fact that he had won three national championships. And this year they disliked the fact that he had another national contender.

Kentucky-Indiana has always been a big rivalry to the people of both states. In Lexington, they still like to talk about the 1975 Mideast Regionals at Dayton. In that game, Kentucky spoiled Knight's perfect season, winning 92–90. Earlier that season, Indiana had beaten Kentucky by 24 points.

Kentucky fans from every small town from Florence to Crittendon to Williamstown to Georgetown came out to cheer the team that night as the bus drove back down I-75 to campus. There were signs, banners, cars driving past the bus honking their horns. People were just standing along the highway waving.

I had no relationship with Knight, one way or another. We played golf together for the first time last summer. Our paths had not crossed too much prior to that date. When I was younger, working as a counselor at Five Star camp, I would say hello to him. But coaching friends are ex-assistants and co-workers at camp. I certainly respect his coaching ability.

Herb admires Knight as a coach. Three nights before our Saturday, December 7, CBS televised game with Indiana at the Hoosier Dome, he scouted Indiana against Notre Dame in Bloomington. He didn't get home until three in the morning because there was a snowstorm. He spun out on the Interstate. But he was back in the office at seven, going over tapes. Mike Atkinson started calling Herb "Patton" and "Major" because he's spent so much time studying the General.

"I feel more like a private," Herb said.

He looked more like a drill sergeant that Thursday afternoon at practice. In the middle of a scrimmage, when Richie Farmer was guarding Chris Harrison, mild-mannered Herb grabbed Richie Farmer's shirt. He was so mad, he screamed. "Chris Harrison didn't even make a move and he went around you," he said. "And you took no pride in stopping him."

The players didn't understand Herb's anger. Or his motive. But I did.

He was motivating them to reach our goal—to play in the NCAA tournament.

But their practice habits had been horrible that week, and preparation is so key to what we do. Because of the NCAA's new 20-hour rule, there's no sense in continuing with a bad practice. When this happens, we end practice in the afternoon and bring them back that night.

Which is what I did.

The coaching staff wasn't surprised at my decision. Herb and Billy had been with me at the 1987 Final Four. They knew how much work was involved to get to the tournament. The night we played Massachusetts, the staff watched film of Indiana until three in the morning. Then they were at my house at seven to break down films again. Herb had broken down all of Knight's clinic tapes, just to get an edge on Indiana's screening techniques.

All the coaches were working on four hours' sleep. The more I thought about it, the more upset I got.

When they arrived back at Rupp Arena at ten that night, I ripped into them. I told them there were people out there who felt the Kentucky work ethic was a fraud. They seemed to respond during the 35 minutes we had left. I even heard Aminu talking on the floor for the first time this year. These were good kids, and they probably felt bad. I was only doing this for their own good. I didn't want them to be embarrassed on national TV.

I didn't know if we were ready to play Indiana. They were a machine, both on offense and defense. They had Butler down, 50–18, at the half. They beat Notre Dame, 76–46. If I had my druthers, I'd rather have scheduled Indiana about three weeks after Christmas. They were so hungry to win, and I knew they were going through double sessions all week for us.

Before our game, Herb had listened to their postgame radio show after they defeated Notre Dame.

"We know Kentucky," Norm Ellenberger, one of Knight's assistants, said.

"What can you tell us about them?" the announcer asked.

"Dig a fox hole," he said.

Kentucky-Indiana is a big game any time, but this meant more to our seniors. It was their last chance to beat them. We had come so close our first two seasons. We went up to Indianapolis with eight scholarship athletes, led at halftime and lost by two. Then, last year, at Bloomington, we lost by three and we were playing our bench the last five minutes because we had so many players in foul trouble. We learned that losing was not failure, but fertilizer for future things to grow.

We took the four-hour bus ride to Indianapolis, Friday. As soon as we checked into the Hyatt, we went over to St. Elmo's steak house for dinner. I had our first-year players get up and give a toast. I told them it was a tradition before the first road game. After Andre, Chris, Dale, and Aminu finished, I got up and made a toast to our seniors.

"Tomorrow," I promised, "we're going to make up for lost time."

Close to 35,000 fans crammed their way into the Hoosier Dome for the game the next afternoon. The promoters gave each school 10,000 seats and put the rest of the tickets on public sale in Indianapolis, so you know who the home team is going to be. At least 20,000 were wearing red.

This was the third straight year we had to travel to Indiana. Next year, the game is at Freedom Hall in Louisville, which seats 19,000. Under the old Big 4 format, Louisville, Notre Dame, Indiana, and Kentucky rotated opponents in a double-header at the Hoosier Dome.

Knight was a gracious host. Before the game, he walked over to Cawood and presented him with a red Indiana sweater.

When we defeated Indiana, 76–74, it was a great win for our fans and our team. I hadn't thought our team was ready to beat Indiana that early in the season.

A lot of our success that day was due to our three-point

shooting. We hit 11 threes against Indiana. They had none against us.

I've been an advocate of the three-point shot ever since the rule went into effect in 1986. When I took the Providence job, I played with the mathematical percentages and felt we needed to shoot the three-point shot. And shoot it in large numbers. We hoped to be the best three-point shooting team in the country. We had to be in order to win, and win big. We did lead the nation in three-point shooting, and it's certainly been a factor in our system ever since then.

At Providence, we were a very good three-point shooting team because we had a good inside game. Dave Kipfer and Steve Wright were two effective low-post players. We did not have a four or five man who could shoot the three. At Kentucky, I dreamed about having five players who could shoot the three on the floor at one time.

I feel if we make a good percentage of three pointers, we will be a difficult team to beat. That's the one statistic that means a lot to me. When we're hitting our threes, it means our motion offense is working and it allows us to get into our press more easily. The other statistic that's crucial is how many three-point shots the opposing team takes and makes. We have very lofty goals in that area. We'd like to hold a team to under 30 percent and we'd like them to take half the number of threes we shoot.

Deron came off the bench, made 5 three pointers and scored 19 points. We wanted to get him the ball because he was being guarded by Eric Anderson. We felt Deron could step outside and get that shot off. We also wanted to get the ball inside to Mash.

Jamal had a big game. He scored 21 points, grabbed 8 rebounds, dominating play inside. Mash scored 10 of his points during a 21–9 spurt that helped us overcome a 55–53 deficit and take a 74–64 lead. We had to sweat out some tense moments at the end. Anderson tied up Mash while the two were scrambling for a loose ball in the final 20 seconds. Indiana was awarded the ball because of the possession arrow.

Indiana had the ball with a chance to tie the game with a field goal or win it with a three. We had to execute perfectly on defense, and we did.

Indiana was looking to go to either forward Calbert Cheaney in the low post or guard Damon Bailey on the wing. But we did a good job denying Cheaney the ball inside and denying Bailey a chance to shoot a jumper coming off a screen. Indiana ended up getting a 23-foot jumper from Greg Graham that bounced off the rim. Richie Farmer grabbed the rebound, tumbling to the floor as time ran out.

I wasn't about to wait for the horn to go off. After Richie grabbed that last rebound, I immediately led the charge onto the court at the Hoosier Dome. "Start the Toyota commercial," I screamed, raising my arms in victory.

I didn't want anything to spoil the moment.

It all goes back to when I was at Providence and we played St. John's in a Big East game at Alumni Hall. They hadn't lost there in ten years. We won the game by two. But a big argument ensued when the clock ran out, yet the horn hadn't sounded. Lou Carnesecca was yelling, "One second, one second!" While the officials were deciding and while the Toyota commercial was running on TV, I told the team, "Get in the locker room. Get in the shower." The referees came running up to me, saying there's one second left. I told them, "Hey, our guys are in the shower. We're not getting out now."

I wasn't taking any chances on losing that game with a desperation shot.

It would have been traumatic to lose to Indiana. We played so well. Indiana's greatest strength is its shot selection. We got them to shoot 39 percent for the half and 43 percent for the game. We succeeded in frustrating Cheaney, who finished with 20 points but had only 6 in the second half.

Our biggest dilemma going into the game was how to guard Cheaney. We had a difficult time matching up John Pelphrey, who is slow afoot, with Cheaney, who is lightning quick. The best way to guard a great player is to not let him catch the ball. Once he has the ball, he then becomes the stronger player. Our strategy was to deny Cheaney the ball as much as possible.

Billy Minardi, Joanne's brother, told me it was worth the trip. He and another friend of mine, Joey Carballeira, bid $4,400 in October for a pair of tickets at the annual America Diabetes Roast honoring me in East Rutherford. Billy is a Wall Street broker for RMJ Securities. Joey is a partner at East Bridge Capital. They sat right behind the bench. It was like old times. Joey C. was a guard at Holy Cross at the same time I played at UMass. We guarded each other in college and later in pickup games at the New York Athletic Club.

This was one of the good times. Rock got so excited, he had the crowd doing a variation of the Tomahawk Chop called the Hammer. As in Hammer Time. When I went out for the post-game show, 8,000 people hung around, even though they couldn't hear me talking with Cawood.

An Indiana state trooper gave the team bus a police escort on the way out of town. We didn't ask for it. He just wanted to do it. He's from Kentucky.

"Wait 'til I show up at work tomorrow," he told Bernadette.

The team called Brassow when they got to the restaurant in Louisville. "I know I'm in the hospital," he told them, "but you didn't have to give me a heart attack."

I didn't travel with the team. I went to the airport to catch an eight o'clock flight to New York. I had to do some recruiting. Billy, Joey C., and I went uptown to 71st Street for pizza at Delicia's. Afterwards, we were standing in a bar called Wild-life, which was packed with people. The music was blasting and ESPN was on TV, recapping the games. When a highlight of our game was shown, one guy in the middle of the crowd started clapping and yelling. "There's my man. There's my man. You should have never left the Knicks. This guy won me a lot of money."

I put my head down. He didn't know I was standing three

people behind him. All of a sudden, he turned around and noticed me. He said, "What the hell are you doing here? You're supposed to be in Indiana, coaching that game."

While I was in New York, I visited my older brother Ronnie in the hospital. He had been mugged in September in Staten Island. The guy hit him over the head with a baseball bat. He had lost a lot of weight, and had been in and out of a coma. When I saw him, he moved his eyes, and gave me a big smile.

It just broke my heart. It was a very touching moment because my mother, who had been living with him day and night, cried over it. Then, Ronnie went back to sleep. We were were hoping to move him to a Westchester hospital, where he could get therapy. He had major brain damage, but we had hope.

Kentucky popped back into the Top 10 Monday night. We were ranked ninth. When I got back to Lexington, I got a chance to introduce the new governor, Brereton Jones, at a fundraiser. I told the people I had more years left on my contract than the governor, who can't succeed himself. I suggested he could coach the New Jersey Nets, because I'm not. See, I was still fighting that rumor.

Jeff Brassow came home from New York that same afternoon. We installed a range-of-motion machine in his room. With four hours' work a day, Rock predicted Jeff would come back in record time.

Chris Cameron told me he did something he never thought he'd do during our next game with Southwest Texas. He escorted Carlos Toomer to the Star of the Game show.

Carlos had been criticized by the fans and media ever since he arrived at Kentucky. He wasn't one of those high school All-Americas. But he played like one against Southwest Texas. Carlos came off the bench to hit 3 three-pointers and scored 12 points as we romped to an 82–36 victory at Rupp. Jamal, Deron, and Junior were going wild on the bench.

My son Chrissy was always bugging me to play Carlos. One

night, on the way out of practice, he asked me, "Dad, if we're up 1,000 points, will you play Carlos?"

He had told Carlos at practice, "If you want more playing time, you got to talk to my dad." We got home. It was after eleven o'clock. The phone rings. It's Carlos, asking what he has to do to get more minutes.

I played Carlos more during that game because Junior came to me at halftime and said, "Don't worry about my minutes, coach. Play some of the younger guys."

There are times when I'm really touched by this team's unselfishness. I made it a point to go over and congratulate Sean Woods afterwards. Sean didn't score a point but he played within himself. Three assists and no turnovers in 20 minutes. He would have never done that two years ago.

After the game, Chrissy came into the locker room. I saw him high-fiving Carlos and telling him, "You got to listen to me more often."

The unbelievable thing was, Carlos was listening to him. That's a scary thought.

This was the only route we'd have all season. I told Mike Atkinson to pump Southwest Texas up in the scouting report. Lie about the offense. Even if the offense stops at a certain point, exaggerate the motion. I remember one time when I was at BU, I told my little guard Brett Brown he was guarding a guy 6' 4", 200 pounds. The kid came out, he was 5' 8", 150. Brett asked me if it was the same guy. "Yeah," I said, "he looked it from the stands. But I was up top."

When the bus left for our game with Morehead State at Louisville's Freedom Hall on the afternoon of December 12, Aminu Timberlake wasn't on it. I suspended him indefinitely. Bernadette, who is the liaison between our program and CATS, the Center for Academic Tutorial Services at Kentucky, told me she reached a boiling point with him. Aminu is a bright young man, a Fine Arts major who had a high score on his ACT. But he was underachieving academically. He cut three classes.

When someone cut a class before the 20-hour rule, I would have made them get up and run at six in the morning. So I did the next best thing and hoped it would send a message to the rest of the players.

Normally, we would travel to Louisville the night before a game. But this was exam time, and I didn't want the players missing class. It made for a long day. And a long night. We won 101–84, but we struggled.

We hit the wall in the second half. The building was hot and, even though we scored 62 points in the first half, our press took a lot out of us. Jamal looked washed out after having played 37 minutes. We've asked him to be the man over and over, and he needs some rest. I told him he could have the bus ride off.

On the way home, I had planned to show the team the tape of the game on the overhead TV. Herb informed me it was against NCAA rules to run a film after a game. But I didn't need a film to see we needed another big man who could defend in the post and rebound. We were involved with two players—Rodney Dent, a powerful 6' 10", 240-pound center from Odessa Junior College, and Conrad McRae, a 6' 9" 235-pound junior from Syracuse.

McRae was declared ineligible by the NCAA. The eligibility committee ruled that the Syracuse staff, along with Rob Johnson, who has been described as a New York City "street agent," had several contracts with McRae and his family during his junior year at Brooklyn Tech—a period when contacts are illegal.

If McRae transferred, he would be eligible right away and have one and a half years left to play. Jim Boeheim, his coach at Syracuse, called and told me it was down to Maryland and Kentucky. I liked our chances because McRae was a Gaucho—just like Jamal and Andre. As for Dent, he told me we were one of three schools, with Arkansas and Auburn. We made a last-second call to have him visit during the weekend of our game with Arizona State, Saturday, December 14.

When Dent was in high school in Georgia, he verbally committed to Auburn, but he didn't meet the Proposition 48 guidelines and had to enroll at Odessa. He played two years there and then enrolled at Howard Junior College this fall in an attempt to earn his degree.

We had been recruiting Dent all fall. Just before the early signing date, I got a call from Auburn coach Tommy Joe Eagles, complaining that Herb had been negatively recruiting. He cited as examples Rodney Dent and Mark Hutton. I said, "Wait a second, you got the wrong guy here. What Herb Sendek told them was 'Auburn looks like they're going on probation. Why don't you wait and see before you make your decision.' That's all he said. Meanwhile, your people have been telling Mark Hutton that Mashburn is a small forward. It works both ways."

We stopped recruiting Mark Hutton once he verbally committed to Auburn. But I told Tommy Joe we were still going to recruit Rodney Dent.

"But, he's committed to us." Eagles said.

"Rodney Dent has told us he is not committed to Auburn. I will call him tonight. If he tells us he has committed to Auburn, we will stop recruiting him."

We called Dent, who told us he was wide open. The next day, I was on the phone to Tommy Joe and I relayed the message. The communication lines were open and there were no hard feelings.

Four games in eight days. I felt like I was back in the NBA. We decided to go through a light workout Friday afternoon, but I still had a busy day. Aminu came to my office in the morning. He apologized. He said he understood why I suspended him. I accepted his apology but I still wasn't going to play him against Arizona State.

I rushed right home after practice to get dressed for a dinner Joanne and I were throwing for twenty-eight of our friends at Bravo's. Joanne's father and mother were there, along with her brother and her friend Lillian LaPenta. Joanne told them the big news. The baby will be a girl. That should put an end to all those jokes about us producing a basketball team. With four brothers, do you think that baby will be spoiled?

The guest list also included some of the former players from my 1987 Providence team. I had not seen Dave Kipfer since then. He was there, along with Billy Donovan, Donnie Brown, and Bill Cramer.

The party lasted until three A.M. and ended with Jodi DiRaimo's wife Kathy singing show tunes at the piano downstairs. Jersey Red, who showed up wearing his Mickey Mouse tie and madras pants, stole the show. Jersey has become a big celebrity in this town. He did an interview for local TV, a radio interview with Cawood, and made a cameo appearance on my coaches show.

As I said before, Jersey has never been afraid to speak his mind. For the last three years, he had been needling Billy Donovan and me on his nightly telephone message. He claimed Johnny Joe Idaho, a friend of ours who works as a mutual clerk at a Massachusetts dog track, could beat us in a shooting contest.

I beat Johnny Joe from the foul line and from the three-point line. Billy shut him out. Ever the sport, Johnny Joe challenged me to a rematch the next day and I beat him again. It didn't take long for the excuses to start. My arm. My wrist. My ankle. I told Johnny Joe that shooting against Billy and me was a lot different than shooting against former Brown University guard Billy Reynolds, who works as a columnist for the Providence *Journal.* We led a fairly sedate life. Reynolds did not.

I discovered some of our players—John, Deron, Junior, Sean—had been experimenting with a Ouija board. They claimed they had made contact with a spirit named Eve, who informed them we would beat Arizona State by 30 points. She told them Kentucky was going to the Final Four and Duke wasn't. Weird stuff.

Before the game, I told the team I had a dream we were playing for the national championship. One official made a call that could have really hurt us, but he was overruled by another official and we went on to win the game. The players began whispering among themselves, "Eve. Eve." Apparently they couldn't get in touch with her Friday, but they figured she must have spent the night at my house. It was all good-natured fun.

I wonder if Eve knew Dale Brown was going to have a big game. Dale had a reputation for being a great shooter in junior college, but he had struggled ever since he arrived. I called him into my office Friday.

"Every time you miss a shot, you think the game is over," I told him. "Shooters miss. Shooters get on a roll. You can't let whether a shot goes in determine whether you're playing well or not."

I told him to go out and play with reckless abandon. And he did. Dale scored 24 points and made six straight three-pointers as we defeated Arizona State, 94–68. Herb had to feel vindicated. He had recommended Dale and had worked with him since practice began. He took Dale out for an extra hour's shooting practice the afternoon of the game.

I had been worried about Arizona State because we had so little time to prepare for an athletic team. But we played well. We shot 60 percent and played excellent half-court defense. Our supporting cast raised its level of play.

Gimel was getting better, and Andre Riddick seemed to have benefited from Aminu's suspension. Andre played 17 minutes and had three more blocks, including one where he swatted a jump shot by Lester Neal with such force that his momentum carried him over the Arizona State bench and into the stands.

The biggest problem I had was coming up with 30 tickets.

I produced ten. I got eight apiece from Luther Deaton, who's second in command at Central Bank; and four from L. D. Gorman. I also got four from the staff.

It made for a fun evening for the crowd, who gave Jeff Brassow a standing ovation early in the third quarter when he hobbled out to midcourt to raise his hands in a Y to supply the last letter of our "K-E-N-T-U-C-K-Y" cheer. It also left an impression on Rodney Dent, who sat up in the stands with Rock. Rock told me Rodney liked to be called "Moon." It's a nickname he picked up when he was eight because he liked to eat Moon pies. He still has a big appetite.

Dent called Sunday night and told me he wanted to come. But he is such an impressionable young man. I knew he still had to call Tommy Joe Eagles and tell him he wasn't coming. He had to get over that hurdle.

Then, within the hour, I got a call from Conrad McRae. He wanted to come, too. I told Conrad about suspending Aminu Timberlake for underachieving academically. I'd been told he had a similar problem. Conrad McRae scored like an Ivy Leaguer on his SATs but he wasn't doing well at Syracuse. I told him we wouldn't tolerate any missed classes. I wanted to make sure he was aware of it.

Monday afternoon, I held a team meeting. The players voted unanimously to take Conrad McRae. Jamal said he was a good person, and that carried a lot of weight. I had met privately with Andre and Gimel to discuss the subject before we had the vote. They were the two players who might be most affected. I didn't want to disrupt our chemistry.

I said to Andre, "You're the future. If you say you don't want me to take him, I won't even bring it up."

"No, coach," he said, "Competition's good for me."

I then spoke with Gimel and he told me he had no problems, as long as it made us a better team.

The seniors admitted they were probably being selfish, but they felt the addition of another big man would help us in the tournament. But John Pelphrey was sensitive about Gimel, who had been starting and had begun to show progress the last few weeks.

Then we discussed Rodney Dent. Jamal said there was one thing he hadn't liked. "Coach," he said, "when he visited, he walked up to Junior and said, 'What's up, fool?' I don't like anyone making fun of my teammate."

I think Rodney was just trying to be macho so he could fit in. Or he was making a joke. He'd gone through two traumatic experiences in the past year. He lost both parents, a brother, and a sister in two separate fires. His mother had died just two months ago.

Rodney and Andre have suffered personal tragedies at a very young age. They are both going to need a close friend.

Life is such a roller coaster. One hour, you hear your wife is going to have a baby. Two hours later, you hear your brother is in a coma. Ronnie had taken a turn for the worse. His temperature was up to 104 and we couldn't move him to the other hospital. I was really worried about my mother, too. My nephew Randy went up there after he finished his examinations at Villanova. It was in God's hands.

# -- 12 --

# *HOLIDAY GREETINGS*

I made a pre–New Year's resolution ten days before Christmas. My wife overheard me cursing up a storm at our last game, so I resolved to tone down my language.

It took some restraint Monday during our intrasquad scrimmage, especially after Travis Ford and Richie Farmer took two bad shots for their team in the final minute and a half of a close game. But I was trying to be on my best behavior, at least until Saturday, when we played Georgia Tech on ESPN in the second game of the Kuppenheimer Classic at the Atlanta Omni.

This was a big game for us. I felt Georgia Tech had Final Four potential. They had everything—size, depth, balance, and quickness—you need to get there. With those two 6' 11" guys—Matt Geiger and Malcom Mackey—they looked like an NBA team.

If I were just starting out in this business, I might not have accepted this game. I would have scheduled an easier one due to all our tough league games. But now that I'd been in the NBA and was getting closer to 40, I wanted to go the other way. I'm at a point where I want to experience the excitement of the big challenge.

If nothing else, I felt it would tell us if we needed more size.

We locked up one big man for next year when Rodney Dent officially committed on December 16. He said Auburn would be like home, but he liked our style of play better. He called our local media. Rob Bromley of Channel 27 had him on a live hookup from Texas. He needed to pass two courses to graduate. Warren Heagy, an Odessa attorney who adopted him, told us Dent planned to take a three-hour correspondence course in history at Texas Tech and a three-hour class in ocean ecology from Odessa. The correspondence course began the same day, and the class at Odessa involved a field trip to Mexico from December 27 to January 2. If everything worked out, he planned to enroll January 15 for the second semester, sit out the rest of the season, and have two years of eligibility left.

Conrad McRae didn't call back.

It was tough arranging practice around exams that week. We worked out for an hour and a half Monday and just two hours Tuesday. We still found time to celebrate Bill Keightley's birthday. We surprised him with a cake at the end of practice Tuesday and the team sang "Happy Birthday" to him. Bill is 67. He's seen it all.

But I guarantee he never heard of this one.

I got a call Wednesday from Warren Heagy. He told me Rodney had gone out to celebrate after he committed to us and he developed an acute case of appendicitis. He had to be rushed to a hospital and had to wait six hours before an operating room became available. Heagy said Rodney wasn't going to be able to complete his courses in time to graduate and enroll second semester. I placed a call to see if Rodney could do his work in the hospital. We wanted him on campus so he could practice and learn our system.

I also received a call from Jim Boehiem about Conrad McRae. He told me McRae was worried about playing time and was going to make an official visit to Maryland. Jim did not know Maryland was on probation until I told him.

After we finished watching the personnel splice on Georgia Tech in the lounge that day, I told the players I was giving them Christmas Eve off after practice, and also Christmas day. But there would be practice Christmas night. I made sure everyone had some place to go and then I invited Jamal Mashburn, Aminu Timberlake, Carlos Toomer, and Andre Riddick over to my house. I said I'd fatten them up. I gave Mike Atkinson two days off so he could visit his wife and three children in Long Island. I gave Bernadette Christmas night off so she could rendezvous with her husband in Cleveland, Tennessee. See, I'm not Scrooge.

Aminu told me he had finished his finals and I told him he could come back to practice. He looked like he had turned it around. His tutors told me he spent five to six hours a day in study hall.

I could see the effect the time off had on our practice. If we wanted to beat Georgia Tech, I knew we had to outrun them. But we looked tired during a three-hour workout. At the end, we ran a layup drill. Full court, four balls. The players had to make 85 baskets in two minutes. It took us five attempts to reach that goal. At least I didn't swear. That's three days now. If I didn't do it watching John Pelphrey play defense, I'll never do it.

That night, I arranged a pickup game for our staff. I had to get our coaches back in shape. I was feeling feisty. I even blocked a couple of Bernadette's shots. Hey, I told her not to come in the lane, but she wouldn't listen. I wish we had taped that game for our staff Christmas party Thursday night. It would have produced some laughs.

I had spoken with Jim Boeheim two, three times that week. He was all set to help Conrad McRae pack his bags. But the NCAA stunned everyone late Thursday afternoon when it reversed its decision and declared Conrad McRae eligible to play for Syracuse. The NCAA had claimed that on two separate occasions Rob Johnson had driven McRae to Syracuse. While there, he had been fed illegally by the coaches at an off-campus restaurant.

The reversal came after the panel on eligibility learned that NCAA investigators had spoken with McRae about his recruitment while he was still in high school. They had learned about the alleged violations then. But they still allowed him to play. The same committee decided a ruling had already been made and so reinstated McRae. I'm glad. McRae did not want to transfer. He was enrolled in the Newhouse School of Communications and was scheduled to graduate in four years.

The picture looked a little brighter with Dent, who had been released from the hospital after a day, and had immediately enrolled in both of his courses.

The players from Penn State, Georgia, and Georgia Tech showed up for the Kuppenheimer banquet at the Omni Convention Center Friday night wearing beautifully tailored suits and sports jackets. I told our guys to dress casually and they did, wearing sweaters and shirts. Henry Thomas looked like he was on his way to the casino in the Bahamas with his short-sleeved white shirt. Travis didn't even bring a pair of shoes or dress pants on the trip. He ended up wearing a pair of Herb's shoes and borrowing a pair of pants from our manager Vinnie Tatum.

I tried to make light of it when I got up to speak. "We at Kentucky are not wearing any double-breasted suits, and I just wanted to let you know why. The NCAA took away everything, and that includes the clothes off our backs."

A lot of our guys do not own sports jackets and ties. It's not that they're from poor or disadvantaged backgrounds. It's just that they haven't purchased that type of clothing. The players were embarrassed. They wanted to go back to their rooms and change. But I told them our dress code was to be neat and clean and carry ourselves in a proper manner. It was the same way in the NBA.

"Coach, in the old days, Kentucky was the best-dressed team in the country," John Pelphrey reminded me.

We received bad news even before we took the floor against Georgia Tech the next night. Sean had been sick all Friday night. He had food poisoning; we had to hook him up to an IV Saturday afternoon. He played only six minutes during our 81–80 loss to Georgia Tech at the Omni. So much for our plans to press their freshman point guard Travis Best.

I had hoped we could harass Best into turnovers with our press, and force their big people to run the floor more than they had in the past. As it turned out, the only good thing about this tournament was the certificates for dress suits our players received.

We found out what the road was all about. We were supposed to have neutral officials for the Tech game. That's what the contract required. The Tuesday before, I had checked to see who the refs were going to be. As soon as I saw Rusty Herring's name, I called John Guthrie, the director of officials in the SEC. I said, "Wait a minute. I thought the officials were to be mutually agreed upon and that we'd use officials from both conferences."

All three officials were from the ACC. Guthrie tried to tell me the SEC had picked up two of those officials as backups.

I told him I had a major problem with Rusty Herring. I call Herring "Red," because I feel he really did a number on us last year when we played North Carolina, another ACC school, in Chapel Hill. Incidentally, Rusty was from Durham. The other two referees had never worked an SEC game before. Guthrie called me back and said, "Look I can take Herring off the game, but it would make you look bad because we don't black-ball." I agreed to the officials listed. But in my mind, Fred

Barakat, the director of officials in the ACC, had pulled a fast one, or else he did not read the contract. We play Georgia Tech next year at Rupp. I want to see what happens when John Guthrie assigns two SEC officials who have backup affiliation to the ACC.

I felt that, true to form, Herring did another number on us against Georgia Tech. Forget about taking the charge. We tried to take three in the first half and never got a call. The officiating changed from minute to minute. One minute, they weren't calling over the back. The next, they were calling hand checks. By the end of the half, Jamal, Deron, and Gimel each had three personals and John had two. I was forced to play a combination of Aminu, Andre, Sean, Junior, and Dale the last minute of the half. We blew a seven-point lead. Junior came down two on four at one point and threw up a wild three-pointer.

It all started unraveling at the beginning of the second half. We fell behind by 20 points. We made a game of it at the end, but I wasn't around to see it. I was ejected after Herring whistled me for a technical foul with 14:18 to go. I got hit for being out of the coaches' box when I stormed onto the court after Matt Geiger went over the top on Gimel and there was no call.

"You stink," I yelled.

I wanted that T. I figured I had to fire our players up some way. But then Sam Croft, another official, blew a second technical on me from across the floor. I don't think he realized Herring had already called the first one. I really believe officials don't want to be embarrassed on TV, but I gave Herring a piece of my mind on the way out. I machine-gunned him: "You stink. You screwed us at Carolina and you screwed us tonight."

Many coaches have problems with certain officials. At times, we imagine they're out to get us. When we calm down and realize how absurd that is, we realize that an official's job can be impossible. I do believe certain coaches and officials would have trouble getting along in church on Sunday.

It was just as well that I left. If I had stayed around, we might have lost by 20. When I left, we were down 52–41. Jon Barry, Rick Barry's son, hit all four technical foul shots. Travis Best made a three-pointer. All of a sudden we were down by 18.

I told Herb to run the team and watched the rest of the game on TV in the locker room. Herb did a great job holding things together in my absence. We got within two points twice in the last minute, getting as close as 79–77, when Gimel made a layup with 14.5 seconds to play. But Barry made a pair of free throws in the final 5.5 seconds to put the game away. If we had had another minute or two, it could have been our game.

We had blown a golden opportunity. Ohio State lost. Arizona lost. If we had won, we could have been in the Top 5. We shot poorly in the first half, just 35.3 percent. We didn't rebound, and we allowed Barry to have a career night—24 points and 11 assists. The only good thing about defending Barry was that John Pelphrey took him down early. Other than that, we played soft on him.

Barry is such a cocky kid, but a hell of a basketball player. The rest of our players should have followed John's example and hit him at least five more times. We had recruited him when he played for Paris Junior College in Texas. He was supposed to visit, but canceled the trip at the last minute. He stayed in Texas to receive the school's athlete of the year award at a team banquet. He never bothered to call and tell us, though, so we stopped recruiting him.

A lot of people wanted to see this game as a valiant comeback for Kentucky. But I thought it was more Dale Brown's great play and Georgia Tech's fatigue rather than our legendary hustle. Dale scored 13 of his 21 points in the last 11 minutes. He had three steals in just over a minute. He took Barry to school. And Dale did it in front of his mother. This was the first time she had ever seen him play. Anywhere. A mother can do so much by coming to a game. There's no better motivational tool than a mother's presence.

When we finally got back to the hotel, the Kentucky fans in

the rooms facing the atrium came out on the balconies and began chanting, "Go Big Blue" as we walked across the concourse to a conference room where we had a late-night snack.

I didn't have to worry about eating the next morning. The service at the hotel was awful. The syrup for the waffles at our team brunch never arrived. The rolls were so hard you could play softball with them. To make matters worse, the videotape machine we ordered never materialized, so we couldn't show films of our next opponent, Ohio U. I think the only good thing that came from this tournament was that a lot of the proceeds went to charity for the needy children at the Scottish Rite Hospital in Atlanta.

The manager tried to apologize on the way out. I told him if my restaurant ran the way his hotel did, it would go under within a year. Sometimes, I revert to being a New Yorker.

When I got on the bus, we did a head count and I spotted Aminu wearing a North Carolina hat. I snapped out. I told the players I never want to see them wear a cap from North Carolina, Georgetown, or any other school.

"You play for Kentucky," I told him. "You don't see a player from the Pistons wearing a Chicago Bulls cap."

C. M. Newton felt the Omni would be a neutral site because we would have 5,000 fans there and the Georgia fans would probably root for us against Tech. The problem was we sold only 2,200 tickets and most of our fans were seated behind the basket or in the bleachers. The Georgia fans did get on the Georgia Tech players as the Yellow Jackets made their way to the locker room prior to the game. The fans chanted, "Dawg Meat, Dawg Meat." But they weren't about to stay around for a 9:40 game. When our game finally tipped off, they were in their cars headed back to Athens.

Sunday we flew to Cincinnati for a game with Ohio University at Riverfront Coliseum the next night. We were all in a foul mood. When I reviewed the tape of our Georgia Tech game, I saw that the officiating was worse than I had thought.

The officials' rating system in the NBA is much more efficient. They don't care whether you're at home or on the road. If a coach starts arguing, they walk to the other side of the court. They have a contempt for coaches who try to intimidate them. They don't have to answer to any coaches. They report directly to Darrell Garrettson, the head of officials, in the league office. Finally, there's a uniform set of rules. Right now the college game is called differently in different regions. Hank Nichols, a veteran official who works with the NCAA, is trying to standardize calls, but it's an uphill battle.

It's difficult winning on the road in both the NBA and college. In the NBA, it's fatigue. When a team is on a four- or five-game road trip, the home team has a distinct advantage. But the officiating is fair. That may not always be the case in intersectional college games. When a team plays on the road, they take their chances with officiating. Familiarity does not favor the visiting team.

Anytime a team wins on the road, it's usually because it brings its own officials or has neutral officials working the game. To win on the road, a team has to be ten points better than its opponent.

After a loss, most coaches can't wait to get back on the practice floor. And I was no exception. We practiced for a good three hours Sunday at Riverfront Coliseum. By the time we got back to the hotel, I had stopped being upset with the players. I cracked up when Chris Harrison pulled out his front teeth and began imitating Herb demonstrating defensive slides.

Joe B. Hall always used to refer to the state of Ohio as O-High-a with that southern drawl. O-high-a U. gave us all we could handle. We won, 73–63. It was one of those old-fashioned games when your heart is in your mouth on every play. When I first started coaching, before the NCAA instituted the three-point shot, it seemed every game was like this contest. One-point games. Overtime. Double overtime.

Everyone circles Kentucky on their calendars. We're their

biggest game of the year. They all play at a different level emotionally.

We were fired up, going on all cylinders. For 40 minutes, it was a war. Ohio is a Mid-American Conference team, caught in the shadow of the Big Ten. They may not be Top 20 right now, but they were a senior-dominated team that stayed within five against Ohio State at Columbus until the final six minutes. They executed as well as any team we had played so far. It was good for us to play against their ball-control style.

We shot 50 percent. Even though we made only 5 of 20 three-pointers, we came up with the big plays when needed. Our defense broke it open. With the score tied at 53–53, Deron dived on the floor to tip away a long inbounds pass and Richie picked up the loose ball, making a three-pointer. Then Deron helped put the game away with a spinning three-point play. That move must have pleased many in the crowd of 15,390 who had watched Feldhaus and his brothers grow up just down the road in Maysville.

I was surprised the place wasn't sold out. Once we had packed the place with 17,000 for one Blue-White scrimmage. This was a rare chance for our fans in northern Kentucky and Cincinnati to see us play. But I guess it was a sign of the economic times.

After the game, I was asked if I wanted to play Ohio U again. "Yes, in about 1999," I said. We might play them again, but I won't enjoy it. I'd rather go to the dentist.

We dropped from eighth to 17th in the week's AP Top 25. No one could figure that one out. We lost to a ranked team by one on the road. But I wasn't about to let that affect my holidays. I had Andre, Mash, Carlos, and Aminu over for Christmas dinner. I did the cooking: salad, Italian bread, lasagna, and meatballs. Then I went out and barbecued some steaks in the garage. I knew Andre liked steak. Everything was fine until I set off the smoke alarm in the garage from the smoke.

Mr. Handyman, I'm not. My father could fix anything. He built our second home, brick by brick with my uncle Joe. They did all the electrical work and plumbing. His talents went to my brothers Bob and Ron.

My mother left me her skills. She was an extremely organized woman who started out as a hospital clerk at Bellevue Hospital. She worked her way up the ladder, passing test after test to become a senior administrator. She finally retired after the commute from Long Island to New York became too much.

My father continued working. He was a blue collar worker supervising an industrial building, two blocks away from Bellevue. I worked for him during my summer vacations from college. I learned how to punch a clock and served as a night watchman. I played ball at McBurney's Y on 23rd Street and 7th Avenue during the day and read everything I could get my hands on at night. Novels, magazines, newspapers.

My dad worked until he was 67 and retired. He died six months later of bone cancer. To this day I become squeamish when someone says they are retiring.

# --13--

# *THE RIVALRIES*

You could tell the Louisville game was getting close—Bill Keightley was getting uptight. We were in the Atlanta airport the Sunday before Christmas, waiting for our flight to Cincinnati, when he spotted one of their players, Everick Sullivan, talking to Sean Woods.

Sullivan was headed home to South Carolina for the holidays, but Bill was not exactly filled with the Christmas spirit.

"Louisville's here," he said. "They're too close. Woody's close friends with all their guys. He's down there all the time. That's why we lost Cliff Rozier."

Bill would blame everything on Louisville if he could. The Gulf War. The recession. He's disliked them for over 40 years.

Cawood Ledford and most of our players claim our biggest rivalry is Indiana. But Bill knows better. We played Louisville December 29 last year in Freedom Hall and he wouldn't celebrate Christmas until after we beat them. We were up 21 at halftime and he came in, sweating like a son of a gun. "Twenty minutes' 'til Christmas, Twenty minutes 'til Christmas," he kept saying to me.

This year's game was scheduled for Saturday, December 28 at Rupp Arena. Bill was in a lather most of the week because Louisville was undefeated.

The Kentucky-Louisville series does that to the people of the Commonwealth—and to most of our office. Marta has a bumper sticker taped to the wall behind her desk that reads, YOU'RE UGLY AND YOUR MOTHER SENDS YOU TO LOUISVILLE. There is also a mimeographed sheet that reads "Will the lady who left her five children in Freedom Hall, please pick them up. They are beating the Cardinals, 84–76."

For 60 years, from 1922 until 1982, Kentucky refused to have anything to do with Louisville. Kentucky ruled basketball in the state. Adolph Rupp and Joe B. Hall had no desire to share any headlines, paydays, or border-to-border fan support. Even in the city of Louisville, there are as many Kentucky rooters as U of L fans.

For years Kentucky refused to play Louisville. The Wildcats always felt Louisville was not in their class, even though the Cardinals had won two national championships in 1980 and 1986. Kentucky felt it had nothing to gain and everything to lose. During that period, Kentucky and Louisville met just three times—in the 1948 Olympic trials and in the NCAA tournaments in 1951 and 1959. After trying to match the two teams up several times in tournament play, the NCAA finally succeeded in 1983. Kentucky played Louisville on March 26, in the Mideast Regional finals at Knoxville, in what has since come to be known as "The Dream Game." Louisville won the right to go to the Final Four, defeating the Wildcats, 80–68, in overtime.

Governor John Y. Brown, ever the politician, wore a blazer at that game, half red and half blue. The entire state came to a standstill and gasped when Kentucky guard Jim Master hit a jump shot as time expired in regulation to send the game into overtime. In the end, Louisville's press was too much and Denny Crum, who claimed he wanted a piece of the Cats "anywhere, anyplace," finally got his wish.

Later that spring, under pressure from Louisville, state legislators, and fans of both schools, the Kentucky Athletic Association finally relented and agreed to schedule Louisville on a regular basis, beginning in 1984. The teams have played nine times since then. Kentucky holds a 6–3 edge, but I could see how relationships between the schools could be strained. Louisville is starting to pressure UK into a football game. It won't happen as long as C.M. is athletic director. UK has everything to lose and nothing to gain, especially in the recruiting world where Kentucky must come up with the best three or four players in the state every year.

Eddie Sutton didn't ease the tensions when he said Kentucky looked at Louisville as a "little brother." That just incensed the Louisville fans.

Dwayne Morton, Louisville's best player, didn't help matters this year. In an interview that ran in the *Herald–Leader* before the game, he said he never really had any interest in Kentucky. The only reason he had visited Lexington was because his high school coach thought it could help his chances of becoming Mr. Basketball if it was thought he had considered the state university.

I never felt a deal was cut for Dwayne, but I don't buy this token visit nonsense. Dwayne loved his visit to UK, and he told every member of our team he wanted to be a Wildcat. I'm puzzled as to why he would say otherwise.

Bill Keightley kept poking his head out of the tunnel near our locker room at Rupp Friday afternoon, waiting to see if Jock Sutherland had left Rupp Arena following my press briefing. Jock is a former high school coach from Lexington who does color on Louisville games on WHAS radio. According to Bill, he has made his living from attacking one school, Kentucky.

Sutherland coached Dirk Minniefield, an All-State guard at Lafayette High. When Minniefield signed at Kentucky in 1979, the story around town was that Jock thought he could parlay that into an assistant coaching position for himself. When that didn't happen, Sutherland began attacking Joe B. Hall on a local sports talk show he did on Ralph Hacker's radio station. The attacks became so vicious, Hacker had to let Sutherland go, and Jock took his show to Louisville.

Jock had been C.M.'s assistant at Alabama, and C.M. asked if I would do a special interview with him. I said I was busy because I thought Bill Keightley would break out in hives if Jock showed up on campus. Bill spent most of the week prior to the game sitting in the equipment cage, taking phone calls from friends, who wished him good luck. Jersey Red, who flew in for the game, and I didn't improve his nerves when we went down to the cage to egg Bill on about the Cardinals.

Kentucky basketball is Bill's life, and he was not about to let Louisville rain on his parade. When Kentucky was put on probation, he died a little bit. He was really disgusted, upset with administration because they hadn't fought it. He felt the probation had taken two years from his life. When we took over, he saw us playing hard and overachieving. He felt rejuvenated.

Bill didn't need much to juice himself up for this game. The way he remembers it, Louisville trashed the visiting locker room at Rupp Arena two years ago after they beat us, 86–79. Actually, they had left the showers running and some tape on the floor. But you'll never convince Bill otherwise.

His finest hour occurred in 1986 when Kentucky defeated Louisville, 85–51, giving Crum the worst loss of his career. That was the season some enterprising Kentucky businessmen printed up shirts that said CREAM GAME, a takeoff on the Dream Game concept.

On Friday, during final preparations for Louisville, C. M. Newton casually dropped his bomb. "We may not be able to take Rodney Dent," he said.

What? I was stunned. Then C.M. explained that our compliance office had made a mistake. The office miscalculated the number of scholarships we had to give our athletes. They never checked with the NCAA. At the beginning of the year, the basketball office was told we could give a semester scholarship to our walk-on, Junior Braddy, with the stipulation that we could pull it back if we signed Dent. Although scholarships in all other sports are renewable on a semester basis, scholarships in basketball and football are renewable on a yearly basis.

We were stuck. We had a great player, and no scholarship. We filed an appeal to the NCAA. We sought an exemption, claiming we had kept Henry Thomas on scholarship even after doctors had told him he would risk permanent knee damage if he tried to play again.

I know all about North Carolina-Duke, Syracuse-Georgetown, and UCLA-USC. I think Kentucky-Louisville is as big as any game in the country. Sean called it Army-Navy. To Bill Keightley, it's the one that sticks with you all year if you lose.

There were fans looking for tickets as early as eight in the morning. They were standing in the pouring rain near the Hyatt with home-made signs. Jersey Red told me tickets were going for $500 apiece. I was so preoccupied with the game Saturday afternoon that it wasn't until I was in the car on my way home after shootaround, that I realized I had left my son Ricky and his friend at Rupp arena. I made a quick call to our managers. I tried to comfort Joanne: "Hey, we have four more at home." I don't think she was amused.

By the time I came back for the game, Rupp was already a sold-out sea of blue and white, with just one little patch of red over in the corner. It was a wild scene, with Dick Vitale mugging for the ESPN cameras up in the student section and Louisville and UK cheerleaders standing side by side at midcourt while our pep band played "My Old Kentucky Home."

The bitterness came out as soon as Dwayne Morton trotted onto the court during introductions. Morton had spent most of the warmups trying to psych himself up. But I don't think he was prepared for the thunderous boos he received. Or the sign that said, MORTON: DID YOUR MOTHER HAVE CRUM CAKE FOR DINNER?

Speaking of dinner, one of the chefs in our restaurant was there rooting for Louisville. Would you believe I even got him four tickets? I told him he had better cook us some good pasta when Joanne and I got back to Bravo's.

We celebrated there after our big 103–89 victory.

Joanne could put away the rosary beads for now. She's had them ever since I was coaching at BU. For this game, she carried every religious relic she owned.

Fortunately, we didn't need a miracle. Just Pel. John stuck it to Louisville pretty good, scoring 26 points and making 5 of 8 threes. He told me he had been motivated by a column that appeared in the Louisville student newspaper. It not only guaranteed a big Cardinal victory, but also suggested the Doctors of Dunk would be playing "the lowliest of creatures." And then it said that they were "starving for some in-your-face-dunk-on-you-pointy-little-head-don't-bring-that-limp-stuff-in-here-Pelphrey basketball."

Someone sent John the story with the pertinent passages highlighted in red. Our managers kept running off copies and placing them in his locker every day. I didn't know about it until game night. I guess I should thank the writer for getting John out of his slump. He had made just one of ten threes in our last two games, but he banged out four in the first seven minutes.

John found out where he thought the writer's seat was on press row, then went over to give him a mouthful at the end of the game.

"Get your limp stuff out of here," he yelled.

Later on, John discovered he had the wrong guy. He apologized to him in the locker room.

Aside from Pel, the guy who hurt Louisville the most was Mash, who had his way inside and scored 25 points. They both had nights you dream about.

There was only one ugly incident. It occurred when Sean drove the lane for a layup with 9:03 left and was fouled by James Brewer. The two collided with such force that Woods landed on top of Brewer's left shoulder. Instead of helping Sean down, Brewer simply dropped him to the floor. Woods glared at Brewer and the two had to be separated. The officials hit Brewer with a technical, and we used that as a springboard to score five straight points and increase our lead to 83–71. When I did our TV show the next morning, we showed a tape of the play. I had to bite my tongue.

Bill Keightley would have been glad to escort Louisville out of town. He was wired. You should have seen him. The top of his head was completely red. His blood pressure must have been 200.

We didn't make him sweat this one out too much. We shot 54.2 percent and made 11 of 21 threes. Denny Crum claimed all week that his team had embraced the three-point shot and he was correct, but we got in their faces defensively the entire game and they made only 3 of 17.

Morton was not a major factor, scoring just 13 points and grabbing 4 rebounds in 23 minutes. His attitude toward Kentucky had changed since he enrolled in Louisville. He taunted the fans quite a bit during the game. It must have been hard for him, coming into Rupp carrying all that baggage.

This was the first time since the resumption of the series that a Kentucky team had scored over 100 points on Louisville. We stopped their ball reversal, holding them to just 8 assists. Most of the 24,295 fans—the third largest crowd in the history of Rupp Arena—loved it. So did Tony Delk and Walter McCarty—Tony was so excited, he had his barber shave the initials "UK" into the back of his head.

This was one game everyone on our team helped win. Carlos, Aminu, Chris. Rock told me Travis was ready, and we even brought him off the bench for two brief rotations. He made four free throws. I had wanted to rest Travis for two weeks, but I didn't have much choice. I put him in late in the first half. Sean was in foul trouble, Richie was tired, and Chris was over his head at that position. It was either Travis or Bill Keightley.

I was so relieved at the end of the game, I gave the team Sunday off. I figured Bill Keightley would probably need it.

We were 7–2 and ranked 17th in the poll again this week, even though we won four games against teams that received votes in the Top 25. I felt there were six or seven teams in the poll that might be good, but it was difficult to tell. Take Kansas or Georgetown: they hadn't played anybody, but were talented teams.

Our next game wasn't until Thursday against Notre Dame, but I wasn't taking any chances. We practiced double sessions the next three days and spent New Year's Eve in the gym.

That's right.

Films at 9:00; stretching at 9:45; and practice from 10:00 until 12:10.

As a coach, New Year's is the one holiday I'm concerned about because people get careless. They don't act like themselves. They drink and drive. If our players went to parties on campus, it would be different. But our students were on break.

We tried to make it festive. We hung up THE BIG BLUE NEW YEAR sign we used a couple of years ago at Midnight Madness. At midnight, my sons Chrissy and Richard, who had been watching the ball drop at Times Square on the TV in my office, came out waving pom-poms. Our players went over to the water cooler to toast in 1992.

Now nobody on the team has any girlfriends left to hug.

But it worked out okay. I promised the players pizza after practice.

Our series with Notre Dame had been going on for 49 years. For 32 of them, the game was held at Freedom Hall in Louisville. This was always a big holiday treat for our fans there.

This was the first time Notre Dame had ever come to Rupp Arena.

I thought Notre Dame was going to be very good this year. They had four senior starters, including LaPhonso Ellis, who Herb claimed was the best rebounder in college basketball; Daimon Sweet, Elmer Bennett, and Keith Tower.

But their record was only 1–4. They hadn't played since December 11 when they lost by 20 points at Boston College. They were scheduled to be on the road for nine straight games until January 23. And then they would play Missouri, who I felt would be about 15–0 at that time. Notre Dame also had to face DePaul, USC, North Carolina, UCLA, Duke, and St. John's.

I felt sorry for their new coach, John MacLeod. He's a nice man, but he was in a difficult situation. He had been away from college basketball for almost 20 years. The recruiting and the game itself are so different these days. Everybody thinks it's difficult going from college basketball to the pros, but it's just as difficult going the other way.

We know. We've done it.

After the current seniors leave, it will take Notre Dame's program four to five years to achieve its former prominence. I'm not sure if they can ever come back unless they get into a conference. It's tough to get a schedule as an independent. Notre Dame football can get away with it because they're one of the premier teams in the country. But basketball's different. Some teams use conference tournaments as a way to get to 17 or 18 victories and make themselves more attractive to the NCAA tournament selection committee. Notre Dame does not have that luxury.

I broke my New Year's resolution one day after New Year's. We defeated Notre Dame, 91–70, but I was disappointed at the way we played. I thought we shot well. We made 12 of 22 threes. But we got off to a slow start, played poorly in the second half, and never made Notre Dame pay for its mistakes. Get this: the Irish shot 58.6 percent.

Notre Dame had a reputation for being a patient, ball control team, but John MacLeod turned them loose in the opening minutes and they grabbed a 14–5 lead. Richie doused the fire. I put him in after Dale Brown suffered a minor ankle sprain two minutes into the game. He lit up the arena for 22 of his 28 points in the first half when we grabbed a 48–32 lead. Richie shot 8 for 11, made 5 of 7 threes and was 7 for 7 from the line.

"The basket looked as big as the Pacific Ocean," he said later.

Still, when he put up a 25-footer in the second half, I lost it.

"What are you trying to do Richie?" I screeched. "Go for the scoring record?"

I wanted to get upset at Mash, too. He had only 5 rebounds. Then I looked at the rest of his line. He scored 25 points and took over the game after Notre Dame cut a 19-point lead to 63–55. Mash settled the issue when he hit 2 three-pointers and posted up Notre Dame's center Jon Ross for a field goal to give us a 83–67 lead with just over four minutes to play.

We also got some productivity out of the center spot for a change. Andre came off the bench to score 8 points and grab 8 rebounds in just 15 minutes. He threw down three hellacious dunks. Andre had been coming on in practice—he had dunked over Mash and Pelphrey and sent Pelphrey flying on one slam. He still needed more work at the foul line. He missed all four attempts. At least he hit the rim.

"Kentucky was game ready, and we hadn't played," Mac-Leod said. "Having 21 days off in the middle of the season was too much to overcome."

We had no time to rest. We were scheduled to open our SEC season Saturday, January 4, at South Carolina. I figured we'd be going into a hornet's nest. South Carolina was 8–1. They had just joined the conference and this was their first SEC game ever. They had sold out the Kentucky game by December 20. The Gamecocks were planning all kinds of commemorative ceremonies. I knew the atmosphere at Frank McGuire Arena would be emotional.

Plus, I wasn't sure whether we'd have Dale Brown back for

the game. I goaded Dale into practicing the morning after the Notre Dame game. I told him it was nothing more than a candy sprain, and NBA players play with them every day. See, he didn't die. By the way, NBA players would have been out a week.

When we charter to games, we use a twin-propeller plane that must be 45 years old. I think the last time I saw one like it was in the movie *Casablanca.* I keep looking for Humphrey Bogart and Ingrid Bergman when I ride in it. Rock affectionately refers to it as the *Enola Gay.* That line is certainly a bad joke, but buckle your seat belts.

The trip to Columbia gave me a chance to see the two horses I co-own—Rail and Tourney—work out at Aiken, South Carolina. I got up at six Saturday morning and drove down there with Seth Hancock, Billy Minardi, and Joey C., who had flown in for the game. Aiken is like a basketball camp for horses. It's where they go to learn the fundamentals and become champions. Seth had high hopes for Tourney, who is a filly out of 49'er. He thought she was physically the best filly he had ever seen.

He also nominated Rail for the Triple Crown series. When I first bought part of Rail, I thought he was a Deron Feldhaus type of horse, just a hard worker. But Seth told me he had really come on.

We'll see.

# --14--

# CONFERENCE PLAY

Somebody once said there were only two sports in the Deep South: football and spring football.

I had a hard time believing it until I came to Kentucky. College football is a way of life in the Southeastern Conference. We put 60,000 fans in Commonwealth Stadium for every home game. It is not unusual for football budgets at SEC schools to run in excess of $8 million.

At least where we coach, basketball has a fighting chance.

The other coaches in our league do not have the same feelings.

The first thing I noticed in the SEC was that the basketball was good, but many of the basketball coaches were treated like the second-sport coaches. I heard it at our SEC coaches' meetings: "Oh, my AD is never going to go for this. He's a football guy." That was the first thing they said. Where I came from, it was just the opposite: "Oh, my AD will go for it. He's a basketball guy."

Fortunately, at Kentucky, C. M. Newton is open to anything that makes the program better. In fact, there are times, if he had his wish, he'd rather be in the Big Ten. He feels that Kentucky has more in common geographically with the Big 10 than the SEC. He feels our football program would be more competitive. He doesn't have any problems with basketball in either conference.

Kentucky has always been been a pioneer in basketball. It has dominated the SEC for almost 50 years, simply because it took the sport more seriously than other schools. It found a vacuum and filled it.

Back in the '30s, when assistant football coaches took turns coaching the basketball teams at other SEC schools, Kentucky was always one, two steps ahead. The university capitalized on a steady stream of state-supplied talent and innovative coaches like Johnny Mauer and Rupp. Their trademark was a fast break that simply wore down opposing teams.

Kentucky has always been the most disliked team in the SEC. We win. We have 36 banners to prove it. But it's always a fight.

It doesn't matter how long a school has been in the league. Take South Carolina. Last year, they were an independent in football and they played in the Metro Conference in basketball. But when they were invited to join the SEC, they jumped at the chance because they felt it would increase visibility in both sports.

South Carolina tried to be as visible as possible when they hosted Kentucky January 4 in Columbia during their SEC debut. The school pulled out all the stops. The game had been sold out for more than two weeks. The administrative staff showed up wearing tuxedos.

The only thing missing were party hats and horns. They even honored Frank McGuire. McGuire had coached South

Carolina from 1965 to 1980, and produced a number of nationally ranked teams with players he brought down from the New York Catholic League. The sellout crowd gave him a standing ovation when he made his way to half-court to present the game ball to referee Don Rutledge during pregame ceremonies.

Jamal Mashburn spoiled their party. He popped all the balloons. Mash scored 33 points and grabbed 11 rebounds during an 80–63 victory. He shot 14 for 27.

Going into the game, Mash was making close to 59 percent from the three-point line. If he shot that percentage against South Carolina, he could have had 50. As it was, he shot just 5 for 15 from the three-point line. At one point, after he missed a couple of threes, he wanted to stop taking them. He told me he didn't want to be a ball hog. I told him if he stopped shooting, he was coming out. Mash's biggest problem was he couldn't believe he was that wide open. South Carolina's coach Steve Newton decided to play his seven-foot center Joe Roulston on Mash, and it was a definite mismatch because Roulston was too slow to guard Mashburn outside.

I could see it coming. The night before, he had stayed out on the floor for an extra half hour of shooting practice. He would have never done that last year. Jamal had not been a good three-point shooter as a freshman. He shot 27 percent. But this year, he's like a weightlifter who's suddenly discovered he has muscles and wants to work out all the time.

I was really pleased with our effort. We fell behind early, 25–13, but we never panicked. We outscored South Carolina 35–12 over the last 12 minutes of the half. Mash, Pel, Junior, Richie, and Gimel each made at least one three-pointer during that run.

We shot 59.4 percent for the half and 52.5 for the game against a team that had been leading the NCAA in field goal defense. We wore out South Carolina's guards with our pressure. We had three point guards now that Travis was healthy, and we just threw waves of pressure at South Carolina's point guard Barry Manning. We even got a good whistle from the officials.

When we got back to Lexington airport, I picked up my car and Pel immediately jumped into my seat on the bus. "I'm going to be coaching here someday," he said. "You all better be nice to me if you want tickets."

Believe me, our conference games won't all be this easy.

I felt the SEC had the best talent in the country this year. Dick Vitale said if you selected an All-Star team from our conference, we could beat any other conference. Center Shaquille O'Neal of LSU, forward Todd Day, guard Lee Mayberry of Arkansas, guard Allan Houston of Tennessee, forward Robert Horry, guard Hollywood Robinson of Alabama, and Jamal are all destined for the NBA. The competition is only going to get tougher too, because of new coaches like Lon Kruger of Florida, Wade Houston of Tennessee, and Tommy Joe Eagles of Auburn. Kentucky, Georgia, Tennessee, Arkansas, LSU, and Alabama all had the Top 20 recruiting years in the country.

No wonder I started jogging again to relieve some of the stress. I jog up to ten miles a day in the summertime. I'm not a marathon runner, but I enjoy it. I convinced Rock to go for a run with me in Columbia, but I lost him somewhere around the stadium area. He said if he hadn't run into the officials, he might have never found his way back to the hotel.

Now that conference play had begun, sleep was out of the question. I began turning into an insomniac. As of Monday, I hadn't slept much for four straight nights. I stayed up until three o'clock, watching West Coast Sports Center, a rerun of *Zorro*, and a black-and-white Gregory Peck western. Gregory Peck looked like he was about 25 years old. God, was it bad.

I was edgy at practice Sunday night. I got all over Dale because I felt he was milking his ankle sprain. He had to get tougher. When he was in junior college, he was treated like he was in a country club. The team even had a month off after

Christmas. He wasn't going to find it that easy at Kentucky.

At the end of practice, Dale came up and apologized to me for not fighting through it. I felt it was a step in the right direction. Dale was going to have to come up big Tuesday, January 7, when we played Georgia at Rupp Arena. We assigned him to guard Litterial Green, who had just scored 38 points against UCLA on national TV. Green got 32 in the second half and made 7 of 10 threes during an 87–80 loss on the West Coast.

Dale was very familiar with Green's game. The two grew up in neighboring communities in Mississippi. Dale is from Pascagoula. Green is from Moss Point. They'd been going at it ever since they were kids and were matched up against each other a lot over the summer at the Pascagoula rec center.

We were going to treat Litterial Green like we treated Michael Jordan when I was with the Knicks. We wanted to just tire him out and hope he shot a low percentage. When he was defending our players, we wanted him to fight over our screens. We wanted to run him into screens two or three times each possession. Then we wanted to press him full-court without trapping. When they crossed half-court, we wanted to deny him the basketball.

Junior and Dale gave up their bodies to stop Green during a 78–66 victory. Sean did a great job helping out. Green had only 11 points. He shot 3 for 15 and had only one field goal in the first half.

Junior had slipped in the lineup after the Georgia Tech game. We were scrambling to get back into the game when he told Herb he couldn't run because he felt like God had taken all his oxygen. For a while, he slipped to about the last man on the team. He wasn't working hard in practice, not on the level we wanted. Then he realized nothing is a given and he started working harder. He had his second consecutive strong game, coming off the bench to score a career-high 15 points as we ran our record to 11–2 and 2–0 in the SEC. Junior played with a broken nose he'd suffered in practice.

We hadn't been in this type of game for a while. We shot only 39 percent and made just 6 of 25 threes. Georgia had come in with a great game plan. They wanted to isolate on Mash and take it inside. It worked. Mash was called for his fourth foul with 12:24 to go. But our other players really picked it up. Especially Deron, who came out of a minislump with 15 points after missing double figures in his previous four games. Georgia is a great defensive team, great at shooting the gaps. We played smart. We went with a smaller lineup with Deron in for Jamal, and their big people had to chase us around screens. We spread the floor and got a lot of backdoor layups. The lead went from 8 to 15 before we put Mash back in with 4:46 to go. We made every clutch free throw down the stretch. At one point, we were working on 24 in a row.

The most interesting thing I have in my office is a piece of the Berlin Wall. A coach who worked at our summer camp sent it back from Germany. I received a piece of coal from a fan Wednesday with the Wildcat logo pressed on the back. I couldn't resist playing a practical joke on Bernadette. I convinced her it was valuable. "This is called the perfect chunk," I said. "A piece of coal like this is worth between $1,500 and $2,000 on the open market. Look at the way it's cut." Bernadette swallowed it. So did Suzetta. They're so trusting.

After three games in five days, it was nice to get back to practice at Memorial Coliseum. Remind me to keep bugging Gene DeFilippo about getting a new scoreboard. I don't think Rupp will mind. We have to reset the one we have now every time we start a new drill.

This was the last week we were allowed unlimited practices before the NCAA started counting hours again for the second semester. I wanted to make the most of it. We had a two-hour film session, followed by a two-hour practice. Deron shot the ball well in our scrimmage. We felt he'd have a big game against Florida Saturday because he thought he couldn't miss. It was in his profile.

I watched the Arkansas-Alabama game that night. There were 14 pro scouts at Tuscaloosa. I saw Jerry West of the Lakers and two scouts from Portland on the tube. There must have been six pro-draft choices on the floor. I knew Arkansas was good. But Alabama won the game, 65–63. Todd Day made a baseline jumper with seven seconds to go that would have given Arkansas the lead, but officials called him for charging. Nolan Richardson said afterwards that nine out of ten times that play would have been called a block and they would have counted the basket.

I felt like saying, "Welcome to the SEC, Nolan."

I knew the SEC was good, but I had no idea Alabama was this good. I could see why the writers voted Robert Horry to the preseason All-SEC team over Jamal. As a matter of fact, I thought Horry would go high in the first round of the draft, but his temperament was questionable. As for Hollywood Robinson, he may be the most talented guard in America. He got 20 on Arkansas. He was doing it against Lee Mayberry and Day.

When I got to work Thursday, I decided we had to become a good rebounding team, or die trying. We went double sessions. I had the players tape up at 11 and then again at 3:30. I jumped all over our freshmen big men during a scrimmage. When Andre didn't block out on one play, I sent him over to work out for five minutes on the stationary bike.

When he didn't sprint over to the weight room, I told him, "Ten minutes."

When he kept walking, I tacked on five more. Andre will a difficult time reaching his potential if he doesn't work hard. Basketball has to become important to him. Unfortunately, he will look back someday and wish he could do it all over again. We're staying positive with him, but he needs more motivation.

Andre and Aminu were a year and at least 20 pounds away. They are never going to be great players until they learn to love the game. I had some hope for Gimel, who was developing better hands and more refined moves in the post. He was better conditioned and was becoming a much better shooter. When he shot three-pointers in practice last year, five out of every ten would be air balls. This year, he had already made one three against Louisville and another against South Carolina. He still gets into foul trouble.

Gimel had finally persuaded his mother and sister to move out of Miami. She's now working at a hospital in Jessamine County near Lexington. His sister Barbara enrolled at Jessamine County High.

I was planning on making Rodney Dent our center of the future, but the NCAA threw us a curve Friday. They ruled against our appeal on Henry Thomas, our injured player on a medical scholarship. I couldn't believe it. This could lead to coaches running off injured players so they could give their scholarships to healthy players.

We had to tell this story to Dent's legal guardian, Warren Heagy. C.M., Herb, and I spoke to him in a conference call Saturday before our game with Florida. Heagy felt the school had made an honest mistake. He said, "I want him at Kentucky." Rodney still had to get his grades. But it looked good.

Besides, I liked his attitude. When we were recruiting Rodney, I asked him about Matt Geiger and Malcom Mackey from Georgia Tech. "Coach," he told me, "I played against those guys. I will handle them on the backboard."

I glanced at Travis Ford's stats after our 81–60 victory over Florida that afternoon. A career high 8 points, 8 assists, and only one turnover in 20 minutes. That's what a point guard should do in a game.

I had put Travis in the lineup in place of Sean Woods at the start of the second half and he helped turned a one point lead into a blowout, triggering a 21–6 run with a pair of three pointers.

"He's like a fly you can't kill," Rock said and then started impersonating a fly. "Call the Orkin man. He's a pest."

For the first time, Travis looked like he might be coming on. He had been ten pounds overweight most of the year. We gave him additional playing time because Florida decided to play a zone—they were dropping off any time Sean got the ball. Travis was a better shooter than Sean, and was able to constantly penetrate the lane. He made some great passes to the open man whenever he was double-teamed.

Travis can be spectacular. He made a behind-the-back pass to Andre for a layup in the first half, then he hit Gimel with a 30-foot pass for a breakaway layup at the beginning of the second half. He conducted a clinic on how to take the three pointer. He went inside, then outside—and once, he went inside a second time before taking it.

Travis was still bothered by his knee afterwards. He had an ice pack on it. He may need an operation after the season.

We shot 51.1 percent, the tenth time this season we shot better than 50 percent. We also played good defense. Florida had only 3 assists, which means we forced them to go one-on-one and break their patterns. They were a pretty good three-point shooting team and we shut them down. We were 7 for 19. Florida was 0 for 6. That's a 21–0 difference.

Despite the final score, I was concerned that John and Sean were paying more attention to the pro scouts than the game. Sean was trying to score off his dribble penetration. He had only 3 points, and Pel shot only 2 for 7. He wasn't moving without the ball. I'd seen this before. Some seniors have an hour glass. They turn it upside down and see the sands running out on their year. They think they must put numbers on the board instead of contributing to the team. Deron and Richie knew they weren't going to the NBA, so they just played.

We jumped back into the Top 10 two days later. We went from 15th to tenth in AP and from 11th to ninth in CNN.

I thought we were a pretty good offensive team, but the score that jumped out at me over the weekend was Troy State's 258–141 victory over DeVry Institute. Troy State was

102 for 190 from the field, including 51 of 109 from three-point range. It was bizarre. Nobody could have played any defense. You don't see that even in summer league games. The teams must have had an agreement. I think they wanted to be in the Guinness Book of World Records.

I had been in my office about two hours Monday when Sam Wyche, who had just been hired by the Tampa Bay Bucca-neers, called and told me he wanted to bring Rock Oliver in as his strength coach. Rock was going to stay on until the end of the season. We'll miss him and the comedy routines he does on our bus trips. We can always find another strength coach, but Rock was also a great recruiter. He was an awesome presence on campus when kids made their official visits. Every prospect we signed felt he was a factor in their decision.

This was an opportunity he couldn't turn down. He would be getting a $35,000 raise. In the old days at Kentucky, the school would not have let him go. Five guys from eastern Kentucky would have put up the money to keep his talents at UK. But this is a new regime.

For a while, it appeared Rock was having second thoughts. He was very close to the staff. Billy was his best friend. When Billy was on the road, Rock would take Billy's wife Christine, who was eight months pregnant, to Lamaze classes. But it's always been a dream of his to work in the NFL, so he decided to take the offer.

It didn't take long for his family to adjust to the idea of life in Florida. Rock showed his four-year-old daughter Ashley a map of where they were going to live. When he told her about the weather and the water, she ran over to the closet and got out her bathing suit.

I immediately started thinking about replacements and came up with the idea of hiring Reggie Hanson, last year's captain. Reggie has a great personality. Always smiling. Al-ways laughing. He always played hard. He was the glue to our team last year. Reggie spent this year playing for the Louisville Shooters in the Global Basketball League. Before we could hire him, Reggie still had to complete work for his degree. He was taking a correspondence course and was due to graduate in May. Maybe this would push him along.

Nashville has always been considered the capital of country music. I joked about that with Cawood before we bused down there for our January 15 game with Vanderbilt.

"We're off to see Bobby Joe Sinatra perform," I said.

We arrived in town Monday night. Bill Keightley showed me a copy of the *Tennessean.* Dan Hall, one of Vandy's players from Gilbertville, Kentucky, had blasted me for criticizing the officiating in last year's game there. Vanderbilt had shot 51 free throws and we shot only 7.

"He will make a big show out of it, like he does everything else. He'll try to get a few calls out of it," Hall said of me. "He hopes the officials will read it. Well, I hope he reads what I've said."

He wouldn't have said that if he was coming to Lexington. I had no idea who Dan Hall was until this year. Vanderbilt's lineup is always filled with players from Kentucky who weren't recruited by UK.

What bothered me was I had been very complimentary about Vanderbilt last March when I was an analyst for ESPN the night the NCAA bids came out. I praised the Commodores. I said they definitely deserved to be in the tournament. Dan Hall would someday learn that his remarks would come back to haunt him. Players and coaches gain nothing by mouthing off, and we all learn that from experiences.

Vanderbilt's Memorial Coliseum has never been one of my favorite places to play. The fans are tough. I had been ejected from our game there last year. To add insult to injury, a 60-year-old woman started beating Bill Keightley over the head with a pom-pom as he accompanied me to the locker room. I wonder if they treat people this way in the Grand Ole Opry.

Chris Cameron was walking up the three flights of stairs that lead to the press box at the top of Vandy's arena the night of the game. He heard the PA announcer reminding all the Vanderbilt fans to get their "Memorial Magic" T-shirts, on sale at the concession stands. The T-shirts listed the scores of Vanderbilt's four consecutive wins over Kentucky at home. They left a line blank for the score from this year's game.

Chris brought one to the locker room. He wanted me to show it to the team before the game. I told him, "No." I didn't want to remind our team of the losing streak. After all, Vanderbilt hadn't won at Rupp in 17 years. I didn't think their coach Eddie Fogler would bring that up.

Thanks to Mash, the line on their T-shirt remained empty. We could have produced one that said Kentucky 84, Vanderbilt 71. Mash had 21 points, 15 rebounds, 6 steals, and 4 assists. He scored 9 points in a two-minute stretch as we opened up our lead from 58–57 to 67–62. Vanderbilt had no one who could guard him in the low post. Last year, Vandy outscored us from the foul line, 40–4. This year, we shot 17 free throws. They shot only 16.

I saw Chris again outside our locker afterwards. I playfully threw the T-shirt against the wall and stomped on it a couple of times. "We finally got the monkey off our backs." I thought the only people there were Chris, my friend Brent Rice, and our staff. We were just joking around, but there were also two writers in the hall who witnessed this private moment.

The media would love nothing better than to create a feud between Eddie Fogler and me. In his post-game interview, Eddie suggested we were trying to rub it in when we called two timeouts with 33 seconds left.

The first time, John was trying to avoid a ten-second call and the other, Mash couldn't get the ball inbounds. Eddie made a sarcastic comment about it in the press conference. He claimed the most strategic point of the game was my time-out with 33 seconds left. I still don't know why they were pressing on the floor. If they couldn't understand us calling a timeout, why were they denying the inbounds pass?

I did not call a timeout; the players did. Eddie should have known it. Besides, I was so far away, the officials couldn't have heard me. The benches at Vandy are located on the baseline instead of the sidelines.

I thought Fogler's comment was bizarre, especially in the age of the three-point shot. I also think he has a very short memory. When he was Dean Smith's assistant at North Carolina, he was in a similar situation. The Tar Heels came back from eight points down in the final 17 seconds to win a game against Duke. But Ed is an outstanding coach who, like most of us, has a tendency to say things after a loss.

Our team decided to stay over rather than make a late night, four-hour bus trip home. It was snowing back in Lexington and there were reports of at least two tractor-trailers jackknifing on the interstate. Just what I needed. I had to be in Louisville the next morning for a speaking engagement. I couldn't use the weather as an excuse because I had already sent part of my fee to my old high school. Van Florence, who drove in for the game, offered to drive me there after the game.

The team went out for pizza. On the way back to the hotel, our bus driver Bobby Wombles went the wrong way down a one way street. "That's okay, Bobby," Billy Donovan yelled out, kidding. "We own this town."

I don't mean to get down on Nashville. We had a very heartwarming experience there the day of the game. Our four seniors, Chris, and I made a special trip to the Vanderbilt Medical Center to see George Owens, a London, Kentucky, man who had just undergone a lung transplant.

His sister Inez Nicholson wrote Chris and asked if someone from the team could visit him. She said her brother had gone through three rejections, several infections, and had caught pneumonia. She was afraid he was starting to give up.

I took Sean, Deron, John, and Richie over there after our morning shootaround. We went up to the seventh floor, washed our hands in special foam disinfectant to wipe out the germs and went into the room. His nephew brought along a camera to catch the expression on his uncle's face. He was so nervous he had trouble shooting the picture.

George was surprised. I could see the tears. The nurses told us later his stats were almost 100 percent while we were there because he wasn't thinking about breathing. George had his UK hat right by the bed and I put it on him. Then I told him he needed to get out of Tennessee and back to Kentucky. "If we can get Richie Farmer to lose 20 pounds, anything is possible," I said.

George lives less than 20 miles from Richie's hometown. Like everyone else from eastern Kentucky, he was a big Richie Farmer fan. He wanted to know if Richie had shot a deer this season. I asked him how many points he thought Richie would score against Vanderbilt and he said, "Twenty." Then, he changed his mind. "Thirty," he said.

I asked him what he thought about John Pelphrey's defense and he had the perfect answer. "Let him shoot the ball," he said.

Speaking of shooters, while I was in Nashville, I saw a newspaper clipping on one of our recruits, Tony Delk. He had just scored 70 points against Munford. He shot 21 for 36 and made 8 of 11 threes. I'm sure there were Kentucky fans in the stands when he did it.

According to Tony's brother David, shortly after he had signed with us, our fans had begun making the pilgrimage to Brownsville, Tennessee, a town of 10,000, 50 miles northeast of Memphis. On several occasions, Haywood's 2,000-seat gym couldn't handle the crowds. The fans who couldn't get in bought tickets to watch the games on closed circuit TV in the school cafeteria.

One Kentucky fan told David Delk he came because he hadn't been able to get Kentucky season tickets for 11 years and he wanted to see Tony play at least once. David coordinated all Tony's recruiting and accompanied his brother on an unofficial visit to Rupp to watch a game. "When we walked in," David said, "people knew him. I thought I was with Michael Jordan."

Tony and Rodrick had both made the McDonald's All-America game, which was scheduled to be nationally televised from Atlanta on April 19. Walter McCarty was named an alternate.

I was sure our fans would be watching.

When the team finally arrived in Lexington the next day, it was 3:45 in the afternoon. We called a practice at 8:30 that night, but I didn't use Mashburn or Pelphrey in the scrimmage. They'd both been playing a lot of minutes. After viewing the films, I decided I had to cut Pel down to 30 minutes. He played very good defense for a while, then he wore out. I thought about experimenting with Junior as our backup small forward. As for Mash, he had played 35 or more minutes in eight games. I didn't want him to droop like asparagus by the end of the year.

Our next game was against Eastern Kentucky. When I first arrived, I had said not only should we play Louisville, but we should also play the other teams in the state. Mike Pollio of Eastern was the first one to take me up on my offer. He had seen me at the Las Vegas high school tournament that summer and he said, "Rick, we'd like to play you."

I said, "Sure, Mike. First opening, it's yours."

When I got back, it was a headline in the Lexington *Herald–Leader*. Major news. C. M. Newton walked in and said, "Rick, what are you doing? We never play those teams."

"Why not?" I asked.

"What if you lose?" he replied.

"If we lose, so be it," I said. "Give them the credit." For this season, we scheduled Eastern Kentucky, Western Kentucky, and Louisville at Rupp and Morehead in Freedom Hall. We'll play Murray State in the future. We'll rotate it to let those schools share the revenue from a big game.

Looks like we've started another tradition in Kentucky.

Eastern Kentucky, our next-door neighbors from Richmond, had given us a tough time at Rupp a year ago. We won the game, 74–60, but they outrebounded us by 20. They had a one-point lead with ten minutes to play. We didn't help matters by making only 5 of 30 three-pointers.

One person who hoped we would play well was Bill Curry, our football coach. Curry had brought in 40 prospects for a recruiting weekend and they were all going to the game. I spoke to the recruits at a dinner at the Hyatt Friday night. I told them that when I was with the Knicks, Sonny Werblein, who ran the Garden, used to say that when the Knicks and Rangers both made the playoffs, it was good for the stockholders at Gulf & Western. It's the same concept here.

Looking at it selfishly, we need football to succeed from a recruiting standpoint. I'd like to see bigtime football. Bill Curry is a super guy. I'd love to see him do well. If football does well, maybe the reporters will concentrate on Kentucky basketball primarily during basketball season instead of all year round.

I was driving to Rupp for our game with Eastern, listening to the radio. I got the biggest kick out of all these people calling up our pregame talk shows, coming up with all kinds of wild predictions on how many points we were going to win by. It was like a comedy hour.

I was praying for a one-point victory and they were coming up with all these crazy numbers. We must have at least two million Kreskins out there. As it turned out, we did win convincingly, 85–55, to run our record to 14–2 and break Eastern's four-game winning streak.

Mash had 18 points, but only 3 rebounds. He wasn't really challenged. I had some concerns about that area of his game. He has super hands, great timing, and good jumping ability, but I felt he needed to take off about eight or ten pounds to improve his quickness to the offensive glass. John scored 14 points, including the 1,000th point of his career when he scored a breakaway layup with 17:17 to go in the first half.

It took him long enough. He started the countdown two weeks ago and the other players constantly kidded him about it. "He can probably tell you most of the names on that list," Deron said, laughing. Deron finished the game just six points away from his 1,000th point.

John's girlfriend Tracy Lyons thought he might break the

barrier against Vanderbilt, so she took a sign to Nashville to commemorate the moment. She had to rip it up afterwards. It was quite a milestone for a kid Kentucky didn't even want. Our PA man announced it during a timeout, but I decided not to stop the game. I planned to present him with a ball after it was over. I guess I should have told his parents. After we built up a 12-point lead at half, they left to go watch his brother Jerry play at East Tennessee.

I got upset only once. In the first half, I picked up the phone on the scorer's table and slammed it down. Soda and ice went everywhere. When I was at Providence I picked up the phone once and handed it to a referee. "It's for you," I said. "It's refereeing school."

We played well with only one day to prepare. We held them to just 31 percent and we had a chance to play some people who normally don't play. Andre Riddick had 7 rebounds and 7 blocked shots in 16 minutes. He also missed three more free throws.

I've tried changing his free throw but it's going to take some time. It's going to take some patience. He was a 37 percent foul shooter in high school. Before the season is over, we're going to get him up to 60 percent. He'd be there now if it weren't for this 20-hour rule. We would have him shoot an hour a day, because foul shooting is all repetition. I don't know, I may even bring in Rick Barry to teach him to shoot underhand. I'm willing to try anything at this point. One of the greatest players ever—Wilt Chamberlain—wasn't a great foul shooter, but he could play a little offense and defense.

Chris Harrison came off the bench in the second half to score ten points and hit a couple of three-pointers in nine minutes. Chris wears No. 3 because that was the number his hero Rex Chapman wore when he played for Kentucky. Rex came to the game with his wife Bridget and sat three rows behind our bench. Chris didn't know he was there until halftime.

But Chris told me he was thinking about changing his

number to 32 next year, because that's the number his room-mate Richie wears. Those two are close. They're both from the mountains. The No. 1 question on the Big Blue Line each week has always been, "How many minutes is Richie Farmer going to play?" I thought that would stop when Richie gradu-ated. But I can already hear it next year. Those fans from eastern Kentucky will be calling me up. "When are you going to play Chris Harrison more?" If we had 13 kids from eastern Kentucky, we wouldn't have a call-in show.

Mike Pollio was the first person to mention what everyone in the Commonwealth was thinking. He said we were the best team he had coached against in seven years of Division I. He felt we had a chance to get to the Final Four if we got the right draw. We jumped to eighth in both polls by Monday.

It seemed like everyone in town was talking about our up-coming game with Arkansas the next Saturday. There was only one problem. We still had to play Tennessee first on ESPN Tuesday night in Knoxville. That subject rarely came up during the Big Blue Line. Cawood received a call from a woman who claimed she had gone to high school with him up in Harlan County.

"Was he a good student?" I asked.

She assured me he was.

"Cawood," I said, later, "she was probably after you in high school."

"If she went to high school with me," he said, "she's too old for me."

I even did an impersonation of Richie Farmer. I'd like to know what he thought of my Clay Country accent.

When we arrived in Knoxville, everybody was still in a good mood. We went to Calhoun's on the river for dinner. After we finished eating, the players gravitated to the TV to watch Oklahoma State play Oklahoma. The seniors, particularly John Pelphrey, who was close with Sean Sutton, seemed in-terested in how they would do in Norman. Oklahoma State won, 92–89, to run their record to 17–0. When the camera cut to Byron Houston, I turned to Andre and said, "Dre, next year, you're going to look like that."

"If he does," Rock said with a chuckle, "there'll be an investigation."

Tennessee is the oldest of Kentucky's SEC rivals. The two states are very similar. Knoxville has always been a tough place to win. When Joe B. Hall coached Kentucky, the Wildcats were 1–11 at old Stokely Athletics Center. Their only win came during the 1978 championship year.

Tennessee has since constructed a new arena, Thompson-Boling Arena, which has a capacity of 24,535. When they built it, they wanted to make sure it was larger than Rupp. Usually, when we play there, the place is half-filled with Kentucky fans, who travel down I-75 because they know they can get tickets. When we played Tennessee last year, the lower section was all orange and the upper deck was all blue.

I left this year's game seeing red. Tennessee beat us, 107–85, before a crowd of 19,416. Allan Houston had a special night for the Vols, scoring 36 points, but we were our own worst enemy. We shot only 41.4 percent and made just 6 of 32 threes. We weren't patient enough in our offense at the end. We committed 24 turnovers.

We were in serious foul trouble and couldn't play as aggressively as we'd wanted. The officials called us for 41 personal fouls, which equaled a school record. Five of our players fouled out. There were a total of 67 personals and 91 free throws. Anytime officials call it close, all that stop and go action affects the success of our press. We're a much better team in an ebb and flow type of game.

We're also a much better team when Mash is on the floor. Jamal scored 28 points before he fouled out with 3:32 to go. But he didn't have a field goal in the last 13 minutes. Without Mashburn, we're just a good team. Nothing special.

Deron, who had 23 points, finally scored his 1,000th point on a three-point play with 10:57 to go in the first half. But he had the assistants in our sports information department take the ball home because he didn't feel like carrying it on the airplane.

There was complete silence on the bus to the airport. After we arrived in Lexington, I kept the players on the plane. I really got on the seniors. They were the ones who weren't getting it done fundamentally. None of them were having a good year. You know why? They had all been in supporting roles last year. Now, they were being asked to step forward.

It was not a fun trip. We got hit with a double whammy earlier that day. I got a call from Warren Heagy, telling me Rodney Dent had flunked his correspondence course in history that he needed to get his junior college degree. Heagy said Dent was still going to come, but he couldn't enroll until fall semester. If he had showed up now, it would have given us a leg up on his development. But he only had ten days to prepare for the final exam. That is one of the reasons he failed.

My biggest concern was still the center position. Gimel had contributed nothing against Tennessee. He hadn't scored a field goal and he picked up a foul a minute. The other players picked up on it and started mimicking the PA announcer, "Foul, Martinez. Foul, Martinez." It was a problem that wouldn't go away. We had to give Andre a look. He had been grabbing almost a rebound per minute and I felt he would give Jamal some help with post defense. Mash got his points against Tennessee, but he had also allowed the Vols' 6' 7" forward Carlus Groves to score 23 points and grab 11 rebounds.

We had to find some help up front, so I went to Jackson, Mississippi, to watch Othella Harrington practice at Murrah High School. I flew down with Brown Badgett, a semiretired multimillionaire from Travis Ford's hometown of Madisonville. Brown made his money in coal and construction and has a Lear jet he allows us to use. He has been associated with the Kentucky program for years. He was best man at Frank Ramsey's wedding in 1953.

When Brown arrived at Sprite Flights that afternoon, an

ambulance had just left the parking lot. "Rick," he said, "for a second, I thought you were in it." Brown loves to play cards, and I took it out on him for the next two hours in gin. Write it down: he owes me $28.75, and still hasn't paid up.

Brown had gone with me on other recruiting trips in the past to see Aminu Timberlake and Greg Ostertag, a 7′ 1″ prospect from Duncanville, Texas, who eventually signed at Kansas. But he had never seen anything like Othella.

We didn't have anyone remotely close to him in our program. Othella was the No. 1 player in the country. Athletic, graceful, a 6′ 10″, 220-pound post power player, who could step out and hit a jumper. He had good leadership qualities. He threw down some hellacious dunks during a half-court scrimmage. I told the Oklahoma assistant, who was also there, I wanted to take Othella home with me for our game with Arkansas. I wouldn't mind taking most of their entire state championship team. They had four bigtime prospects. They wouldn't finish last in the SEC.

When I got to the gym for the 4:30 workout, Othella was nowhere in sight. My heart sunk. I thought he might be sick. That had happened to me before. He eventually showed up— wearing an Arkansas T-shirt. I didn't know what to think, but I felt a lot better when he quickly took it off.

Othella had already made official visits to Georgetown, LSU, and Arkansas, and an unofficial visit to Mississippi State. I spoke with his coach Osmond Jordan afterwards and he told me Othella was considering a visit to Kentucky after the season. But I doubted whether he ever would take a step onto our campus.

# --15--

# *HARD TIMES*

T he T-shirts read PIG ROAST IN
RUPP, JANUARY 25.

Although the official nickname of Arkansas is the Razor-
backs, most of our fans refer to them simply as the Hogs. This
includes members of our student athletic council, who un-
veiled the latest in clothing for the Wildcat fan at the end of
our game with Eastern Kentucky.

It was their way of welcoming Arkansas to the SEC.

Arkansas was a Top 10 team, and it hadn't taken long for
the hype to start.

I received a letter from Jennye Curtis, a Kentucky fan from
Forest City, Arkansas, who sent along a copy of a column by
Wally Hall from the *Arkansas Democrat* in Little Rock. Hall
claimed that Rupp would not be the toughest arena Arkansas
would visit during their first season in the conference. Hall
described Rupp as "a rich man's playground."

"Like Indiana fans," he wrote, "Kentucky fans are so accustomed to victory, they don't make much noise."

Hah.

He must have confused Kentucky with Palm Springs. I'll bet the average salary of the season ticket holders at Rupp Arena is about $12,000.

I had Cawood read Hall's description over the air on the Big Blue Line. The crowd at Bravo's booed.

The Arkansas players, particularly their All-America forward Todd Day, seemed intent upon turning their first trip to Lexington into a feud. Day had been mouthing off all week. He was upset by statements he attributed to Sean and Dale. He claimed they had suggested he and teammate Oliver Miller liked to talk trash.

Day was tired of hearing how difficult it was to win in the Southeastern Conference. He was tired of constantly hearing how difficult it was to win in Rupp. He said there had been some bad blood drawn between the two teams.

I wrote that off as media talk. I don't believe in using newspaper clippings to motivate a team. I don't believe in bringing up what other people say. That may work in the first two minutes of the game, but at times it can backfire because it gets the players too high emotionally. It tires them out quicker and it stops them from focusing on what's important. What we did talk about was stopping Day and point guard Lee Mayberry, trying to make sure we stayed ahead because we knew Arkansas had a very good spread offense at the end of the game.

I admit I was interested to learn that Arkansas coach Nolan Richardson considered his team's visit to Lexington as the biggest game played in Rupp in 16 years. I agree that Arkansas was one of the best four teams in the country then. But, the biggest game ever at Rupp? We are talking about Kentucky tradition, now.

I don't think Nolan understands what Kentucky basketball is all about. He had one big game a year in the Southwest

Conference—Texas. There were 18 pro scouts coming to watch Day, Miller, and Mayberry. But Georgia, Alabama, LSU were just as talented. We were going to be sky high, but we'd be sky high for our last home game against Tennessee, sky high for Alabama. Arkansas had to understand—this was not Louisville.

Nolan has been at Arkansas since 1986. He's carried on a tradition started by Eddie Sutton in the '70s. When Sutton first arrived at Arkansas, basketball was drawing only 800 fans to home games in Barnhill Arena. The court was set up on a dirt floor and the only seats were beat-up bleachers.

Sutton turned it around once AD Frank Broyles gave him $9 million to spruce up the place. He recruited great players like Sidney Moncrief, Marvin Delph, James Brewer, and Alvin Robertson. His teams made nine straight trips to the NCAA tournament, including one to the Final Four in 1978.

When Sutton left to take the Kentucky job in 1985 and Broyles hired Nolan, it took a while for the fans to adjust. For one thing, Nolan played an up-tempo style, which was a radical departure from Eddie's game. For another, he was the first black coach in the Southwest Conference. But Nolan eventually won the fans and media over, even Wally Hall, who had been a big fan of Eddie Sutton. He coached Arkansas to the NCAA finals two years ago and has put them back in the national spotlight with his "Forty Minutes of Hell" defense.

Our players were getting edgy in practice as the game approached. We worked for three hours Thursday night and went hard for two more hours the next afternoon at Rupp. I spent some time working on post defense, trying to get Andre ready for Oliver Miller, who was 6' 9" and weighed 300 pounds.

On the teleconference for SEC coaches earlier in the week, I was asked if I thought the Arkansas game was a tough environment for Andre to break into the starting lineup.

I said, "What did you say? What was that word?"

"Environment," the writer said.

"A tough environment is where he grew up in Brooklyn. I don't know if you'd call this a tough environment. We are at home, after all."

Rupp Arena was anything but home sweet home Friday. Toward the end of practice, Jamal went to throw a pass and experienced a sharp pain in his arm. JoAnn Hauser bandaged him up with an ice pack. That was just the beginning. On Saturday morning during our final workout, we were going full speed. Then Richie ran into one of Jamal's elbows. He was knocked out cold.

I was worried about the weather the day of the game. Originally the national weather service had predicted four to five inches of snow. I was afraid our fans would have trouble making the game. As it turned out, the roads were clear and a record crowd of 24,324 squeezed into Rupp.

The crowd was loud and boisterous. The game had a Final Four atmosphere. Nolan Richardson wore his cherry cowboy boots for the occasion and Glen Campbell, who is from Arkansas, sang the national anthem.

However, the pig roast never took place. The Hogs overpowered us, 105–88. Arkansas was the better team that day, and it showed.

All things considered, I thought we played fairly well.

John and Deron did their best to keep us in it. Each scored 22 points. We made 12 threes. But Mash, who had scored double figures in our first 17 games, was nowhere to be found. He finished with just 4 points and didn't get his first field goal until 17 minutes before the game ended.

Jamal played just 21 minutes. He spent most of the game in foul trouble. He picked up three personals in the first ten minutes and never got into the flow against their matchup zone. Against a team like Arkansas, with all those big bodies, that was fatal.

We stayed as close as 78–77, with 8:07 to go, but Arkansas just overpowered us in the last five minutes when they went to a spread offense.

They took advantage of their one-on-one quickness and isolated Miller inside. Miller finished with 19 points. His 6′ 8″ teammate Roosevelt Wallace had had 17 points and 11 rebounds. But the key to Arkansas's success was Mayberry, my favorite player in the country. He scored 23 points and controlled the game down the stretch. He was constantly looking to push the ball up the floor after we had scored for strike back baskets at the other end. He ran their spread offense to perfection. It was one of the few times I had ever seen anyone just blow by Sean.

We did a pretty good job on Day. We held him without a field goal for the first ten minutes of the game. He finished with 18 points, but this was the same player who had already torched LSU for 43 points and was averaging better than 25 points.

After the game, the Arkansas players sprinted past our players without shaking hands. Later, they said they were just trying to avoid the fans. Some of the local writers suggested that was a slap in our face. We didn't take it that way.

Mash avoided the media for the first time in his career. He hid in the trainer's room. I called him into the office Monday and had an interesting conversation with him. He was really down. I told him not to worry, everybody has a bad game. I told him he had to be more assertive and make his presence known on the floor.

I told him, "Look, Mash, there were nineteen pro scouts there. I think you can be the best player in the country. But it doesn't matter what I think. In their eyes, you're a great talent who doesn't work hard. You may think you're working hard, but you're just laid back. If being laid back makes you the fifteenth pick in the draft instead of the fifth, shame on you. If I were you, I would stop being laid back. I would create an aura like Charles Barkley presents. You have to keep up that image of being the Monster Mash, because reputation means something."

He took it well. He said, "I'll do whatever you say."

I said, "Don't do what I say. Do what perception calls for. Perception calls for you to be much more aggressive." Mash wouldn't hurt an elementary school kid. "If you're going to commit a foul, take somebody down and make them pay for it."

All he talked about was playing Arkansas again.

We put together a splice of the game—the things we did incorrectly. Normally, we make from 20 to 25 mistakes in a game. We did 45 things wrong against Arkansas. Our shot selection was horrible. Dale took four shots with a guy in his face. Richie took bad shots. Sean took three bad shots. We took about 15 bad shots. That number normally ranges from two to seven.

The callers to the Big Blue Line felt the officiating had been lopsided. Most of the callers were angry at Don Rutledge, who whistled me for a technical foul after I complained about the lack of a five-second call with 56 seconds left. One fan claimed he had charted the calls made by the officials during that game. He said 90 percent of Rutledge's calls were against Kentucky. Another asked where he was working next. Better not travel anywhere near Clay County, Don.

I had planned on recruiting for three straight days after the Arkansas game. As it turned out, I did get to New Orleans Sunday, but, instead of going from there to New York, I came back to Lexington Monday for practice.

I vowed to make Andre a better foul shooter. Andre missed two more free throws against Arkansas and was shooting just 3 for 18 from the line for the season. The crowd at Rupp actually gave him an ovation when they saw him make a free throw in warmups.

I told Andre I'd had it with his foul shooting. His technique was terrible. I told him we were going to try the Rick Barry underhanded way. Andre did not want to shoot free throws underhanded. He did not know anything about Rick Barry. It was the funniest thing. He shot five. They landed on the dotted line, not even close to the rim.

Then, I said to him, "Okay, Andre, now we're going to shoot them one-handed, like Don Nelson." This seemed to work better. At least, he wasn't shooting air balls.

I called the Golden State Warriors' office to have them send me tapes of Don Nelson as a Celtic, so Andre could study his free-throw technique. I found it interesting that Don didn't keep any tapes of his playing days. I've always felt Don Nelson has one of the most creative minds in basketball. He's one of the few coaches who'd be great at any level—high school, college, and pro.

We had lost two straight games and had given up an average of 106 points in them. We were 14–4 and had dropped to 14th in the AP poll. The media asked if I was concerned about the way our team was playing.

"No," I said. "We did a lot of great things against Arkansas."

I proceeded to list them. Several players had gotten their chances to emerge from Jamal's shadow. John had his best offensive game since Louisville. Deron had his second straight 20-point game. Sean had his best assist-turnover ratio of the season with 8 assists and only one turnover. Gimel had his best game as a Kentucky player, coming off the bench to score 10 points and grab 7 rebounds in 23 minutes. We also forced Arkansas out of their press and forced them to abandon their man-to-man.

The next morning, Jerry Tipton opened up his column by suggesting I would have taken a rose-colored approach, even if I was handling publicity for Arkansas governor Bill Clinton.

Clinton, who was running for the Democratic presidential nomination, had been defending himself against allegations of marital infidelity made by Gennifer Flowers, a Little Rock TV reporter. Flowers claimed she had had a 12-year affair with Clinton.

"If Rick 'Positive Spin' Pitino managed Bill Clinton's campaign, he would have convinced the candidate that yesterday brought good news," Tipton wrote.

"Pitino to Clinton: 'Yeah, I heard Gennifer Flowers say she was your lover for twelve years. Your name recognition will go through the roof, my man.' "

I had to laugh as I boarded my flight to New York.

As soon as I arrived at LaGuardia Airport, I went right to the hospital to see my brother. Ronnie hadn't been showing any improvement for weeks, but he finally had started to come around in the past week. My mother called me. She was excited. Ronnie still had a trach in his throat, so he couldn't speak yet. But if you asked him a question, he'd shake his head yes or no. He could now sit up and drink something. The doctors moved him to a different section of the hospital after Christmas, and that was the difference. The care was much better. The nurses were getting him up, dressing him. They were watching what he ate. It was a miracle. He had gone from a point where everyone thought his brain would never function again, to where he could eat a piece of pizza and understand what I was saying when I told him about the Knicks.

Billy Donovan's fantasy was to be Jamal Mashburn for just one night against a team like Ole Miss. "I'd make national headlines," he said. "I'd score 65, and they'd need a bulldozer to keep me out of the lane."

Jamal busted loose for 24 points and 7 rebounds in 29 minutes as we defeated Mississippi, 96–78, Wednesday, January 29 at Rupp. Nobody kept him out of the post. He was much more aggressive and so was the rest of the team.

We outrebounded Ole Miss 48–34—29–10 in the first half when we built a 49–28 lead. I thought everyone played well, particularly Sean Woods, who finished with 9 assists and had only one turnover. He really looked to distribute the ball.

Sean seemed to be recapturing the efficiency he had as a sophomore, when he averaged 2.1 assists to every turnover. As a senior, his ratio had fallen off to 1.4 assists to every turnover. I had tried to drum it into Sean's head what a point guard's responsibility was. Certain nights, a scorer. Other nights, a passer. There's one common denominator—a point guard has to make other players better. Sean had been doing that lately.

Ole Miss hadn't won in Lexington in 65 years. We kept the streak alive as we improved our SEC record to 5–2. The victory, coupled with Tennessee's 20-point loss at LSU, gave us a one game lead over the Vols in the Eastern Division.

Andre was feeling more confident with his new style of foul shooting. Andre made only 3 of 10, but at least he looked good shooting the ball.

He missed three free throws in the first half. When he went to the foul line for the first time early in the second half, our entire team got off the bench and crouched on the sideline, just to watch. Andre missed the first, but made the second and the fans exploded, giving him a standing ovation. He got more applause when he made two more later in the game. I didn't mind. This is a fun game, and he needed to laugh at himself.

I had made a decision to start Richie instead of Dale at the two-guard position in an effort to create more scoring balance between our two units. Richie responded with 10 points, 6 rebounds, and 4 assists. He also avoided any more wild elbows.

Dale understood he wasn't playing well. He was shooting just over 50 percent from the foul line and 30 percent from the field. I knew what was coming. His mother called me at the office and told me Dale wanted to come home. I asked him to come see me. He told me things weren't going well. I said, "Dale, when things don't go well, whether it's your shooting or your ball handling, you don't take off and go home. That doesn't make things get better. The only way to make things better is by working harder and taking a positive attitude."

Once again, I talked him into staying. I hoped we could teach him to handle adversity.

We had planned to start preparing Thursday afternoon for our upcoming February 2 nationally televised game against LSU. Everything was put on hold when Joanne was involved in an accident.

She was driving down Euclid Avenue when a Cadillac slammed into the left side of her car. Neither driver was hurt, but both cars were totaled. Thank goodness, the air bag opened. I ran out of the office and rushed over to pick her up. When I arrived, she was so upset, she was almost hyperventilating. She was afraid she might lose the baby. Fortunately, everything was okay. The ambulance took her to Central Baptist Hospital.

I was a nervous wreck. The doctors assured me she was okay, but they decided to keep her overnight, just to be on the safe side. When I got home, I rescheduled practice for nine that night. By the time I walked out of the gym, I felt like I hadn't slept in three days. I was completely washed out.

The last time we had played LSU at the Deaf Dome, their coach Dale Brown turned the game into a three-ring circus, complete with indoor fireworks and a guest appearance by Mike, the 1,200-pound Bengal Tiger who lives in a cage outside the building. The fire marshal had outlawed fireworks this time, but Dale joked that he was still planning to bring in a bear to wrestle the officials.

Baton Rouge has always been a tough place for us to play. I don't have that many fond memories of it, either. Two years ago, I almost got into a fight with Dale. It was late in the second half when their guard Maurice Williamson shoved Jeff Brassow in the face. I immediately charged the officials to complain. A moment later, Dale approached me. The two of us started shouting at each other and had to be forcibly restrained. Dale claimed afterwards that Jeff and I were the instigators. He claimed I had faked my anger to motivate our team. I questioned his account.

"Dale has said some ridiculous things in the past, but this tops them all," I said. I also said Kentucky would not be intimidated by anyone.

"I was in a situation like this before with John Thompson when I was at Providence," I told the media. "I was worried about what he might do. But I'm not concerned about Brown unless he wants to fight me with his mouth."

The SEC reprimanded both of us and there was extra security a month later when LSU traveled to Lexington. Dale and I have since made up. It was really silly for both of us to stoop to that level.

Last year, I came down with food poisoning the night before the game. I had to be connected to an IV in my room. I had a 104-degree fever and almost missed the game. As it turned out, it wouldn't have mattered. Shaquille O'Neal ripped us for 33 points and 16 rebounds during LSU's 107–88 victory.

This season, Shaquille started off slowly. But he had really come on in the last five games. He had just blasted Tennessee for 30 points and 17 rebounds during a 97–82 victory Wednesday in Baton Rouge. He also blocked two more shots, giving him 329 for his career, an SEC record.

Shaquille is an awesome talent. Larry Bird of the Boston Celtics said Shaq was the second best player on the planet right now, just behind Michael Jordan. I think he'll be the next Wilt Chamberlain, but I doubt he'll develop any more in college. There simply isn't enough competition for him.

He doesn't have an up-and-under move. He doesn't have a jump hook. He doesn't need them. He can get away with just dunking over opposing players. Once he gets to the NBA, I feel he'll develop all these moves. Then watch out. There are lots of good college players, but he's an NBA franchise.

When Billy and Mike were breaking down film on LSU, they were blown away by some of Shaquille's dunks. Herb, who had scouted LSU, told our guys if they were just going to stand there with their hands up and not try to body him out on the floor, they may as well go to the football office and ask for helmets. Shaquille was going to be dunking on their heads.

I told the players we couldn't be macho about our style. We had to play this guy in a special way because he was special. We planned to surround him with with our center and power forward and send a third player from the opposite side whenever he went baseline to prevent him from getting the basketball. It was a gamble. I just hoped some of their other players didn't break loose for 30.

I juggled the starting lineup again. I decided to shift Deron, who had played well against LSU last season and was a good shooter, to center. I knew if we started Andre, Shaquille would never come outside on defense.

Normally, Herb is the nervous one on our staff. But Billy had been pacing for a week. Everytime he picked up the phone, he thought it was his wife Christine. Their baby was due any day. I told him to stay in Lexington. "He thinks the stork is going to come," Rock said, "like in one of those Loony Tune cartoons, and drop off a little bundle of joy."

Just before we left for the airport Saturday, I held a press conference. One Baton Rouge reporter asked me if I planned to watch what I ate this time.

"It wasn't the food. I should have been suspicious when I got complimentary room service and Dale Brown's name was signed to the check," I joked.

I wasn't taking any chances on getting sick this time. I ordered chicken for dinner and made sure I had a large supply of vitamin C on hand. I had dinner that night with Dr. Wethington and his wife Judy, who had come down with us on the charter. At the end of the meal, the management at the restaurant sent over some complimentary champagne. We toasted to a great victory. "And here's to Shaquille spraining his ankle," I added, with a smile.

I hope Dale Brown didn't hear me. He and Dick Vitale, who was doing the game on ABC, were having dinner in the other room. Dale and Dick Vitale? I wonder who got more words in at that table. Dale came back to see us and meet our Dale Brown, who was actually born in Baton Rouge.

Only our Dale Brown is much better looking and certainly doesn't talk that much.

We got off the bus for our shootaround on Sunday morning and were greeted by about two dozen LSU students. They had slept out all night, waiting in line for tickets. They were stand-ing on the walkway above us, chanting, "Tiger Bait, Tiger Bait," at our team. One guy even mooned us. They just love Kentucky down here.

"Hey, pal," I yelled to my son Michael, after we got inside. "Would you help me out if they come after your father?"

"You're on your own," he said, with a grin, and walked away.

Before our game at LSU last year, they had their Tiger mas-cot descend from the ceiling on a rope. Chris asked Cawood whether he thought they might lower him to the floor in the same manner since this was Cawood's last broadcast from Baton Rouge.

"Sure," Cawood said. "Head first."

I felt like I had landed on my head later that afternoon. LSU celebrated Dale Brown's 20th anniversary as a coach with a giant cake and a 74–53 victory.

We tried to milk the clock, tried to keep our players out of foul trouble and tried to turn it into a 20-minute game. Our offense was impotent. We shot 19 for 69 and were an ugly 8 for 44 from the three-point line. Deron shot 1 for 10. Sean was 0 for 7. Richie was 2 for 9. Dale was 2 for 7 and Travis was 1 for 9. It wasn't like the Pitt game, where we were taking bad shots. We were wide open on 31 of those three-pointers. I felt we could hurt LSU with our press, but we never made enough field goals to get into it.

Our interior people played like we were scared to take it to Shaquille. Even Mash, who finished with 21 points, looked like he didn't want any part of him. He had three or four opportunities to dunk on Shaquille, but instead of taking him on, he just tried to finesse it.

Shaquille finished with 20 points, 20 rebounds and 6 blocked shots. He also had the play of the game when he dribbled the length of the floor on a break, then took off like some giant 747 just below the foul line. Travis, who was back-pedaling on the play, thought about taking the charge. If he had, he might have ended up looking like a pancake. Shaquille missed the dunk. The ball ricocheted so hard off the rim, it flew out of bounds over our bench.

In the past, if a team stopped Shaquille, it had a pretty good chance of stopping LSU. But this year, the Tigers had enough good shooters—Clarence Caesar, Justin Anderson, and Mike Hanson—to take some of the pressure off Shaquille. Caesar, their freshman forward, scored 21. Anderson had 16.

At the end of the game, T. Lynn Williamson, our cheerleading coach, went over to LSU AD Joe Dean to complain about the LSU band playing while our players were trying to shoot free throws. His complaint fell on deaf ears. Joe told him—in language that would make a sailor blush—to get out of his building.

To me, this was the low point of the season. I just hoped there are no bridges in Kentucky. I might have been tempted to jump off. But Junior Braddy saw it differently.

After the game, Junior tried to lift everyone's spirits. He handed out an essay he had composed earlier. It was hand-written on double-lined yellow paper. Entitled, "Chance of a Lifetime," it read this way:

"Every child in America dreams of becoming someone famous or just doing that special something that sets you apart from the rest of the world. It is impossible not to dream. Everytime we go to sleep at night or just daydream in class, we enter another world where no goal or achievement is impossible. Most of us wake up, but a select few dream on until one day they realize that their dream has come true.

"Fifteen people share the same dream, with each person striving to make that dream come true, but knowing that with one mishap or twist of fate you can be rudely awakened never to dream that dream again. But with determination and hard work, we can dream on, until truly we become one of the select few on this earth.

"We have the chance of a lifetime. And I believe that we can do it. Not by might or by power, but by faith. And I do believe.' "

# --16--

# *PICKING UP THE PIECES*

$I$ don't own a crystal ball. But when I was coaching Providence and we got into a slump midway through the 1987 season, I went on my radio show and predicted we would go to the Final Four.

Two months later, we were in New Orleans.

The Friars knew they weren't the most talented team in Division I, but they made up for it with incredible hustle, incredible mental toughness, and an incredible desire to win. Once they felt that, they dominated everybody.

I wanted to send the same message to this Kentucky team.

To do so, I called a special meeting on the day after our loss to LSU.

I told the team we still had the capability of going to the tournament. But to get there, we had to work much harder to overcome our deficiencies.

I used our first Kentucky team as an example. That team

was supposed to have been a disaster, but they ended up 14–14. If this team worked as hard as that one, I wouldn't be so worried about our future. The tournament was less than two months away. We needed a minimum of 20 wins to get a decent seed. Anything less and we might sneak in with an 11th or 12th seed, but we'd meet one of the best teams right away and the season would be over.

There was a lot of work to do.

We weren't back-tipping on the press. We weren't working together on the traps. We weren't drawing the charge. We weren't coming up with every loose basketball. We weren't dogging it, but at times we were playing like we had more talent than our opponents. And that wasn't the case. We had arrived in the comfort zone and that is where all players start to underachieve.

We had one point guard who didn't dribble very well. Off his knees. Off his ankles. We had another who didn't shoot with a lot of range. We had a couple of freshman who were very weak and didn't shoot very well. We had a guard who was very soft on defense. We had two seniors who were making a lot of mistakes. A *lot* of mistakes. And we had a forward who was playing like he was a two-guard and acted as though he didn't want to dominate.

Every team goes through these periods. Only remaining positive and instilling a stronger work ethic gets you out of these doldrums.

Rock said he would even buy us a win at K-Mart. He had just returned from Tampa, where he spent the week looking for a house. When Rock put up the FOR SALE sign outside his home in Lexington three weeks ago, his neighbors took it down. After we lost to Tennessee, he said some of them playfully put up two FOR SALE signs in his front yard.

But the fun had ended for him.

And for Herb, as well. Herb had a listed phone number. He had to take his receiver off the hook at night because he started getting crank calls at 3:30 in the morning.

"You tell that Pitino . . ." the voice would say.

Herb never waited to hear the rest of the message.

We were 15–5, but had lost our fire and weren't playing with the effort we had the year before. A fan wrote me a letter to that effect after the LSU game, and I read it to the team two days before our game with Auburn.

We were ranked 19th in AP and 15th in the CNN Coaches' poll. But part of me wished we had dropped out of the Top 20. At least that way, we wouldn't be fooling ourselves into thinking we were better than we were.

We had a week to prepare for our game Saturday afternoon at Auburn. I split the team up Monday and Tuesday. We had the white team—our subs—practice Monday and gave the blue team—our starters—time off. Then we reversed it the next day. The white team looked great. The blue team looked terrible. If I had any guts, I would have started the white team against Auburn, but we needed the win. For the first time since I had been here, I felt our backs were to the wall.

I also felt we had to take two steps back to move ten steps forward. This was a motivational technique I brought back from my days in the NBA. In the NBA, if a coach makes spontaneous decisions, they come back to haunt him. I try to stay away from such kneejerk reactions, sleep on it, and come away with a much better perspective the next day.

I was tired. I needed a second wind. At least, I didn't lose my sense of humor. I found time to play a practical joke on Joanne. Two ladies from a hospice sent me flowers because they thought I might be down after our LSU loss. I forwarded them to Joanne, with a note from a secret admirer. At first, she thought they were from me, but I got Marta to convince her they were from "Bill Robinson" from Louisville, a good-looking divorced guy who was in his mid-30's. She bought it.

Ed Carpenter, my former SID at Boston University, came by to see me later that week. He was in town making preparations for a national convention the Sports Information Directors were holding in Lexington in June.

He brought back a lot of memories of my first head-coaching job. That job served as a laboratory during my early years in the profession. It afforded me the luxury of making mistakes without anyone second-guessing me or covering the team. I would learn what would work and what wouldn't. It was trial and error and helped teach me all the basics on the Division I level.

Believe it or not, take away Jamal Mashburn, and my last few BU teams were better than this team athletically. But no one ever saw them play. We used to play South Carolina, Purdue, Cincinnati. I would look out my window at the Case Center and see who was walking in. You could count the number of people at the games. There would be less than a hundred before some games. It's so different here.

Every season has its streaks. But we were caught up in a typical Kentucky syndrome, where everybody in the Commonwealth thinks the world is coming to an end because the team has lost a couple of games. They should experience an NBA season to really understand peaks and valleys.

I felt the *Herald-Leader* played on the feelings of our fans when we were struggling. In Jerry Tipton's story that Friday, he suggested the most talked-about question among Kentucky fans these days was why Richie wasn't playing more. He took me to task because I said it wasn't an issue.

Tipton quoted Robert D. Smith, the editor and publisher of the *Three Forks Tradition,* a tiny weekly in Beattyville, Kentucky. Smith had written an editorial in January that claimed I was jealous of Richie's popularity. As a result, I had limited his minutes on the court, despite his obvious talents.

I felt the *Herald-Leader* had waited for this opportunity to print that opinion. Richie *was* starting. If the paper really wanted to say something about it, they should have printed it during our winning streak when Richie was on the bench.

I blasted Tipton at a pregame press conference. "That article you wrote is good for one thing," I said. "Coffee grinds."

After I told him he wasn't an authority on anything, it turned volatile. I was going to ignore it at first, but I'm glad I didn't. If I was really worried about my popularity, I would play

Richie Farmer 40 minutes. But this is about winning and losing. I'm not a politician. I play the players who are going to win ballgames. I don't care if they're from Antarctica. In our program, playing time is determined by performance and defensive matchups.

I felt the *Herald-Leader* was trying to drive a wedge between me and the fans of eastern Kentucky. I wasn't going to let that happen. I find the newspaper's sports editor, Gene Abel, extremely cynical.

Everyone connected with Kentucky basketball was upset. Even Cawood. "You know what gets me mad?" he said to me. "He took some obscure little paper that probably has a circulation of 500 and doesn't cover the team on an intimate basis, and placed all the blame on them instead of saying, 'This is what I believe.' "

When Joe. B. Hall was here, he banned Jerry Tipton from his office. Tipton was not high on Eddie Sutton's list, either. Eddie was talking to Ralph Hacker and told Ralph to congratulate me.

When I was coaching the Knicks, the team was in a rut and faced a big game with Dallas. I let the players vote on how we wanted to play them.

I did the same thing with this team. I gave them three choices of how they wanted to play Auburn—full-court pressure, triangle and two, or man to man.

John and Gimel wanted to play a triangle. The rest of the team voted to press. I wanted to put the onus on them. They responded, smothering Auburn, 85–67. It was our best defensive effort in three years. We held Ronnie Battle, who had 43 points against Alabama two weeks earlier, to just 11 and held Wes Person, Auburn's leading scorer, to 9.

The players who put the clamps on Battle and Person were John and Richie, two guys the critics said couldn't play defense. We held Auburn to just 57 shots and 10 three-point attempts.

We played intelligently on offense, too, powering the ball

inside. Mash and Gimel, who room together, ran wild. Mash, who had lost a toenail and was playing in pain, scored 13 of his 19 points in the first half. Gimel had 15 of his career-high 17 points in the second half.

That had to please the large group of Kentucky fans who made the trip and helped fill up the normally half-empty arena. A number of Kentucky grads attend Auburn's vet school, which is one of the biggest in the country. They purchased a block of tickets at midcourt, right in front of the student section. Some of them painted their faces blue and white and held up "3" signs.

I noticed a big difference in the team. They picked up their focus and their alertness on defense. They were attentive to the game plan. They understood how to attack Auburn. They knew who they had to stop.

The only negative was that someone had broken into our locker room after halftime and stolen some of our warmup shirts. The thief also made off with a pair of John's undershorts.

Everyone was in a good mood on the bus ride to the airport. I didn't even get upset when they told us our charter was 45 minutes late. I just plugged in a tape Terry Meiners sent me.

Terry Meiners is the afternoon disc jockey at WHAS. He and his staff are famous for his parodies of our Big Blue Line, which he dubs "Cat Calls." If you have an ability to laugh at yourself, you'll find him funny.

I like it when he makes me sound like Marlon Brando, with a mouthful of cotton.

Some of his fictitious callers include "Big Stan Curtis" of Flynn County, who can always predict Wildcat victories because his pig jumps through the window before the games. Then there was "Mary May Stone" from Paintsville, who drove down in her pickup truck to "give the coach a New Year's kiss, but was rebuffed when coach saw my lip fungus."

And, finally, there was "Lucius Bedwetter" of Park City, who sent Cawood a box full of dead cardinals for Christmas in honor of Kentucky's victory over Louisville. Lucius had only one question. "How come coach Pitina don't let Richie Farmer spit when he's playing ball?" he wanted to know. "You know, my boy played ball with Richie and Richie could really get his stroke going when you let him spit. You know, chew a big ol' chunk of Redman and spit and shoot. Chew, spit, and shoot. It works everytime. Hit that three-pointer like a blind man."

For the record, Richie scored 16 points in 28 minutes against Auburn—without spitting.

We had another great practice the next day and I finished early, so the players could watch the NBA All-Star game. A lot of the players were discussing whether Magic should play. It was two months after he had gone public with the fact he had tested HIV positive.

I felt he should play. I admired his candor and courage. The more we know about AIDS, the better our chances of finding a cure and preventing future transmissions. I had already taped a commercial for Magic Johnson's project on AIDS Awareness. Right now, there is tremendous paranoia surrounding this condition. There are probably five or six other players in the NBA right now who might have the HIV virus. The statistics probably hold for major league baseball and pro football, too.

Magic put on a show later that afternoon. He scored 25 points, had 9 assists and was an easy choice for MVP.

Billy watched the game from home. His wife still hadn't delivered. "By the time that baby's born," Richie Farmer said, "it will have a beard."

Christine went into labor at 3:30 Monday morning. Herb, Mike, and Rock went to the hospital that morning to visit the expectant parents. They found Billy—where else—in the cafeteria, ordering lunch. Marta and Suzetta went over after work.

Twenty-three hours later, Christine gave birth to William Conner Donovan. Mother and baby were doing fine. I immediately nicknamed the baby Billy the Kid, Jr.

I think Christine went in a little too early. Billy was one of the best basketball players I ever had, one of the brightest players on the floor, but I'm not sure he knows how to time contractions. Dad, by the way, looked like a zombie Tuesday. He hadn't slept, but he was back in the office by noon, splicing film with Mike and Bernadette for our game with Alabama.

Billy's brain must have been like scrambled eggs later that afternoon as he went over the personnel report for a group of students we had invited into Memorial Coliseum to watch practice. We were trying to get the students more involved as the season wound down. I even gave them the names of the officials for the game. Yes, one of them was Don Rutledge, who had done our Arkansas game. I detected some groans from the audience.

There might have been another series of groans if they had seen the ugly red plaid sports jacket I planned to wear to the game in honor of Alabama coach Wimp Sanderson. In Tuscaloosa, they call Wimp "The Man from Plaid" because of his fondness for these particular garments. I had my newest piece of clothing delivered to my office early in the afternoon. It needed to be upholstered. It was a size 42 and looked like a horse blanket from Claiborne Farms.

Last year, before we played Alabama in a big home game, I decided to take some of the edge off the game by purchasing the most hideous tan and blue plaid sports jacket I could find. I normally wear suits to a game. When I walked onto the court in a plaid jacket, the fans went wild. Kentucky not only won, but the idea was a money maker. We wound up auctioning off the jacket for charity and made $2,000.

I picked up the idea from the Big East. Back in 1985, when St. John's was ranked No. 1, Lou Carnesecca loved to wear his "lucky sweaters" on the sidelines. When Georgetown played St. John's in the Garden that year, John Thompson showed up in a sweater of his own.

Georgetown won.

This year, my fashion show will benefit a Catholic elementary school in Paintsville. I planned on auctioning the jacket there March 5 as part of a charity dinner.

With all due respect to the manufacturer, I wore the jacket for only about six minutes during our February 8 game with Alabama. It was like a steambath in Rupp.

It didn't take long for temperatures to boil over during our 107–83 victory. We made a decision we weren't going to back down from anybody anymore. Gimel took those words to heart. He took it to Horry, scoring a career high 26 points and grabbing 10 rebounds. Gimel shot 8 for 15 and was 10 for 11 from the line. He looked like his body was possessed by Kevin McHale with those up-and-under moves. If that was the case, I hope Kevin's spirit stays around a while.

Last year, Gimel had been booed, and Kentucky fans questioned why we had recruited him. They felt he wasn't on Kentucky's level. But it's been my experience that big men need time to develop. There are very few Mashburns and Chris Webbers out there.

Gimel was just starting to come into his own. Normally, when he goes into the locker room, no one from the media comes over to see him. But, this time, they surrounded him like he was Michael Jordan.

Or Evander Holyfield.

Gimel got into a scuffle with Horry with 16:24 to go in the second half. Horry had blocked his shot and Gimel fell over his legs. The two went to the floor. I didn't see it, but Gimel said Horry punched him in the chest. "I just grabbed his legs," Gimel said. "I didn't want to get kicked. Then, I felt a punch in the face. Not a hard blow or anything. I don't think he should be a boxer."

The officials didn't see a punch, which would have called for an automatic ejection and suspension from the next game. But Rutledge did hit Horry with a contact technical. Then, as both teams rushed to the scene, Gimel walked several feet to shove Horry in the chest. That resulted in another contact technical. As the teams milled around the bench, Rock had some serious words with Wimp.

Wimp came over to me afterwards and said, "Who is that guy?"

"You don't want any part of him."

I was more upset at Gimel at the time. Instead of two shots and our ball, we ended up trading off two and two and it was a jump ball.

It was an intense, physical game. For Gimel, that type of game, where there were a lot of tempers flaring, was just another typical day at Miami Senior. Horry picked up a second technical and was ejected with 13:32 left. This time, he exchanged words with Sean during a dead ball and the two appeared to bump.

"He talks trash to everybody," Sean said.

Sean was terrific, finishing with 16 points, 6 assists, and just two turnovers in 30 minutes. He also helped Richie limit Alabama's leading scorer Hollywood Robinson to just 12 points. Sean had to work 94 feet. He had to deny the ball for four or five seconds, then guard for 75 feet. Then turn around and deny again. He had to work the whole night. I'll bet he lost seven or eight pounds of water weight.

When Horry was ejected, we were ahead, 52–43. Alabama got within four before Deron got hot, scoring 10 straight points for us. He made a pair of threes during that stretch as we jumped back to a 72–61 lead.

Cawood couldn't resist teasing me about the sports jacket.

"Are you going to buy a pair of matching pants next year?" he asked.

"Sure," I said. "The Pee Wee Herman look is in."

Whenever we win a big game, I get energized. I don't feel like sleeping, and my mind starts racing. I can't wait for practice. I hadn't eaten all day, but I went over to the restaurant to spend some time with the 1974–75 Kentucky team that was being honored. I also wanted to see Dick McGuire and the Scout, who were in for the game. Dick was a great playmaker with the old Knicks and he was going to have his jersey retired March 14.

I was on my way to the terrace when I was stopped by Chris Gaspari, who owns a pizza shop in Yonkers, N.Y., and his girlfriend Jennifer. Chris told me he was a fan of my coaching style at Providence College and had bought season tickets when I was with the Knicks. He and Jennifer had driven 13 hours just to watch us play. They didn't have tickets when they arrived. They paid $275 for seats from a scalper. They were all set to drive right back home after the game. I was so touched, I called the Hyatt and paid for a room for them for the night.

The afterglow continued the next day. When Ralph Willard called, Marta knew it was he and answered the phone, "American Boxing Federation. Are you our next opponent?"

Billy and Suzetta conspired to cut out a picture that had appeared in the *Herald-Leader* of Rock going jaw to jaw with Wimp. They wallpapered our office with copies. Billy penciled in a cartoon bubble coming out of Rock's mouth. "Yes," it said, "I'm interested in applying for the position of strength coach."

Wimp apparently didn't get the joke. He complained to the *Herald-Leader* and the SEC office that Rock had pushed one of his players. Rock said he was only trying to separate both teams. John Guthrie of the league office later backed him up.

Rock was scheduled to leave for Tampa March 7, the day before the first round of the SEC tournament in Birmingham. For his sake, it was probably just as well. He didn't want to be within 150 miles of the Alabama campus.

# -- 17 --

# *PLAYING POLITICS*

**O**kay, I admit it. I called Ralph Willard deceitful. I said I didn't trust him and predicted he would bring along a bag of tricks Saturday, February 15, when we played Western Kentucky.

But I was only kidding, honest.

Ralph waited a week for his revenge. He brought along an article that had appeared in the Oyster Bay *Guardian* in 1987, the day I was named head coach of the New York Knicks. He distributed copies to the media when we did our pregame press conference together at the Lodge the day before the game.

The story, which referred to me as "the round faced kid from Bayville," included my senior class picture from St. Dominic's Yearbook along with a list of activities I was involved in during my high school career.

Let's see: Bowling Club, Glee Club, Chemistry Club, Dance

Committee, Student Council, the Debate Club, and the Future Scientists of America. Debate Club, I could buy. But Future Scientists? Below my name was a quote, "Why Should the Devil Have all the Fun?"

I want to see the original copy of that story. Look. They spelled my name "Patino." That was definitely a doctored job.

As long as I've known Ralph, he could never resist a little good-natured ribbing. It was a good thing I came prepared with some comedy shtick of my own. I just happened to have some highlights of a tape that I swear appeared on Jersey Red's telephone answering machine just the other day. Ralph revealed his true feelings about our program.

Listen to this:

On Jamal Mashburn: "He's overrated. If our star Jack Jennings played at UK, he would get more publicity."

Deron Feldhaus: "He's living on memories. Hasn't hustled much this season."

John Pelphrey: "He gets emotional only for big name teams."

Sean Woods: "Western Kentucky's backcourt players will go by him as if he's standing still."

Gimel Martinez. Get this one: "His game was there all along, but Rick kept him hidden for fear Gimel would be more popular in the Cuban community of eastern Kentucky."

C. M. Newton: "Like Digger Phelps, he knew the schedule was too tough at Vandy the following year, so he left coaching to become an AD."

And, last but not least, Cawood. "The man is faking fatigue. He should not retire because he hasn't paid his dues."

But, seriously, folks, it's never easy playing your friends, and sometimes a little laughter can ease the tension. When Ralph left my staff to become head coach of Western Kentucky two years ago, we agreed to schedule a two-game series. We thought it would help create interest in Bowling Green and help him with in-state recruiting.

Ralph had done a good job getting the program back on

track. He was 16–7 coming into our game. His team had just beaten Louisiana Tech, 79–77, in overtime Thursday during an important Sun Belt Conference game. I felt Ralph had a chance to win 20 games and go to a tournament.

But Ralph was growing impatient. Despite the fact Western had won 25 of its last 35 games, he was upset that attendance at Diddle Arena was just over 5,200. I told him, from past experience, to be patient, that the grass was not always greener elsewhere.

Ralph couldn't prepare for his game with us. He had gone through a stretch of four games in seven days. Western Kentucky had become a victim of the NCAA 20-hour rule that dictates all teams must take one day off a week.

"It's almost criminal," Ralph said. "We drive up here Friday for a game against the 18th-ranked team in the country and the NCAA says not only can we not practice, but we cannot show film. We can't even go over a scouting report. If the Japanese were five inches bigger, they'd dominate basketball."

Ralph had been on the phone all week, trying to come up with enough tickets for his family and friends. Western had received only 50 tickets and most of them went directly to the president's office. Even Joe Iracane, a close friend of both coaches and the chairman of the Board of Regents at Western, was having trouble getting tickets.

Joe is an excellent cook. The night before the game, we gathered at the home of Barbara Ricke, where he prepared an Italian feast. Barbara is one of the leading interior designers in the country, but her local claim to fame is that she designed the interior of Wildcat Lodge.

It was just like old times. Ralph played at St. Dominic's before I did, and came back to coach at the school. We coached together with the Knicks and Kentucky. It was good being with Ralph and his wife Dottie. We laughed a lot and eased the tension of coaching against one of your best friends. I wish all our state rivalries could be so friendly.

Joe Iracane was the man responsible for hiring Ralph at Western. He had been embroiled in an ongoing, bitter struggle with Western Kentucky president Thomas Meredith for almost a year. A group of 30 to 40 local businessmen were trying to force Joe and vice chairman Patsy Judd to resign from the Board.

Joe and Patsy had pushed the Board to ask for an independent audit of some university payments to president Tom Meredith's wife. Also at issue was money spent on the president's house, which is owned by the university-related College Heights Foundation. They wanted to investigate the allocation of various funds. But Joe was being painted as a person who was after the president at Western.

Here's a guy from Brooklyn who played football for Western, married a Kentucky girl, raised his children in Owensboro. He had been there 30 years and was now more of a Kentuckian than a New Yorker. But, when the going got tough, his opponents suddenly started referring to him as "this Italian from New York" and a lot of people in the local media started ridiculing his ethnic background. Ralph and I found this to be ridiculous. I told Joe the best thing for him to do was ride off into the sunset and forget about Western. But he wanted to leave the school in good financial shape.

Stay tuned.

The governor's office had passed cost-cutting legislation that eliminated duty pay for any state trooper who wanted to work our games at Rupp Arena. But security behind the scenes was still much tighter the day we played Western.

Three days before, Wimp Sanderson had gone into a rage after our game with Alabama. His anger had nothing to do with the final score. Or his confrontation with Rock. Wimp was enraged after he heard that Brett Bearup, a former Kentucky player, had gone into the visiting team's locker room and tried to pitch an agent to Robert Horry. Bearup received a press pass from Kentucky's office of administrative services.

Wimp had every right to be upset. Bearup should have known better. He should not have been in the locker room and the University of Kentucky had to take the responsibility for his presence there.

Chris Cameron and Van Florence, who were in charge of access, came away from guard duty with headaches. So did I, but for a different reason. I spent part of the second half of our 93–83 victory throwing my towel in the air in frustration. Once, when Western's Harold Thompkins split a trap by Jamal and Gimel on the way to the basket, I hurled it toward the ceiling. Bill Keightley caught it and neatly folded it up.

"I got it, coach," he said, sounding very much like a center fielder for his favorite team, the Cincinnati Reds.

He'd seen these kind of tantrums before. My first year here, I told him not to let me out of the coaches' box. He would always stick out his forearm. One time, I told him, "Bill will you get out of my way, please."

"Coach," he said, "you told me under no circumstances was I to let you out of the coaches' box."

Then I told him, "Don't pay any attention to what I say. Get out of my way."

He did.

I composed myself long enough to congratulate Ralph's team for a job well done. Then I lit into our players, particularly Jamal, John, and Andre.

We had been flat. Mash scored 26 points, but had only three rebounds. John scored only five points. He continued to take bad shots and eased up on defense. Travis had problems containing Western's 5' 8" point guard Mark Bell, who penetrated at will. Bell scored 21 points and combined with Thompkins to pick up the slack after Ralph pulled Jack Jennings. Jennings was issued a technical for flipping a ball at Gimel's face with 4:28 remaining in the first half. Ralph refused to put him back in for the rest of the game.

I was really upset with our hustle stats. We keep charts for each game on back-tipping, steals, loose balls, offensive rebounds, and assists. I was also upset with Mash's quote to reporters that it was difficult for the team to get up for Western after they had just played Alabama.

I had Mash come into my office the next day for a special meeting to discuss this. I told him when I was an assistant at Syracuse in 1977, I thought we had a Final Four team. But we lost in the second round to an obscure team from North Carolina–Charlotte, which then went to the Final Four. The next year, Syracuse lost to Western Kentucky, the only team in the tournament with a losing record.

"You don't ever want to put your foot in your mouth," I told him. "Because when an NBA scout sees that comment, he's going to cringe. What you're telling him is you just want to play against the Lakers, Bulls, and Knicks and not worry about the rest of the teams on your schedule."

When I was an assistant with the Knicks, I loved coaching Bernard King because he would play just as hard against an expansion team as he did the Lakers. "You have to get thirty-five points and eighteen rebounds against teams like Western, because you're not going to have that type of night against Shaquille," I said.

Last year, Mash said, "This is Reggie Hanson's team." This year, he said it belonged to the seniors. I told him the current team, and every team, would react to what the most talented player does. Mash was our best player. He was a player who had gotten a chance to become a versatile offensive player. He had pro skills. I was a coach who wanted millions for him, but he was acting like a player who wanted pennies for himself.

I also told him to stop making the statement that he would stay at Kentucky for four years. I told Mash he didn't know how long he would be anywhere. If he is a lottery pick next season, we'll talk about certain options. "I say that as if you were my son," I told him. "If you leave Kentucky after three years, the fans will be delighted you're a lottery pick. You came to Kentucky when the school was on probation and most players wouldn't even consider us."

He just listened and agreed with everything I said.

Then, I had Pel come in and told him I was going to start Deron in his spot for our next game at Mississippi State. I told John he wasn't having a good season and predicted his reaction would be: "Well, I don't know if I'm in a slump, but I haven't been scoring the way I should."

I told him that in every film I watched, there was something missing in his game.

"John, you're never going to realize it unless it's pointed out to you. What's missing is what stops businessmen, athletes, politicians, from ever duplicating successful years. They get too comfortable in a role that should challenge them, make them better. You're not hustling anymore. You have not worked hard."

Then, I asked him a number of questions.

"How have you trapped this year?" I said.

He admitted he had been late.

Then, I asked how he had back-tipped, whether he had drawn any charges. I knew the answers. So did he.

I went on to tell him he was getting beat a lot defensively. He hadn't denied his man the ball and hadn't blocked out well. On the offensive end, I told him he hadn't moved without the ball well and hadn't thrown many good, solid passes.

"What you've tried to do," I said, "is make look-away passes, make difficult shots, make the home-run pass and tried to develop into something you're not."

John wasn't dogging it, but he wasn't working to the same threshold he had last season. All of his hustle stats were down, and he wasn't a good enough athlete to overcome that. I told him it wasn't too late to recapture the work ethic that made him a good player and rid himself of that comfort zone, once and for all.

Pel was down, but he realized everything I said was true. Part of the solution to any problem is understanding what the problem is and the methods to solve that problem.

"Part of the problem is we've never made it uncomfortable

for you and Mash," I said. "It's been uncomfortable for Richie at times, Sean at times, Gimel at times, and for Deron. But not for you and Mash."

Mash had five dunks and John had a great practice Sunday night, but it was only one day. He had to do it in the games.

Andre didn't practice at all. I had suspended him after the Western game for a bad attitude. I told him I had treated him with kid gloves in the past because of his family background, but he was 19 and it was time for him to grow up. "I can experience firsthand what you're going through," I said. "I lost a son, and I have a brother who has suffered brain damage and right now can't get out of a wheelchair." My sympathy was with him but, in two years, if he wasn't ready for this world, it was both my fault and his fault. And, right now, he wasn't preparing himself.

Andre is intelligent. He thinks a lot, but he is afraid to show it. He wanted people to perceive him in a different light, and I wouldn't allow that to happen. I told him I would say his suspension was for academic reasons; but until his attitude shaped up like that of a Kentucky player, we weren't going to tolerate it. He apologized, and I told him he would be back on the team Thursday.

The news wasn't all bad. We were 18–5 and had jumped to 12th in the CNN ratings. We moved from 19th to 13th in the AP poll. When Georgia upset Arkansas Tuesday night, we were tied with the Hogs for the best record in the conference at 8–3. I told the players they could control the team's destiny if they won the rest of their games.

Chris Cameron likes to refer to the small college town of Starkville, Mississippi, as "Stark Vegas." But I wasn't about to get involved in any more controversies with the local Chamber of Commerce there.

When we had played Mississippi State down there the year before, the fans at Humphrey Coliseum wanted to lynch me over some comments they thought I made about their town.

An AP writer asked me why I was becoming an insomniac and I told him in New York, you could always go out at one in the morning, go to a diner, stay up, watch shows.

"Well," the reporter said, "you're going to get plenty of sleep when you go on the road in the SEC. Some of those towns roll up the sidewalks at nine in the evening. When you go to Starkville, you're going to go to bed early."

"Then I guess I'll get a lot of sleep," I said.

That could be why the fire alarm at our hotel went off at three in the morning this time.

The students seated across from our bench at Humphrey Coliseum have always been wild. When Rupp was here, they once planted a dead skunk under his bench. And another time, they hung a funeral wreath on the Kentucky locker room door. This year, the Bulldog fans threw M and M's at our players in honor of Mash and Martinez. But we kept the crowd under control until the final moments of an 89–84 victory. Then, we went cold from the foul line, missing eight straight free throws and nine of ten in the final four minutes to make the game much closer than it should have been.

For the first time since I'd been in the SEC, the game reminded me of Big East play. Nine thousand foul shots, coaches who wouldn't let five seconds run off the clock. That's the way it was every night. It was nerve-racking, totally nerve-racking.

I didn't think our marathon with Mississippi State would ever end. It lasted two hours and 25 minutes. The Bulldogs, who had been down 10 with 3:17 left, pulled within 4 points with 1:20 to play. Then Richie made 8 free throws in the final 50 seconds to save the day.

Richie and Dale also combined to shut down Mississippi State's leading scorer Tony Watts as we won there for the first time since I had been at Kentucky. Watts finished with 14 points, but he shot only 3 for 12. One of his field goals was a lucky three-pointer at the end of the game. It was the best job we had done containing the other team's best scorer. Watts didn't touch the ball.

I've always thought that on defense, you must stop what the other teams practice. I don't subscribe to the theory of letting the great player score and stopping the others. Simply put, stop the options they practice. Press the teams that don't have a press themselves. Zone teams that don't use one. Even if they practice against certain defenses, it won't be beneficial due to the lack of practice and intensity.

Deron scored 18 points, including a pair of three-pointers. He scored on a three-point play when we came back from a 47–46 deficit to take a 58–49 lead. John had 17 points, 5 assists, and 5 rebounds in 27 minutes off the bench.

By the time we finally chartered back to Lexington, it was 2:30 in the morning. Scores from around the country had filtered in. North Carolina, Kansas, Missouri, Michigan State, and Oklahoma State—all teams ranked ahead of us—lost. After Oklahoma defeated eighth-ranked Oklahoma State, 70–67, in Stillwater, Eddie Sutton had to be taken to a hospital in Tulsa. Doctors discovered a slight blockage of an artery. He was kept overnight for observation.

I didn't get much sleep, either. We were beginning a brief ten-day observation period and I was going to use every minute of it. I had to catch a 7 A.M. flight to New York. From there, I was scheduled to fly to L.A. Friday morning to see three more prospects before taking a red-eye flight back to Lexington.

We gave the team Thursday off. At 3 P.M., they tell me, the only player in the gym was former Kentucky star Adrian Smith. Smith was the MVP in the 1966 NBA All-Star game with Oscar Robertson, Jerry West, Wilt Chamberlain, and Bill Russell. He still had the Ford Galaxy he received as a prize. Smith had played for the Fiddlin' Five. He had come in to visit Bill Keightley and asked to borrow some gear to work out.

He also wanted to set the record straight about the best guard ever. "Everybody talks about Magic," he told Mike. "He's a very good player. But I played with Oscar on the Cincinnati Royals and he averaged—*averaged*—a triple double in scoring, rebounding, and assists his rookie year in the league."

I finally arrived back in Lexington at six Saturday morning.

I was going to kill Herb. I hadn't slept more than four hours for the last two days. Part of it was my own fault. I stayed out until 1:30 in the morning in New York. But I did get to watch three prospects who could play at Kentucky.

I also brought back a videotape featuring a 6' 2" eighth grade phenom named Jarrett Lockhart. Jarrett attended St. John's Elementary School in the Bronx, which had won the New York City CYO championship. He was a high priority recruit of every Catholic high school in the city. His father had been the leading scorer at Manhattan 15 years ago. Doctors had told ABC and WPIX-TV in New York they expected him to be 6' 8". His mother, who worked for the *Live with Regis and Kathie Lee* show, made sure he had good grades. Who knows? We may start a file on him.

Billy and Mike had been living in the film room, preparing a scouting report for our next opponent, Georgia, which suddenly had become the hottest team in the SEC after victories over LSU and Arkansas. Georgia was only 12–10, and needed a win over us to keep their NCAA hopes alive. I felt Litterial Green, whose stock had vacillated with pro scouts, would like nothing better than to do a number on us, especially since we had contained him earlier in Rupp. But, according to form, we had to stop their major component in practice.

Sunday, February 23 was a two-shirt day. I was drenched from the heat and humidity inside steamy Georgia Coliseum. It must have been 90 degrees. I slipped out of my suit jacket five minutes into the game and changed my shirt at halftime. When I met the media after an emotional 84–73 victory, I was wearing a blue short-sleeved Kentucky golf shirt. I should have put on shorts.

Our team was also drenched from an intense performance in which we played tournament-type defense. We held Georgia to just 32.3 percent in the second half and limited them to just 26 points in the last 17 minutes as we rallied from a 47–40 deficit.

Bernadette's homecoming was a successful one. She got a

chance to see her husband. Some of his students at Athens Academy showed up at the game with signs to welcome her back to the Coliseum, where she had made a big name for herself. Bernadette played for Andy Landers. Landers, who owns a farm, had named one of his cows "Pitino." I didn't know how to take that.

I took Jamal's performance as a sign he was ready to step forward. Mash had a great game, wheeling around, going up and under, scoring 26 points and grabbing 7 rebounds. He went strong to the basket the entire game, setting the tone for our big men. Dale also stepped up, coming off the bench to shoot a perfect 7 for 7. He made 4 threes, scored 18 points and helped Richie defend Green. Green scored 17 points, but he shot just 4 for 14 and hit only one three-pointer.

Dale got the best of his old buddy again. I wish I could bottle it. In the past, I think Dale's problem had been the fact he considered only his shooting percentage as a barometer for whether he played well. He played a total game here. He got to the glass, passed well, cut efficiently.

In the first half of the season, there would always be a star of the game, but we really didn't have a second, third, fourth, fifth guy playing well. Now, we had 5' 6" people playing well, and that was a good sign. John, who earned his starting position back, was bringing his game to another level. Dale was bringing his game to another level. Sean was playing well. I liked the way we were coming on.

Sean made the biggest play of the game. He hit a three-point shot with time running out on the 45-second clock and Georgia guard Bernard Davis in his face, to give us a 74–65 lead with 3:18 left.

"Take it, take it, take it," I screamed as the time evaporated.

His shot had a high arc, but it caught nothing but net on the way down and was like an arrow in the heart. We made 11 of 21 threes. Travis made 3 treys, and Junior hit one just before the half that pulled us within 39–38 and left some doubt in Georgia's mind.

Mash put an exclamation point on the victory when he

tossed in a 60-footer just after the final buzzer sounded. "Now, I'll buy a ticket to the lottery," he said.

I figured it would take at least a week for our win over Georgia to register in the minds of the voters in the wire service polls. When the results were announced, we moved up from 13th to 11th in AP but were still 12th in the CNN Coaches' Poll.

I went directly from the game to the Atlanta Airport, 90 miles away, to catch a flight to New York. I had to do some recruiting on the Island. I took my son Michael with me to look at two prep schools—Lawrenceville and Kent.

When I got back Tuesday night, the first thing I heard on the radio was Cris Collinsworth, a former NFL player who was now a talk show host in Cincinnati, trashing Kentucky. He claimed we weren't that good and that Cincinnati, which had finally jumped back into the Top 25 for the first time since 1978, deserved to be seeded ahead of us. Anytime a Kentucky fan would call up to argue, he'd hang up the phone.

I just shook my head. I knew he was just trying to rile up the Kentucky fans. But I thought Rock and Bill Keightley, who also listened to the show, were going to kill him. "His father played ball at Kentucky," Bill said, "and he's married to a former Kentucky cheerleader."

Our guys don't understand what sells.

John, Deron, Richie, Travis, and Sean arrived at Rupp Arena early the night of February 26 to watch the Bud Lite Dare Devils, a group of former gymnasts who use minitrampolines as a springboard for a spectacular dunking exhibition, practice for their halftime performance of our game with South Carolina.

"They got some major rise," Richie said.

John said when he was at Paintsville, they used to have a minitram in the gym. "Before I could dunk, I used to get an extra lift," he said. "If the principal ever caught me, I would have been thrown off the team."

Sean actually thought about trying out the minitram. He made a run at it. Then, common sense took hold. It might be difficult explaining how he suffered a sprained ankle if anything had happened.

That was about as much excitement as there was to report. We defeated South Carolina, 74–56, to improve our record to 21–5 and clinch a first-round bye in the SEC tournament. We had a two-game lead over Florida in the SEC's Eastern Division with just three league games remaining. We were tied with LSU and Arkansas in the overall standings with a 10–3 record.

Deron, who continued to shoot the ball with great confidence, led the way with 19 points and 5 three-pointers. He had been our most consistent player all year. The only things he cared about in order were: 1) getting to the tournament and contributing each day out; 2) playing overseas after college; and 3) getting his golf handicap down from a five.

The other seniors had really picked up their games the second half of the season. We shot 12 for 27 from the three-point line and had 22 assists. At one time, the score was 60–33. We didn't play any of the starters more than 24 minutes and never used the press in the second half. I hope Steve Newton appreciated the fact we didn't run it up.

South Carolina started with an 8–1 record, then lost ten straight and were now just another team struggling to the finish line. Their leading scorer Joe Rhett hadn't played since January 25 because of a heart irregularity.

I had another incident with Dale, who did not score and was complaining about not having enough time to study. I told Bernadette he could spend the next week catching up on his classwork. That included missing practice and our trip to Florida. I couldn't let that explanation hold up. I've always believed excuses were a sign of weakness.

I had a major decision to make the next day after practice. I could choose life, or a trip to Evansville on a small private plane to watch one of our recruits, Walter McCarty, play. A weather front was moving through Blue Grass Airport. It was raining and the winds were gusting up to 30 miles per hour.

"If I don't make it back," I said, "seniors run the team."

"Good," Deron said with a smile, "we'll kill Richie Farmer."

Actually the trip to Indiana wasn't that bad. It felt like Space Mountain for the first ten minutes, but once we got up to 10,000 feet, the ride was smooth. Seth Hancock and Bill Keightley accompanied me, and we spent part of the time talking about which of the seniors we thought would cry at Senior Day the following week.

"It's very emotional," Seth said. "I even cried over Jonathan Davis last year."

Seth and Bill are both big high school basketball fans who live for the Sweet Sixteen state tournament every year. I told them they were in for a treat watching Walter play. But none of us had any idea it would include listening to Walter, who was in the church choir, sing the national anthem a capella on his Senior Night at Harrison High School. Walter went on to score 16 points, grab 11 rebounds, and block six shots as Harrison defeated Jasper, Indiana, 73–45.

I came away thinking he was the most skilled high school player in the country. He had a soft shooting touch and a sophisticated face-the-basket game. He could put the ball on the floor, shoot jump shots from 18 feet, and was a great passer. He also had an outstanding attitude, never showing any frustration when his teammates couldn't get him the ball in the low post. He was constantly patting them on the back.

Evansville is located just five miles from the Kentucky border, and there was a lot of blue in the stands. The cheerleading coach even had on a Kentucky sweater. Spread the word. Indiana's pro-Kentucky, except for Bloomington, of course.

I knew when we left the gym I had a dilemma. Walter would have to sit out next year because he didn't have enough core courses. In one respect, that was good. He could use an extra 20 pounds. But, because the SEC permitted its schools to take only one Proposition 48 and Rodrick Rhodes still hadn't qualified under SAT guidelines, I was concerned we might lose one, and there was no way I wanted to give up Walter. I saw him as the heir apparent to Jamal. We'll just keep praying Rodrick passes his SAT.

Lights, cameras, action. ABC analyst Cheryl Miller, a former All-America and Olympic basketball star at Southern California, was at our practice Saturday, the day before our March 1 regionally televised game with Vanderbilt at Rupp. Jamal wanted to ask her for her autograph.

She probably wanted to ask for his autograph too, after Mash exploded for a career high 34 points and grabbed 12 rebounds as we defeated Vandy, 80–56, to clinch first place in the SEC East with an 11–3 record.

When I finally pulled him with four minutes to go, I gave him a hug and told him, "You're big in New York."

Before the game, we retired three more jerseys—hanging banners in the ceiling of Rupp for Carey Spicer, who was Rupp's first All-America in 1929; Louie Dampier from Rupp's Runts; and Jackie Givens from the 1978 championship team. I fully expect Mash's number 24 to be up there someday. Eddie Fogler called him the most versatile player in the SEC.

I was willing to go a step further. I said he could be the most versatile player in the country. I watched him shoot 12 for 17, step outside to drain 5 of 6 three-pointers and contribute 3 assists. All he had to do was get better defensively.

"I'm a perfectionist," Mash said later. "I want to achieve a grasp of the game that will enable me to play at the next level."

We were getting much better defensively as a team. Mash was averaging 32 minutes a game. To conserve his energy, we moved him to the safety position in the back of the press. We used our centers to guard the inbounds pass. Vandy not only had difficulty with our press, but they also had problems with our perimeter defense. Sean completely locked up their lead guards, and we held Vandy to 23 points in the first half. Their motion offense runs much quicker than most, with back screens being set constantly. Ball pressure is the key to defending motion. You can't allow the passers, who are not continuing to dribble, to see the ball.

Sean had really been coming on ever since he had decided to make his teammates better. He had 7 of our 22 assists and turned the ball over only once. Deron had 17 points and John added 16. But Gimel had a fan club. A group of students showed up wearing fake noses and calling themselves "Gimel's Amigos."

When we got to the locker room, I informed the players they needed to be inoculated against an outbreak of measles on campus. I had already had the measles when I was a child, and I couldn't resist making the players a little queasy.

"Guys, I've seen the needles. They're huge," I said. The only one who cried was Herb.

This is the time of year when a lot of mares give birth. That night, I took Pat Nero and Dan Egan, two friends from Providence, and Chris and Richard over to Claiborne Farm to watch one of them, Jurisdiction, have her foal. The birth occurred just before midnight and it was magical, watching that little 75-pound colt lie there in a stable of straw, struggling to stand up on those matchstick legs.

Spring in the Blue Grass can be beautiful.

Everything looked like it was coming up roses for us as well as we took off for our next game, Wednesday, March 1, at Florida. Six police cars gave us an escort to the airport.

"If it's this way now, I wonder what it will be if we make the Final Four," Jeff Morrow said.

When we left for our trip to Gainesville, we knew what was at stake. We needed to win two more games to clinch a tie for the overall SEC title. Our players looked like they were going on vacation. Dale brought a plastic snake onboard and John and Rock were walking up and down the aisle of our charter flight, seeing who they could scare to death.

It was difficult to concentrate once we arrived. The temperatures were in the 80s and all the students were wearing shorts. When we went over to the arena to work out, we found out we couldn't hold a closed practice because the gym was a public classroom.

We got a taste of what was to come that night. It was Florida's Senior Night. Lon Kruger's team was 15–10 and in a must-win situation if they wanted to make the tournament. They played like it, blasting us, 79–62.

Mash shot 5 for 22. He got beat up in traffic. That's what's going to happen in the NBA. You have to make those shots with players hanging on you. We were outrebounded, 42–27, in a physical game where we let a 31–26 lead slip away. John didn't grab one rebound. Neither did Aminu or Gimel. Deron had only one defensive rebound.

The first half, we ran our offense beautifully, got some back-door layups. The second half, the wheels came off. After we fell behind, we tried to make up the difference in a hurry with three-point shots. But we shot only 7 for 28 from that range for the game.

The game was extremely upsetting, but Lon Kruger did a great job, getting Florida to play at a high level. He's is a bright coach with loads of intregrity and should add class to our league.

# --18--

# *WAVING GOODBYE*

$T$hey had their names up in lights.

Three weeks before Senior Day, Chris Cameron drove John, Deron, Sean, and Richie over to the Hyatt. They took the elevator to the roof, where they had their pictures taken for a special spread in the newspaper.

The city skyline at twilight made for a perfect setting, especially since our four seniors had owned Lexington all season.

That was just a preview. The feature was yet to come.

When the four came back to earth, they changed from their sweatsuits into tuxedos. Then it was off to the old Kentucky Theatre on Main St., where they found their names up in lights on the marquee. Chris had them pose in their formals and tennis shoes for a poster he intended to hand out to the fans at Rupp before their final home game against Tennessee.

"Are we bad or what?" Sean said as a carload of teenage

girls pulled by for the third time, honking the horn and squealing.

Senior Day was their moment, and I arranged with Rodney Stiles, our student ticket manager, to allow the players to purchase as many tickets as they needed for their families and relatives. Richie told me this would be the first time his grandfather—his "daddy's daddy"—ever saw him play in person. He had been confined to a wheelchair, and was unable to attend Richie's high school games because the seats in the old high school were located above the floor.

I realized how important it was to them. I had seen that last year when Reggie Hanson had come out to center court, accompanied by his young nephew, who had a sign pinned to his back that said, "I love my Uncle Reggie." Reggie and his nephew both cried.

I figured John would definitely break down, too. I could envision it happening right in the middle of "My Old Kentucky Home," as soon as the crowd chimed in with "weep no more my lady." I hoped it wouldn't be too emotionally draining for the four since we had a big game to play. I was thinking about bringing some old fight songs to the locker room during our pregame talk.

I had stopped trying to convince Cawood to stay. I couldn't do any better than the woman who came up to him before the Western Kentucky game and offered to stand on her head if he would broadcast our games one more year. Cawood and his wife Frances had decided to go back to his hometown of Harlan, where he planned to settle down on a 20-acre farm. He wanted to be near his 95-year-old father and devote more of his time to raising miniature horses.

Two days before their big day, the seniors and I attended a fundraising dinner held to save a Catholic missionary school in Paintsville.

Our Lady of the Mountains had been in existence for 45 years, but was experiencing financial difficulties. The school was housed in a three-story Victorian building and had an enrollment of 65 students. I found out about its problems through a letter from two members of the board. I was touched because it came from John's hometown, and I am a big believer in Catholic education. I informed the board we would come and bring along several items to auction off at a dinner.

Among them were a set of Kentucky blue road uniforms, the plaid sports jacket I wore at the Alabama game, and a pair of tickets behind our bench to the Tennessee game.

When we arrived, we were led to a reception on the third floor. The room was completely decorated in blue and white. During an autograph session, one of the students asked John to sign a piece of wood.

"What's this for?" he asked.

"Our gym floor," she said.

"Well, make sure it goes behind the three-point line," he said.

When John looked out the window, he could see his elementary school. "I once threw a book out of the window there," he said. "Got grounded for a month."

John knows almost everyone in this town of 5,300. Three hundred of them attended the $100-a-plate-dinner at the Country House. We raised more than $40,000 for the school. The principal told me that was enough to keep the school open for two years.

John's uniform went for $1,300. Someone bought Deron's jersey for $1,200 after I offered to throw in a kiss from him. We got $900 for the sports jacket. Old basketball shoes they wore went for $300 apiece. But the big hit was the two tickets to the game. I raised the ante by promising the winner could also come into our locker room before the game and during half-time. Dave Hutchinson, a local resident and the owner of a string of McDonald's restaurants in the area, won the tickets with a bid of $6,500. That sum blew me away.

At the end of the auction, John said a few words to the crowd. He told them we'd be fine in the tournament, as long as "we got some coaching."

Thanks John.

I laughed. They were such good kids off the court. I wanted desperately for Deron, Richie, Sean, and John to have a SEC championship banner hanging on the wall at Memorial. They had talked about winning it, then had let the moment slip away with a loss to Florida. I couldn't understand these kids. If you have a championship at stake and you're going to lose, pour your heart out, anyway. Maybe it would be a different story in Birmingham, site of the SEC tournament.

One of Oscar Combs's favorite stories involves the day NBC broadcast Kentucky's 1978 Senior Day ceremonies so a national television audience could enjoy the pregame color and pageantry and listen to the late Happy Chandler leading the sellout crowd in the singing of Stephen C. Foster's "My Old Kentucky Home."

The outpouring of emotion was so great as Mike Phillips, Rick Robey, Jack Givens, James Lee, and their parents made their way to half-court, it touched both Al McGuire and Dick Enberg. Enberg, his voice cracking with emotion, claimed "That's one of the most powerful scenes I've ever witnessed." McGuire went on to say, "Senior Day alone made Kentucky the nation's premier basketball program."

Some opponents of the program became so jealous, they complained to the network, suggesting the televising of that event created an enormous recruiting advantage.

They were right.

Senior Day at Kentucky is one of the grand traditions in college basketball. This year, it tugged at a few more heart-strings than usual. John, Deron, Sean, and Richie were saying goodbye. So was Rock, who was presented with a special plaque at halftime. And, of course, Cawood.

Scalpers were getting as much as $400 a pair for tickets to the game. All season, I had kiddingly said, "If you need tickets, call Gene DeFillipo." Gene finally got me back. He came down to Bravo's for our broadcast of the Big Blue Line and distributed a handful of tickets to everyone in the audience. The only problem was they were dated 1987.

Gene had arranged for the local bank to distribute rally rags to the crowd for the grand finale. Most of them turned into tissues. This was a two handkerchief day.

I thought about starting all four seniors. I told Deron I would start him if it meant something to him, but he said it didn't matter. I left it up to him.

During the pregame speech, I could tell the seniors were fidgety. This was going to be their last hurrah. They hoped they could do it dry-eyed. They came onto the floor of Rupp one by one, in alphabetical order, bursting through giant paper hoops with their pictures on the front. Then, they ran to center court to take one last solo bow. Accompanied by their parents and relatives, they walked a victory lap around the court. The crowd exploded into applause. It was a celebration of loyalty for four kids who had hung in there through the hard times.

When Melissa Baber began to sing "My Old Kentucky Home," there was not a sound in Rupp. Finally, when it came time for the chorus, the crowd joined in, like a church choir. The seniors held up fairly well. But as I glanced over to our bench, I could see our freshman Chris Harrison, who is also from Kentucky, wiping away a tear.

"I wanted to cry," Richie said later. "But I knew if I broke down it would be hard to get back my composure."

We won on Senior Day for the 28th straight time, defeating Tennessee, 99–88, to finish the regular season with a record of 23–6. But it wasn't an easy win. We were clinging to a 45–43 lead with just 23 seconds left in the half. Sean and Tennessee point guard Jay Price were involved in an elbowing match and both were ejected after each threw a punch.

I thought Sean might be disqualified from our next game against the winner of the Vanderbilt–Mississippi State game in the first round of the SEC Tournament. But the officials ruled it was a flagrant technical, not a fighting technical. I couldn't help but feel sorry for Sean. He had contributed six assists in the first 12 minutes and had a chance to break the school record of 14, held by Dirk Minniefield and Dicky Beal.

But his absence put us in a bind at the lead guard spot. Travis was hobbled by a sprained ankle suffered at the end of the Florida disaster. And Richie was a true lead guard. In the end, Richie and Travis won the battle of backup point guards.

Sean's classmates wouldn't let us lose. John scored his first points of the game when he hit a pair of free throws with 6:30 left to give us a 77–71 lead. Just 32 seconds later, he drained a three-pointer. Next, he made a steal and split a trap, driving in for a slam dunk that was disallowed because he had been fouled before the shot. The unusual explosion got Rock so excited, he bounded onto the floor and ended up clipping John in the face when he went to high five him. John recovered long enough to make both free throws and we were off on a 15–3 run.

A possession later, Deron fired in a three-pointer from the left side. Richie followed with a pair of free throws. Jamal joined the party with a slam dunk. Richie hit a one-hander off a drive in the lane and Deron downed a dunk off a steal from Richie and a perfect pass from John.

We led 88–77 and won going away.

When the game ended, Sean and Jay Price, who had watched the second half on TV in the press room, hugged each other. Sean was fine in the locker room afterwards. Before I talked with him, I wanted to watch the film. Sean got an elbow in the face. The other guy threw a punch first. And he retaliated.

"Coach, when you watch the film, tell me if you wouldn't do the same thing." he said to me. After watching the film, I agreed. He wasn't innocent. But, what are you going to do, turn the other cheek and run? That works only in the Bible.

I admit I was really moved when they honored Cawood. Chris outdid himself with the ceremony. It had just the right touch. Richie walked out to center court to speak on behalf of the 39 Kentucky teams that were linked through Cawood. Richie had met Cawood for the first time when he was just eight years old. Cawood had come to Hazzard to visit a clothing store.

"When I was growing up in eastern Kentucky, I used to listen to Cawood, and he was Kentucky basketball," he said. "Kids growing up all have their heroes. Some are basketball players, rasslers, and country music singers. Mine was Cawood Ledford. And, now that I've gotten to know him after four years at Kentucky, he's still my hero." The words came from the heart.

Then lights went out. We closed our eyes and there was Cawood's voice crackling across the radio again, broadcasting some of the shining moments in Wildcat history over the past five decades. The ones that got the most applause came after he announced the end of Kentucky's 1978 championship game, a victory over Indiana, and a win over Auburn that ended with Charles Barkley sitting on the floor, crying.

When the lights came on again, C.M. called Cawood and Frances to center court. Then Bill Curry and I joined him as he presented them with two lifetime press passes. The cheerleaders formed a long line for one last singing of "My Old Kentucky Home." Everyone joined in. There wasn't a dry eye in the house.

The scene left tears in my eyes. When I watch *The Lou Gehrig Story*, I still always cry when Gary Cooper says, "This is the happiest day of my life." That's the way it was with Cawood's farewell. When I left the Knicks, I didn't miss the job. I missed the people, like Dick McGuire and Fuzzy Levane. It was the same with Cawood. We had so much fun on the Big Blue Line on road trips. It'll leave a void in so many people's lives, and I don't know if it's going to be the same without him.

Finally, Cawood took the mike to say a few words.

"Hello, band," he said, returning the tribute they always pay him before each game.

His speech was short. "It's a sad time for Frances and for me," he said, "but you fans have made it a special and short thirty-nine years and I'll always love you, and God bless you."

It was the best day I've had at Kentucky. And I'm glad a lot of my friends from New York and New England like Jersey Red, Scout, Fuzzy Levane, and Freddie Klein, who owns a piece of the Carnegie Deli, got a chance to see it.

So did Spike Lee, the nationally known filmmaker, who directed *Do The Right Thing* and *Jungle Fever* and was working on a new film about Malcolm X. Spike is a big Knicks fan. He goes to every home game because he's close with Patrick Ewing and Mark Jackson. He was in Lexington Friday for a speaking engagement at Memorial Coliseum.

"I'm sure Adolph Rupp would be rolling over in his grave," he told the crowd. "But my man Rick Pitino told me he's happy I'm here."

I wish all this talk about Adolph Rupp being a racist would go away. It's useless rhetoric. Whether he was or wasn't is totally irrelevant to the University of Kentucky basketball program today.

Spike is very pro–New York, very pro-black, and he was happy about what we're trying to do at Kentucky, even though Adolph might not agree. I asked if he would like to attend the game. I know he's a big Georgetown fan, but his presence did a lot to help our image because of what he stands for in the black community.

Spike Lee even attended our pregame meal, where he spoke with Junior Braddy, who is another budding filmmaker. Junior gave him an outline of a movie script he had written called "Displacement." Spike told Junior he would read it on the flight home to New York. He also had lengthy conversations with fellow New Yorkers Jamal and Andre.

Spike had planned to stay for only a half because he had to catch a flight back to New York. But he told me if he had known it was going to be this much fun, he would have canceled his ticket. After we made a couple of threes in the first half, he said to me, "Oh my god, this place is going to erupt." Yes, that was him, screaming at the officials. It was hard not to get involved. Before he left, he distributed X hats to our team and gave a pair to Chris and Ricky.

I was hopeful the drama and emotion would help our recruiting. We brought Terry Bynum, a 6' 4" lefty guard from Anderson, South Carolina, Junior College who originally signed with North Carolina State out of high school, in for an official visit. We had invited some of the better underclassmen in the state in for the game.

Rodney Dent also reassured us he still planned on coming. A TV report out of Louisville had made that sound questionable. The story claimed that Dent was thinking about enrolling elsewhere because he felt Kentucky's academic standards were too stringent. It apparently didn't take Louisville long to follow up on it. Denny Crum's assistant, Larry Gay, was actually in Rodney's home Friday night. After Gay left, Dent phoned Herb at home to tell us he hadn't changed his mind.

We had four days to prepare for the SEC tournament in Birmingham. This was Kentucky's first trip to any postseason competition in two years, so interest was unusually high.

I got up at five Monday morning for a 6:30 A.M. practice. We practiced again at three. We were all energized. When the polls came out that day, we were ranked 11th in CNN and we actually jumped a spot from tenth to ninth in AP, despite the loss to Florida.

There was an orgy of basketball on the tube all week. ESPN was running its championship week. Tulsa, coached by my former assistant Tubby Smith, was playing Southwest Missouri. I stayed up until four in the morning to watch the rerun. I was really disappointed when they lost. Hopefully, both Tubby and Ralph, whose Western Kentucky team had won 21 games and advanced to the semifinals of the Sun Belt, will receive NIT bids.

Everett Garrison, a fan from Mt. Sterling, sent me a letter.

Enclosed was a hand-drawn comic strip showing me telling the team, "Now, remember guys, you have nothing to fear going into postseason play."

"Don't worry, coach," Jamal Mashburn replies in the cartoon. "We don't know the meaning of the word 'fear.' "

"I am concerned about our rebounding, though," I say.

"Don't worry, coach," one of the players says, "we don't know the meaning of the word 'rebound,' either."

There was also a nice typewritten note, wishing us good luck in the tournament and urging us to use the comic strip for a little extra motivation, if it would help. I *was* concerned about our rebounding. I knew if we didn't improve in that area, we would have a short stay in the NCAA tournament. I was hoping to iron out the kinks at the SEC tournament.

I could see a surge in adrenaline when we practiced Monday. Deron took off from the dotted line for a slam dunk and Chris stepped in to take the charge. Chris suffered a sneaker print on his face. He also injured his right hand. Richie suffered a shoulder injury in the same workout. It was a good thing we had a few days off before our next game.

Rock came in to say goodbye before we left. He was starting his new job in Tampa, but promised me he would try to be on our bench Saturday.

Rock said he wanted to come dressed in red, white, and blue. "Just like Apollo Creed in the first Rocky movie. I'm going to go up to Wimp Sanderson, point my finger at him and say, 'I WANT YOU!' "

# --19--

# *BIG BLUE IS BACK*

The city of Birmingham has always been a college football hotbed, and upcoming spring practice at Alabama and Auburn still dominated the local sports pages at the beginning of the week.

But, it was hard to keep the SEC basketball tournament out of the headlines. Sixth-ranked Arkansas, which had won three straight Southwest Conference tournaments, was making its first appearance. Three-time defending champion Alabama was there, along with Shaquille O'Neal and Dale Brown of LSU. And Kentucky was back after two years in oblivion.

The other coaches understood what Kentucky meant to the tournament.

"Kentucky is still the aircraft carrier, no doubt about it," Ole Miss coach Ed Murphy said. "They are the premier program in the country. . . . The atmosphere is going to be super, and they play a major role in it."

"It definitely matters, having Kentucky in it," Vanderbilt coach Ed Fogler said. "I think anytime you talk Kentucky basketball, it raises eyebrows from California to New York."

Our appearance did wonders for the psyches of Kentucky fans. They couldn't wait for us to arrive. A group of them met us at the airport Thursday night. There must have been another 500 standing outside the hotel when our bus pulled up.

We couldn't get the Birmingham Civic Center for a practice, so I arranged for a walk-through in the Sheraton ballroom that night and again the next morning, three hours before we played Vandy. We laid down tape to simulate the key. I warned the players to avoid the pillars. We had practiced this way when I was with the Knicks and we couldn't get the Garden floor. They had a little cubbyhole in the back and we used to dummy up, using the garbage can for a basket. There would be fork lifts going by, and I would tell the players to watch out for the oil slick.

About 300 UK fans, who found out we were there, crowded into the hallway and conducted an impromptu pep rally when the players emerged after a half-hour practice.

The SEC tournament had been sold out for weeks and Kentucky had only 1,200 seats, but our fans were out in force when we took the floor against Vandy. The fact that scalpers were asking upwards of $100 a ticket didn't seem to deter them.

Mash gave our fans their money's worth in our 76–57 victory. He finally came to life in the second half, scoring 16 of his 24 points.

All it took was one little threat.

Midway through the first half, I had taken Mash out. I told him that unless he took over, he wasn't going to play the rest of the game. I said he might not play the rest of the season. Then I thought about what I had said. Forty seconds later, I put him back in the game. Mash, who had scored 56 points in two regular season games against Vanderbilt, responded with 7 in a row and 9 of 11 as we put the game away.

I've found that Mash will always respond if you end your lecture with a positive. For instance, pointing out that he's not being aggressive enough and then stating, "How can one of the best players in the country not be aggressive?" End with a positive, and the results will be positive.

The victory put us in the semifinals against LSU, which had defeated Tennessee, 99–89, later that evening. But our game soon took on a different aspect because Shaquille O'Neal was in street clothes after having been suspended for fighting.

The incident occurred with 10:05 remaining. LSU held a healthy 73–51 lead. Tennessee's Carlus Groves grabbed Shaquille around the waist and pulled him down to prevent him from making an easy field goal. Shaquille spun around, then flailed away with an elbow in an attempt to break loose. The two exchanged pushes.

The problem could have been settled right there if LSU coach Dale Brown hadn't rushed onto the floor and headed right for Groves. Brown appeared to shove Groves, who was being restrained by an official. Groves fired back with a punch that did not land.

Tennessee coach Wade Houston went after Brown with a verbal assault. Both benches emptied. I had never seen a melée like that before. When the officials finally sorted through the bodies, ten players were ejected and both Shaquille and Groves were assessed technicals for fighting. NCAA rules dictate that both players be automatically suspended for their next game.

After the game, SEC Director of Officials John Guthrie said he saw nothing on the videotape that merited Dale Brown's being ejected. "Don't make Dale Brown the villain," he said.

The media started laughing hysterically.

Wade Houston took the fifth amendment. But Dale was more than willing to get on a soapbox when he met the media. He claimed the SEC should be embarrassed for having suspended Shaquille. Dale blamed the incident on the physical abuse O'Neal had been subjected to all season. Dale claimed he was within his right, as a head coach, to enter the court during an altercation.

"How you can say I took a swing at anybody is an absolute lie," he said. "Let's not make this a Woody Hayes thing. I'd like you to view the video before you nail me to the cross."

I was in my hotel room at the time, watching the game on TV. It was my feeling Dale aggravated the situation. Groves hadn't tried to hurt anyone. He grabbed Shaquille around the waist. This was wrong and the referee had called a flagrant foul. Shaquille responded. But Dale should have stayed on the bench. He was lucky that Wade Houston hadn't lost his cool, or there would be one less preacher man. Imagine attempting to shove a player and then totally ignoring it. I can't. Nor could the fans. The whole arena was yelling "Throw Dale Out."

Dale said he would never do such a thing with his daughter sitting in the stands. He was making matters worse by the second. We all make mistakes. The only way out of an embarrassing situation is to own up to your mistake, apologize and get on with your life. I really like Dale, but he needs someone whispering in his ear when an adverse situation arises.

I felt this whole tournament was well run. But when the heat was on, the SEC officials did not respond well. Roy Kramer, the commissioner, wasn't here, and that hurt. But the officials did not help themselves by ejecting four players— Jamie Brandon, Vernel Singleton, and Maurice Williamson of LSU and Jay Price of Tennessee—for leaving the bench when, in fact, all four had been in the game when the fight broke out.

Dale continued his crusade Saturday morning. He threatened to have his team boycott our game as a protest. He threatened to sit out the game. He accused the fans who booed him of being "uninformed people." About the only thing he didn't say was that the suspension was a conspiracy hatched in Lexington.

I never thought Kentucky would have a home-court advantage in the SEC tournament. But it happened. Dale had been given a reprimand from the SEC office for his public criticism of league officials. But it was not only the officials who reprimanded him. When he walked onto the court, he was serenaded with another loud chorus of boos.

The officials approached me and said, "If Dale walks off, leave it to us to handle it."

It was a lot easier to attack LSU without without Shaquille, because the Tigers played a different defense. They played a lot of man-to-man and a little flattened-out 2-3 zone. When we had played LSU earlier, we shot 44 three-point attempts. We had planned to go inside more this time, even with Shaquille in the game.

We always talked about the danger of the wounded Tiger. Without Shaq, it was time for the other players to step up. The Tiger could be dangerous if we didn't match LSU's level of emotion.

LSU tried to make up for his absence with 6' 9" Harold Boudreax, 7' 0" Geert Hammick, and 6' 8" Vernel Singleton. We got inside for 14 layups or dunks in the first half of an 80–74 victory.

We matched LSU's intensity, and eventually overcame their emotion midway through the second half. John blocked back-to-back shots and fired in a three-pointer to complete a 13–0 run and give us a 59–50 lead. Pel finished with 17 points, Gimel had 14, and Mash, who shot 6 for 8, added 12. We shot 54.7 percent, 63 in the second half.

I went over to shake hands with Dale afterwards and he told me, "We really missed the big guy."

I just laughed and told him, "We've really missed our big guy for three years now."

Dale dropped another bomb in the press conference. He said he would recommend to Shaquille's parents that he turn pro. I was more than happy to second that motion.

"It's been an exciting day," I said. "Not only are we getting a win, but Shaquille's going hardship. We don't have to play him anymore."

We did have to play Alabama, the team that had stunned Arkansas, 90–89, in one of the best-played tournament games I'd ever seen. Alabama won the game when Elliott Washington, their point guard, made a three-point basket with 1.2 seconds left. The Hogs were finally butchered.

There were more great athletes on display in that game than in most NCAA Finals. Todd Day of Arkansas fired in 39 points, including a wild underhanded scoop shot he banked in off the glass. Hollywood Robinson had 26 for Alabama, including a couple of spinning 360-degree moves that electrified the crowd of 17,869, the largest ever to watch a college game in the state.

As usual, nobody thought Kentucky could play with either of those teams. Even Gene DeFilippo asked me if I thought we could win, when we went out for a jog Sunday morning before mass. You have to have faith.

Before the game, I went over to Wimp Sanderson. "No matter how much you foul Jamal," I told him, "he's not turning pro."

Wimp just shook his head at Dale's latest prediction about Shaquille.

I had told Mash before the game that he needed to be the best player on the floor. "If you're not the best player on the floor, we don't win the SEC championship."

Mash played like the best player in the country, scoring 28 points and grabbing 13 rebounds as we defeated Alabama 80–54 to win the tournament before a crowd of 17,389.

It's a good thing Mash came up big. We played tentatively in the first half, falling behind 32–29 when Robinson made a crossover dribble on Richie and made a three-pointer just before half. Mash gathered the players together outside the locker room before we went back on the court.

"We've got to start playing harder," he said.

For guys like John and Dale, the hard work paid off.

Pel made the all-tournament team after grabbing 8 rebounds and holding Alabama's Latrell Sprewell, who had burned him for 32 at Rupp, to just 6 points. That was one way to silence Herb, who kept referring to John as "Sprepel" during our shootaround.

Dale shut down Robinson in the second half, holding him to just 5 points after Robinson had scored 17 on us in the first 20 minutes. Billy Donovan's father, Bill Sr., who was at the game, was so excited he asked Dale if he had given Robinson the key back. Dale had certainly locked him up when it counted.

Alabama center Robert Horry became so frustrated when we were making our charge, he picked up one technical for throwing a ball at Pelphrey and another intentional foul when he nailed Gimel in the mouth with an elbow. I yelled to Gimel, "Keep your cool." He calmly stepped to the line and made two free throws. In the end, we scored 56 points in the paint and out-rebounded Alabama by two.

Gimel had a fat lip at the end of the game, but it was obvious we had a much better inside game when he was on the floor. I kiddingly referred to him as the High Karate Kid, but he played 34 minutes against LSU and 24 against Alabama. We had worked hard the past three weeks to cut down on his fouls.

We had a film made up to show Gimel why he was getting into foul trouble because he was denying it. He claimed he wasn't touching the guy at all and blaming it on the officials. We wanted him to see his hand go on the lower back of the offensive player. Although it wasn't a big shove, it was getting him into foul trouble. Gimel was concentrating more, moving his feet and getting better position. Whenever we saw his hands go down in practice, we would blow the whistle. We even asked him, when he went to sleep at night, to keep his hands behind the pillow.

I could sleep easier knowing we weren't fatigued after pressing three straight games. We executed our press against Alabama as well as any team I've ever coached.

Midway through the second half, I turned to the official and told him to tell Wimp to sit down.

"Why?" he said.

"That sports coat he's wearing," I said. "It's so ugly. It's distracting our players when they go to the line."

He laughed.

We even managed to suffocate the Alabama fans, who outnumbered our fans, 4–1. When the Alabama cheerleaders kept trying to rally the troops down the stretch with a "Roll Tide" cheer, our fans yelled back, "Beat the Traffic."

All I can say is, it's a good thing JoAnn Hauser brought along that pair of scissors. Our players needed them to cut down the nets after the victory. I don't know if anyone thought we would win the SEC again so quickly, but there were Mash and Pel leading the charge into our locker room wearing necklaces of rope.

Mash had made 26 of 31 shots he attempted during the tournament and had 30 rebounds. But all he could think about were the four seniors. He told them, "This is the only thing I can give you. I can't give you a present. I can give you the SEC championship."

I was so proud of this team. We simply wore Alabama out in the second half with full-court pressure, which triggered a frightening 30–6 run. They took a 38–31 lead, then hit the wall. "That's Kentucky basketball," I screamed at the top of my lungs after we held Alabama to just 22 points in the final 20 minutes.

When the players finally took their seats for a moment of reflection, I was bubbling.

"You turned up the heat like you can't believe. Without question, Mash was the best player in the tournament, maybe the best player in the country. But you all played great. I don't want to leave any person out. But I'll tell you why you won and why you got to this point. It's because of this man here."

Then, I pointed to Sean.

"Eleven or twelve games ago he decided, 'The hell with Sean Woods. Let me make all my teammates better.' And, at that point, we became a great basketball team.

"I can't tell you what a treat this is. This was tremendous

because that's exactly the way you played. You turn up the heat in the second half in the NCAA tournament and teams will come out with a false sense of security. They'll think, "Oh, Kentucky's not that good. They're not that good. And, boom, you'll knock them right out. Today, when you kept the heat on, Alabama got more tired. That is what you must expect to happen.

"Everybody played great. You weren't afraid to shoot the ball and you won it going away. This banner's going on that wall at Memorial Coliseum."

The team applauded, then got together for a final cheer.

"One, two, three. Hard work."

Maybe it was destiny. I didn't find out about it until later, but the home white uniforms we wore had been blessed after our games with Vanderbilt and LSU.

Shirley Friedrich, a member of the Kentucky Alumni Association of Birmingham, was helping set up a reception at the Sheraton Hotel after our game with Vanderbilt when Bill Keightley asked her if she could help him out with the team laundry.

At first, Shirley thought it was a joke, but Bill assured her the hotel wouldn't do the laundry and said he needed help getting the uniforms washed. Shirley volunteered to take them home and wash them herself. When she arrived and told her husband, their house guest, Father Jim Lichtefeld, a priest at St. Stephen Martyr in Louisville and a big UK fan, was particularly interested.

"Father Lichtefeld is one of the biggest UK fans ever," Shirley said. "He tried on a couple of the uniforms and was really in heaven, so to speak," she added.

After the uniforms had been washed, Father Lichtefeld said a quiet prayer to bless the uniforms and the team. He did the same thing the night after we defeated LSU. "Of course," Shirley said, "I think he'd been saying a prayer for them every night before he went to bed."

Birmingham had been good to me again. That was the same arena from which we had started our 1987 NCAA run with the Providence team.

At the beginning of this season, I had called our players wallflowers, players who would be standing in the back of the room while everybody else was dancing. Cawood reminded me of that during our postgame radio show.

"Not bad for a bunch of wallflowers," he said.

I was hoping the dance would last three more weeks. After we packed up, we bused over to a local restaurant for dinner before flying home. The manager wheeled in a portable TV so we could watch the pairings on CBS. C.M., who was on the selection committee, told me earlier that morning that if we beat Alabama, we would probably be a No. 2 seed in the East. But I had no idea who we would play, and I wanted the players to be surprised.

When the brackets were announced, we drew Old Dominion, the Colonial Conference tournament winner and a No. 15 seed, at the Worcester, Massachusetts, Centrum. I originally thought we might open with Delaware, where David Roselle was president. The Blue Hens had qualified for the tournament for the first time ever by winning the ECAC North Atlantic tournament, and I sent along a congratulatory note to him.

John's parents, who ate dinner with us, had a major decision to make. Their other son, Jerry, who played for East Tennessee State, had a first-round game against Arizona in Atlanta the same day as our game. "Maybe we'll just stay home and watch both games on TV," his mother Jenny said.

We flew back to Lexington on a new plane with plush cushioned seats.

As our charter was about to land, we caught a glimpse of around 700 fans, who had gathered by the fence outside the private airstrip. Some of them had been there for two hours, huddling in 28-degree weather, just waiting for the plane to arrive.

When we finally deplaned, I gave the trophy to Bernadette,

who held it up for the crowd to see. She in turn handed it to John, who led the team over to the fence so our fans could get a closer look while live TV cameras recorded the moment. They were like giddy little school kids. Aminu had bought home the SEC banner from the press table. Junior started twisting his body into a "C" to start the C-A-T-S cheer.

Bill Keightley just stood in the background, obviously moved by the scene. "I never thought I'd live long enough to see this happen again," he said, wistfully. "Now I know we're back."

# --20--

# *A TRIP DOWN MEMORY LANE*

 $\mathbf{W}$ e were carrying the honor of an entire state with us.

Cawood and I took a heliocopter to Louisville Monday night for our annual special segment of the Big Blue Line.

When we landed outside the mall, we were greeted by a sheriff's deputy in a limousine. He escorted us 100 yards to the entrance, then cleared a path through the crowd of 3,000 inside just so we could get to the microphones.

For the moment, all intrastate rivalries were forgotten.

The next night, we took the team north to Carlisle, Kentucky, to do a fundraiser for Audra Sparks, a 17-year-old cheerleader at Nicholas County High School who was suffering from liver cancer and was undergoing experimental treatment at a hospital in Camden, New Jersey. We were surrounded by Kentucky fans.

Carlisle is typical of so many small towns in Kentucky. Its

major industries are farming and the Jockey underwear plant. When the Nicholas County girls' basketball team won the 16th region championship last weekend, the team bus toured the downtown streets.

"First time we've been to the Sweet Sixteen in thirty-three years," said the coach who accompanied us. "I think it was the biggest thing to happen here since World War II."

The sponsors had arranged for us to attend a reception at a state park and pep rally at the school. When we arrived at the gym, we were greeted by 3,000 fans, who had filled up every seat.

We even received a cardboard good-luck poster made by a bunch of five-year-olds at the Central Baptist Kindergarten in Lexington. Their teacher enclosed a note that said, "Most of these students wouldn't know whether George Washington or George Bush was the president of the United States, but they can name most of the UK players."

During "News Time," she had asked her students who played for the Cats.

Their answers were what you might expect: "Michael Jordan, Magic Johnson, Richie Farmer, David Robinson, Michael Jackson, Sean Woods, Deron Feldhaus, John Pelphrey, Travis Ford and, of course, Andre Widdick." The coach of the team? "Rick Patuna." They also had some last minute advice for us: "Find a lucky rabbit's foot."

The trip to our first-round game in Worcester, was like a walk down memory lane.

I got a chance to drive down to Providence for dinner at Camille's Roman Garden on Federal Hill with Providence AD John Marinatto, Pat Nero, and Dan Egan from the college, Jersey Red, Cawood, Tom Wallace, Billy Reynolds, Billy, and Herb.

I ordered fried calimari and other Italian delicacies for the table as an appetizer.

I met Cawood in the restroom and he said to me, "That fried calipari was really good."

I cracked up and told the rest of the table the story. Cawood must have had basketball on the brain. John Calipari coaches UMass.

John Marinatto was late for the meal because the Providence women's team was playing in an NCAA tournament game against Toledo. "We lost," he said when he finally arrived.

"Our women lost?" I asked, making a Freudian slip.

Providence College will always be special to me. It's a small Catholic school playing bigtime basketball. The place was a perfect fit for me. A Catholic state, a predominantly Italian city, a school with a great basketball heritage.

I coached Providence for two years in 1986 and 1987. My second year that team was the epitome of everything I believe in as a coach. None of our players were household names when the season started. But players like Billy Donovan, Dave Kipfer, Pop Lewis, Delray Brooks, Steve Wright, Darryl Wright, and Jacek Duda helped resurrect a program. We were on a roll that March. It all appeared to happen so fast. When we finally reached the Final Four, a reporter asked me if this was a Cinderella story.

"No," I said, "because Cinderella never worked this hard."

I'm not close to the program anymore. When I left Providence for the Knicks, I begged John Marinatto to hire one of my assistants, Gordie Chiesa, as coach. I thought that was what the players wanted. Gordie lasted only a year. There was tremendous turmoil in the program when Providence didn't make the tournament in 1988. Center Marty Conlon had quit the team in January. Other players were talking about transferring.

I couldn't understand it. Before that season the players liked Gordie. They thought he had a great sense of humor. He had been a dedicated and hard-working assistant coach. Apparently, things changed when he became the head coach. I'm sorry Providence didn't work out for him. He did a super job for our team. He's now an assistant with the Utah Jazz in the NBA.

After Gordie left, John wanted to hire a big-name coach. Hubie Brown asked me if I could get him an interview for the job. I said, "Hubie, they're not going to hire you, but I'll certainly try my best." Hubie had a five-hour interview. He told Howard Garfinkel, the co-owner of Five Star camps, there was something wrong if he didn't get the job. Hubie felt he'd had the greatest interview of all time.

I called John to find out how it went. He said Hubie was the most powerful man he'd ever met. He sat there for five hours and listened to Hubie talk. But John told me it would never work. He was totally intimidated by Hubie. When Hubie didn't get the job, he told people it was because I didn't want him to have it. I was saving it for myself. That's the way Hubie burns all his bridges.

John wanted to bring in Pete Gillen but, as usual, Pete turned them down, as did some other top coaches. I felt what Providence needed most was a recruiter. The school was a tough sell because of its size and lack of high school talent in its own backyard. I suggested to John he talk to Rick Barnes, then coach at George Mason.

"No," he said, "I can't do that because he's not a name and doesn't have much head-coaching experience."

"Yes," I agreed, "but he's a good recruiter. He's a sharp guy. You should consider interviewing him."

John still wasn't sure, but he finally called him after some other candidates declined. After he interviewed him, he wanted to hire him immediately.

When I was the Knicks' coach, Rick Barnes used to say he appreciated everything I'd done for him. But, once I went to Kentucky, things changed.

My first year at Kentucky, I went to the Big East tournament to see Marty Conlon, Abdul Shasmid-Deen, and Carlton Screen, three Providence players I had recruited, play their last game in the Big East. I asked John for four tickets. The seats he gave me were located right in front of those occupied by the families of the Providence assistants. Dave Gavitt, then commissioner of the Big East, told John, "You should never have put Rick there because of all the jealousies and comparisons that will arise." I could see his point, but I just wanted to root Rick Barnes, his staff and players on to victory.

I can understand how Rick Barnes felt. We caught lightning in a bottle, and he was being subjected to all the same expectations. I learned a valuable lesson from all this: to recommend only your assistant coaches or close friends for jobs. Though you may be helping one person, you will alienate ten others.

While Providence was struggling, Massachusetts was flourishing. UMass not only won the Atlantic 10, but also finished the regular season with 28 victories. They were seeded third in the Eastern regional. Their success was far greater than anyone could have imagined.

The UMass campus at Amherst is located just 48 miles from Worcester. There was an enormous ticket demand for their first-round game with Fordham.

Kentucky fans were just as fired up about our first trip to the tournament in four years. We were alloted only 250 tickets, but that did not stop 300 fans from taking two charter flights from Lexington, even though none of the passengers had tickets.

I had received calls all week about tickets to our game with Old Dominion. I did get one break. John Marinatto, who was hoping Providence might be in Worcester, had purchased tickets from the Centrum three months before the pairings were announced. I saved three for my former Kentucky players—Derrick Miller, Jonathan Davis, and Reggie

Hanson. We took them to Worcester. Even if they hadn't played in a tournament for Kentucky, they could at least experience this one.

We didn't know that much about Old Dominion, so I had Herb call Oliver Purnell's media teleconference Monday morning, just to listen in to their coach. By the time Herb got off the phone, I was concerned.

The NCAA didn't do us any favors, matching us up against ODU. Forget about that 40-point loss to Alabama early in the season. ODU might have been 15–14, but they had really come on late in the season. They had won five in a row and defeated Richmond and James Madison to win the Colonial Athletic Conference Tournament. They had enough athletes to cause us problems. Purnell was touting his 6' 7" star Ricardo Leonard, claiming he was just as good as Mash.

When I voiced that opinion to C.M., he just smiled.

"Coach, right about now, you'd probably be concerned about playing Tates Creek High School," he said.

Convincing our players that Old Dominion posed a problem was not easy. This was not the John Gotti trial where the jury was sequestered. Our players had to have heard some of the questions from the media. Have you heard of Old Dominion? Do you know where it is?

The day of our first NCAA game, the town of Lexington came to a halt. Meetings were canceled. Court dates were moved. Fans gathered round their television sets.

For a while, they must have felt like switching to *All My Children.* We shot just 33 percent in the first half and led by only two points, 34–32, at half.

We jumped all over the players in the locker room, especially Pel.

"John," I yelled, "you can just go back to the mountains when this is all over because they're never going to let you back in Lexington."

I told the team, "It's ridiculous how we're playing right now. We're playing scared, uptight. That's normal. Everybody has the jitters, including me. Now, let's go out and show them the real Kentucky team."

John, who hadn't scored a basket to that point, shot 7 for 7 in the second half and finished with 22 points, 5 rebounds, 4 assists, and 4 steals as we diposed of ODU, 88–69. He and the other seniors made up for the fact that Mash had a rare bad game. Jamal shot just 3 for 13. He finished with only 11 points and was in serious foul trouble most of the game.

When Mash picked up his fourth personal with 11 minutes left and we still hadn't taken control, I called timeout and addressed the seniors. "This is your time," I said. "You four seniors waited four years for this moment. You're going to have to win it. Everybody's tired. You've got to use the press to wear them down."

That's exactly what happened. Sean, who had 16 points, 5 rebounds, 8 assists, and 3 steals, continued to raise his game to another level. He was in such good condition he looked like a fighter who could go the distance. He put so much pressure on ODU's point guard, the Monarchs eventually collapsed. They turned the ball over thirty times.

When Deron and Dale hit consecutive three-pointers to give us a 73–61 lead with 5:03 left, I felt ODU had hit the fatigue wall. They had been challenging our three-point shooters all game. Then, we got as many open threes as we wanted. We played with great intelligence when Mash was out. The four seniors and Gimel were playing so well that, if Martinez hadn't fouled out with 3:46 left, I might not have put Mash back in the game.

There is no answer to the first round. You just have to get through it. Winning and having Mash play subpar would help us in the next round. Mash would come out with a vengeance.

The other top seeds in the East—Duke, Massachusetts, and Syracuse—won easily. The biggest surprise of the day occurred when East Tennessee upset Arizona in Atlanta. John's brother Jerry got a chance to advance to the second round. Jenny Pelphrey, who had flown up here for our games, was trying to be diplomatic the next day. She had on a Kentucky-blue dress and a button that read, "I'm an ETSU Mom."

Life finally got back to normal after the game. Bernadette even arranged for the players to get in a two-hour study hall. "Geez," Travis said, only half-kidding, "Twenty-four thousand Kentucky students are on spring break in Florida and we've got study hall."

I had settled into the lounge with Billy, Herb, and Mike to watch the games on a big screen TV when John Calipari and his assistants showed up. John had come over to our hotel, looking for Rock, who had worked with him at Kansas and Pitt. UMass had a big game with Syracuse, the Big East tournament champion, Sunday.

We watched the end of the Georgia Tech–USC game together. When James Forest hit a miracle three-pointer with 0:8 seconds remaining to give Tech a 79–78 victory, I said I'd kill myself if that happened to us. I wondered if I could handle a loss like that in a positive manner. I forgot about it; that would not happen to the Cats.

I figured we'd be much looser in our second round game with Iowa State. We were playing against a young Big Eight team that liked to run up and down the floor. Iowa State would score 120, if you let them.

They almost did.

We won in a shootout, outscoring Iowa State, 106–98, to advance to the NCAA Eastern Regional semifinals at the Spectrum in Philadelphia.

Sean came up big again. He scored 18 points and had 9 assists. He was the catalyst for a 7–0 run that sent us up 69–59 with 14:57 left. But his biggest moment came with two minutes to play. Iowa State had reduced our 12-point lead to 93–90. Sean looked inside for Jamal, who had been a force with 27 points and 9 rebounds. When he saw Mash was covered and time was running out, he pulled up and made a

17-footer from the top of the circle. This gave us some breathing room.

We held on from there, offsetting an outstanding performance by Iowa State's backcourt of Justus Thigpen and Ron
Bayless. Those two players combined for 62 points and were
responsible for keeping Iowa State in the game. Thigpen and
Bayless made 24 of 25 free throws.

We shot 58.7 percent from the field, made 11 of 22 three-
point shots and had a season high 26 assists, taking advantage of Iowa State's decision to front Mash in the post. But we
needed to make 11 of our final 14 free throws in the last 1:27
to finish off the Cyclones. At the end, I was praying, "Foul
Richie, foul Richie." Richie, our best free throw shooter, made
four in a row to seal the game.

I congratulated Iowa State afterwards. You couldn't knock
them out. At least, we couldn't. They just kept coming back. I
spent the rest of the press conference responding to accusa-
tions from Iowa State coach Johnny Orr. Orr blasted the officials to the media. He claimed I was constantly out of the
coaching box, but the referees never called me for it.

"They violated that thing all day and the referees had no
courage to call it," Orr said. "In the Big Eight, if you step over
that line, it's a technical foul. They have no guts, these guys,
and that disappointed me."

Orr conceded my coaching-box violations may not have had
an effect on the outcome, but said he had pointed out my
indiscretions about 15 times to the officials. He claimed the
officials did not act on his complaints.

I admit I strayed from the box, but I wasn't yelling at the
officials; I was just coaching our team. They had better things
to do. Orr was in the coaches' box, berating the officials. I
don't know which was worse.

Kentucky in the Sweet 16? I didn't know if it was possible.
I didn't think it was probable. I just wanted to savor the moment.

We hadn't gotten a chance to enjoy our 1987 tournament run at Providence because I was more concerned about Joanne and our family after Daniel had died. I was picking up the pieces of our family. Now I was getting a chance to hang out with my friends Billy Minardi, Billy Burke, one of my former assistants at BU; Larry the Scout, Dave Dibble, Fuzzy Levane, and Jersey Red.

After the game, one of the first to congratulate me was my old college coach Jack Leaman. Jack coached Massachusetts for 13 years from 1966 through 1979. He still works for the school and serves as an assistant with the women's team.

Jack was a Bobby Knight type. Playing for him was very difficult, but it was like being in a classroom every day.

When I was at St. Dominic's, I averaged 28 points and I could do whatever I wanted. My high school coach Pat McGunnigle taught me basketball fundamentals, but made sure the word "fun" was always included. But when I came to UMass, Jack plugged me into the point-guard spot and took away a lot of my freedom. I was a traffic cop in his system. I was what you'd call a Philly Catholic League guard, a guy who just directs the attack and plays the best guy on the other team. You just made everybody else better. You were a coach on the floor, but you did not shoot the ball.

I averaged only 8 points, but we won 20 games my senior year and went to the second round of the NIT, back when that meant something special before the tournament went to early-round games on home-court sites. Every year I was away from Jack, I appreciated him more. Jack always thought I would go into politics someday. But he was supportive when I told him I wanted to get into coaching. At Kentucky, I do both.

I spent so much time answering questions after the game, I missed most of the first half of the Massachusetts-Syracuse game. I tried to be neutral. Massachusetts won, 77–71, to set up a rematch with us. Only this time it would be in the Eastern Regional semifinals.

I missed Harper Williams's desperation three-pointer with

30 seconds left in overtime that gave UMass a 75–71 lead because I had to get to the airport. We were on a charter flight back to Lexington that night. We got out just in time. Worcester was expecting six to eight inches of snow and the white stuff had already started to stick to the runway.

For our team, it was a White Christmas in March.

# --21--

# *ALMOST*

Aside from the Liberty Bell, the one attraction most tourists want to see when they visit Philadelphia is the Art Museum. That's where Sylvester Stallone ran up the steps in the famous scene from the movie *Rocky*.

I wanted to run up those steps, too.

So one morning, Mike, Ralph, and I took off from our downtown hotel and jogged two miles up Kennedy Boulevard to the famous landmark. When Ralph got to the museum, he ran up the steps with his arms raised, humming the movie theme from *Rocky*. Then he went out and bought a hot dog and walked back while the rest of us continued on for four more miles down Kelly Drive by the Schuylkill River.

Our team felt a little like Rocky all week. The media had zeroed in on the other three teams in the Eastern Regionals—Duke, Massachusetts, and Seton Hall. We might as well not have been there. That was fine with me.

But I was a little disturbed by the comments from the Massachusetts players. Jersey Red and John Calipari had become good friends during the season. They had watched the NCAA selection show together, along with John's team. When the brackets were announced, the Massachusetts players started chanting, "We want Kentucky. We want Kentucky."

I guess I was naive. I actually thought the Massachusetts fans might pull for us when we played Iowa State. But after Iowa State cut the lead, they started cheering for Iowa State. That was the first sign our game with UMass might be explosive.

Immediately after Massachusetts's win over Syracuse, their players began talking about revenge and suggesting we weren't that good. Harper Williams said the last time they played us, they had just traveled 19 hours from the Great Alaskan Shootout the day before the game.

"We just lost our legs," he said. "We weren't used to the press. With a team like Kentucky, one day of preparation is not enough. Now, we'll have a week or so to prepare. We want to show the nation we can play with Kentucky."

Our players read his comments with great interest.

I took the team to the Palestra for a two-hour workout the day before the game. On the way to the Penn campus, I told them about the history of the building, which was built in 1927 and was the scene of so many great college doubleheaders in the 1960s and '70s. The banners of the five city teams—Temple, Penn, St. Joseph's, La Salle, and Villanova—still hung from the rafters, along with Villanova's 1985 national championship banner.

The Palestra was one of the most difficult places to play at in the country. The fans were right on top of your bench, which was located right on the floor. I still remember coming in with Massachusetts and knocking off Penn in 1972, when the Quakers were ranked in the Top 10 in the country.

Most of our players, who were used to playing in the palaces, probably thought the 8,800-seat arena was small by today's standards. I can still remember getting dressed in one of the locker rooms, which was located just ten feet from the floor, and listening to the roar of the crowd during the first game. After practice, I took the players out to a street vendor and told them to buy a soft pretzel. I wanted them to get a feel for this town.

All week long UMass had been talking about how they didn't get any respect. This was their first trip to the NCAA tournament in 30 years. The school received more publicity with this team than it had when Julius Erving played there in the early '70s.

The media kept trying to turn John Calipari into my clone. John didn't help matters when he kiddingly showed up at a press conference sporting a mask of my face that had been used at a Kentucky promotion. One writer suggested John was even wearing suits that were almost as expensive as mine.

"The difference," John said. "is that his suits are worth one thousand dollars and mine are worth one hundred and fifty dollars. His shoes are Guccis, and mine are Itchys."

I felt I had to end it right there. First, I told the media I received my suits free. I also said I was getting tired of listening to Massachusetts casting itself in the David role.

"They're a Sweet Sixteen team," I said. "They can't claim to be the underdog, anymore. Maybe they're not Goliath, but they certainly aren't David."

When I thought about Massachusetts, my mind raced back to our game with them in December. I had spoken with their team afterwards and told them I would like nothing better than to see them again in the Final Four. But not at our expense.

The Eastern Regionals were held in the Spectrum, where the 76ers and Flyers—Philadelphia's professional basketball and hockey teams—play their home games. Going back there brought back memories of our second season as head coach of the Knicks, when we swept the Sixers in a three-game miniseries. At the end of the third game, Patrick Ewing and Mark Jackson ran into a custodian who was carrying a broom. They borrowed it, went back out and swept up the floor. They were only kidding, but the scene got a lot of national attention.

Mash did everything but sweep the floor during our 87–77 victory over Massachusetts. I told our guys before the game that both teams were similar. We do some things better. They do some things better. But there's one difference, and that was Jamal.

I told Jamal that in order for us to win, he had to play like an NBA All-Star, not just an NBA player.

He did.

Mash scored 30 points on 11 for 15 shooting. We needed all of them. Kentucky had built a 21-point lead in the first half, but Massachusetts whittled it down to 70–68 with 5:47 remaining. Sean had just grabbed an offensive rebound and John Calipari was up on his toes, reaching with his hands, pantomiming an over-the-top foul.

Then, Lenny Wirtz, a veteran ACC official who was standing at the opposite side of the floor, hit Calipari with a technical foul. The call was for leaving the coaching box. It was the turning point of the game. Richie made both free throws, then we stole the ball. Deron scored on two backdoor baskets and we went on to build the lead back to 11.

A number of UMass reporters were irate at the timing of the technical. I've since spoken with a lot of NCAA people who were seated behind the Massachusetts bench. Apparently John had been baiting the other two officials the whole game. So he was hit hard.

The people I talked to said was it was just like the 1991 NCAA semifinals when Pete Pavia called a technical on Dean Smith of North Carolina at the end of his loss to Kansas. Dean Smith had been on Pavia the entire first half of the game. Finally, it was "I've had enough. Technical."

I don't think John should have received a technical at that moment. But, what people tend to overlook was that UMass was never in the lead, never in control of the game. They did have momentum. Although the technical did give us a cushion, we never had trouble scoring in the entire game. We were having problems stopping them, but we were getting every shot we wanted.

I guess I should thank Johnny Orr. His complaints were loud enough to have been heard at the NCAA offices in Shawnee Mission. Before the game, Lenny Wirtz came over and issued stern warnings to both coaches about leaving the box. I was warned more vehemently than I had ever been.

It was fairly calm afterwards when Julius Erving visited the locker room. He made a point of meeting every player on the team. They didn't seem to care he was wearing a Massachusetts shirt and hat.

"Sorry I had to root against you," he told me, "but I enjoyed watching your team play."

About the only person on our staff who wasn't savoring the win was Herb. When Joanne and I boarded the bus back to our hotel, Herb was sitting there, wringing his hands.

"What's wrong with Herb?" she asked.

"Duke," Herb kept repeating. "Forwards, guards, Christian Laettner."

Duke, the 1991 national champions, had routinely disposed of Seton Hall, 81–69, in the second semifinal game. I started calling Herb "Dr. Doom" the next day. Herb, Billy, and Mike didn't sleep the rest of the week, breaking down films at all hours of the night.

Our biggest fear was that the game would turn into a track meet and we would be watching Duke run fastbreaks like the L.A. Lakers. Potential foul trouble was also a major factor. We needed to do certain things defensively to survive.

The day we defeated Massachusetts, another historic event was taking place back in the Commonwealth. Henyrk De-Kwiatkowski, a Polish-born horseman, acquired Calumet

Farm, paying $17 million at an auction for the farm. De-Kwiatkowski said he planned to preserve the 762-acre farm and maintain its red steeples. He also purchased the Calumet name.

A crowd of about 3,000 was inside an auction tent to the rear of the farm. DeKwiatkowski received a standing ovation from the audience when the bidding was completed.

Duke was on everybody's mind the next day. At a closed practice Friday at the Palestra, someone saw a headline in a suburban paper that read HILL OUSTED. They thought the story was about Duke forward Grant Hill. It concerned an aide to the mayor of Chester, Pennsylvania.

Wishful thinking, I guess.

The Duke players were the darlings of the fans, especially their All-America center Christian Laettner, who was the latest teenage heartthrob. And adolescent girls were also squealing at the sight of his teammate, lead guard Bobby Hurley.

The way everyone was talking, Duke was the only team in this region with a shot to get to Minneapolis. When I picked up the New York *Post* the day of the game, it said the only thing that could prevent Duke from getting to the Final Four was if their bus broke down.

In the locker room that night, I sensed an uneasiness among our staff. I always say to Herb before we go out onto the floor, "What do you think?"

And he'll usually say, "We'll be all right, coach, if we do the following things."

I said to Herb before the Duke game, "What do you think?"

And he said, "I don't know, coach."

I said to Bill Keightley, "What do you think tonight?"

He always gives the same answer, "We'll be fine." This time, he looked at me and walked away.

Finally, I said to our manager, Jeff Morrow, "What do you think tonight?" He always gives me the same answer. "We're going to win, coach."

But, this time, he said to me, "It's a great crowd tonight."

We said two things to the players. One, expect to win. And, two, play Kentucky basketball. Duke was the heavyweight champion. I knew if it was close they would get the edge. But our players didn't seem intimidated. It was like Richie had said the day before at the press conference: "We respect Duke, but we're not afraid of them." The one point we drove home was, "Don't be afraid to fail. Take chances and expect to play well."

Before the players went onto the floor, John gathered them together. "Let's play the way we have all year," he said.

The game turned out to be the greatest exhibition of offensive basketball I'd ever seen. When Villanova defeated Georgetown to win the NCAA championship in 1985, it was a great ball-control game. But this was a game for the fans.

Neither team held anything back. Neither played a conservative half-court game. Neither thought maybe we shouldn't take this shot. Both teams extended 94 feet and played all-out basketball. Both teams played great defense, but the offense just took over.

Duke shot 35 for 52, 65.4 percent, and was 8 for 16 from beyond the three-point arc. We shot 37 for 65, 56.9 percent; 12 for 22 from three-point range. We forced Duke into 20 turnovers. Both teams combined for 47 assists on 71 field goals.

Our offense the last ten or 12 games reminded me of Princeton, but at three times the speed. I've never had an offense execute with such precision. It was such a thing of beauty to watch.

In the final five minutes, the lead changed hands six times. There were an incredible five lead changes in the last 31.5 seconds alone.

Individual performances were awesome.

Laettner was a perfect 10, making all 10 field goals he attempted and shooting 10 for 10 from the foul line. He finished with 31 points and 7 rebounds. Mash matched Laettner's brilliance with 28 points and 10 rebounds.

Bobby Hurley said he had welcomed our press. But Sean was his worst nightmare, forcing Hurley into eight turnovers, double his average. Hurley did score 22 points and had 10 assists. But Sean matched him, with 21 points and 9 assists. Dale scored 18 points and John added 16.

I think the most important thing about that game for me as a coach was the fact that we decided to play zone defense. We felt the entire team would foul out if we played man to man. That almost happened, anyway.

I was very proud of the way our players studied the game plan and stuck to it. We believed we could score against Duke, and we did.

When we went down 12, 67–55, with 11 minutes left in regulation, I called a timeout. I said, "Okay, now we're ready to switch. Now, we're going to go to man-to-man. The press is going to take its toll. We're going to win this game. This is our time."

I could see it in their eyes. Down 12, everything was going the other way. In their minds, they felt they were going to win the game. They were totally confident. At that point, it became the most exciting minutes I've ever been associated with as a coach.

There's no question in my mind, we rattled Duke. With 8:06 to go in regulation, Laettner took out his frustrations on Aminu. Aminu fouled him going to the basket. Both players sprawled to the floor. When Laettner got up, he stepped on Aminu's chest.

Laettner was called for a contact technical.

I hadn't known Laettner had stepped on him. I turned to my assistants and asked them, "What happened?"

Herb said, "I don't know. I think Laettner yelled at the official."

If I had seen the incident, I would have gone crazy and demanded that Laettner be ejected from the game. But I never saw the play until the news that night. I don't know why

Aminu was smiling. He should have gotten up and started complaining to the officials.

"It was a tap," Aminu said later. "It didn't faze me. I was kind of surprised. Maybe he thought I was a freshman and he could just play with me."

Laettner said later he was just trying to catch his balance. But the replays appeared to show otherwise.

We forced an overtime when Deron muscled his way inside, following up a missed shot by John with 37 seconds left. Duke had a chance to win in regulation, but Hurley missed a jumper just before the buzzer.

The overtime was just as tense, the lead changing back and forth. We went ahead 101–100 with just 19.7 seconds left when Mash drove baseline and scored on a soft banker. He was fouled by Antonio Lang. Mash made the foul shot and we called time.

I told the players that we would not call a timeout if Duke scored. "Obviously they're going to Christian Laettner. Let's double down hard on him, but don't foul and give up the three-point play." My philosophy in not calling a timeout: if Duke scored I didn't want them to change their defense, because we were scoring at a successful rate.

Duke went right to Laettner after the timeout. He took a pass and went into the lane for a shot, and Mash was called for his fifth personal as he reached in and tried to strip the ball away. Laettner made both free throws, giving Duke a 102–101 lead.

We came down the floor and spontaneously I decided to call a timeout with 7.8 seconds left. Originally, I didn't want to let Duke change its defense, but with Mash and Martinez on the bench, I didn't feel we could stop Duke from scoring with any time left on the clock. I wanted to win or lose the game on the last possession.

Sean almost made our dream come true, banging home an incredible shot over Laettner with 2.1 seconds left to give us the lead.

Duke called timeout.

At that moment, as the players were running to the bench, I felt euphoric inside, realizing that we were going to the Final Four. The players were all jumping up and down, hugging each other. Then reality set in, and I regained my composure. I realized that there were 2.1 seconds to go. The entire timeout was spent discussing whether we should put a defender on the ball, or play five versus four. I felt that the way to play the situation was to have five versus four, and not have a man on the ball.

That's the percentage way to play that situation. I believe that if a team inbounds the ball from the sideline, you have to have pressure, because the man can't move. But the guy can move back if he's inbounding from the baseline. We felt if we put a man on the ball on the baseline, Hill was going to move back and throw it deep. We didn't want to risk a layup or a play going to the basket.

It was also a case of personnel. If Jamal or Gimel had been in the game, we might have put a man on the ball and played Laettner with single coverage. Jamal or Gimel might have been able to body Laettner out. But they had both fouled out and Deron, who is 6' 6", was our tallest player on the floor.

We could have had Aminu or Andre to defend the inbounds pass, but they were freshmen and I was worried that Duke, which had screened on the baseline to free up a man earlier in the game, might try the same thing now. I didn't want to risk the chance of knocking the guy over and fouling.

We decided if we were going to lose with a jump shot, so be it. We felt the ball was going to go to Laettner, and he would take the last shot. We decided to have everybody switch out. We assigned John, who was four inches shorter than Laettner, to guard him. We used Deron to roam the court like a center fielder. Deron was supposed to go for the steal or bat the ball down. John was to make sure that nothing went toward the basket.

The final play of the 1992 season will always be frozen in everyone's mind.

Laettner started out on the right side and broke into the

middle. He just ran up and sealed Deron. John thought he had Hill's pass sighted and moved up to make the interception. But the ball curved away from him. When he went to adjust his position, he had no idea where Laettner was at that moment. The films show Laettner and John both going after the pass and the bigger body winning out. Deron found himself behind the Duke star when the pass arrived.

Stealing a short pass is easy. But there is always more margin for error with a homerun pass. If Deron had reacted too soon and the ball went over his head, Laettner would have had a layup. Deron made the correct move: "Hold your ground. He'll miss the shot."

Once Laettner caught the ball, Deron and John were a little tentative. I can understand that. Laettner hadn't missed a free throw the entire game. Laettner did take a dribble, but people have to realize the clock doesn't start until after he touches the ball. He took a fallaway shot that hit nothing but net.

Cawood was professional to the end during his final broadcast of a Kentucky game, describing the action:

"Hill has the ball two and one-tenth seconds to go. Here we go. The ball is in the air. Ball comes in to Laettner. He catches it. Puts a dribble on the floor. Turns and puts up a jumper. Ball's up in the air.

"It's in.

"That why they're number one in the country."

Then there was stunned silence.

Mike was a gracious winner. Amidst the celebration, he spotted Richie and put his arm around him. "I'm sorry Richie," he said. "I'm so sorry."

"What a tremendous, tremendous game," he told CBS. "It wasn't a game that anybody lost. Whoever had the ball last won. We beat a very determined and great basketball team."

When he finished, he walked over to Cawood and asked to speak to the listeners across the Commonwealth. He wanted to express his feelings for our team.

As I walked off the court, I was looking to shake Mike's

hand, but I didn't find him immediately. My mind was going in a hundred different directions. All I could think about was how to lift the players' spirits once we got to the locker room, after such a devastating loss.

We suffered through an extremely emotional scene in our locker room. I tried to to bring up all the positives our seniors had accomplished over the past three years. But anytime I would mention something, our players started crying and getting more emotional.

I didn't know how to lift their spirits.

The harder I tried, the more they wept.

I was in a fog when I left our locker room to meet with the press. I was totally incoherent. I didn't know what planet I was on. I spoke to the media. I didn't even know where I was. Our players were the same way as we got ready to take the bus back to the Warwick Hotel.

One UK fan came up to Richie and tried to console him. "We'll get 'em next year," he said.

Richie shook his head yes, then walked away.

"Ain't gonna be a next year for me," he said.

His roommate Chris Harrison understood.

"I always have next year," he said. "For the seniors, it's over."

The movie *Rocky* has its final scene at the Spectrum, when Rocky Balboa goes the distance in a 15-round heavyweight championship against Apollo Creed.

"This was a fitting way for our Rockies to go out, since it took place in Philadelphia," I said. "Even though Rocky may have lost the fight, there were no losers. There were no losers in our game with Duke, either."

If anything, we gained the respect of the rest of the country.

When we got back to the hotel, there must have 300 fans there to greet the team. When we arrived home in Lexington the next day, there were more than 4,000 who had driven to Lexington from all over the state. Traffic was tied up around the airport for two and a half hours while cars tried to squeeze their way into the surrounding parking lots.

Cassandra Kessinger, a UK student from Lawrence, and her brother Kyle brought along a present for the team. They topped a tall trophy Cassandra won in a teenage beauty contest with one Kyle received in a basketball tournament, constructing a unique six-foot trophy designating Kentucky as "The Fans' National Champions." She crossed the tarmac and presented the trophy to the team.

The sight of all those fans may have been the first revelation to the seniors that their college careers were over.

The basketball office looked like a funeral home for the next few days. There were flowers and food everywhere.

I had to go to the Final Four on business, but there were still some loose ends to tidy up. I called Dale Brown into the office to find out if he planned to come back next year. He said he did, and things would be much different.

Just before I left for Minneapolis, we received some good news on the recruiting front. Rodrick Rhodes had just received his February SAT scores, and he had achieved a high enough score to be eligible to play as a freshman. What was so good about that was that we could also take Walter McCarty.

Rodney Dent was taking a correspondence course at Southwest Oklahoma. If he received his degree and showed up in Lexington next fall, that would give us four new faces to blend with our returning players. He was supposed to send his official scholarship forms in April 15. The future for Kentucky looks bright.

But it was this year's team that had left an impression on everyone at the Final Four. I ran into John Havlicek, the Hall of Famer from the Boston Celtics, late one night at the Hyatt in Minneapolis.

He said to me, "Boy, my heart broke for you, watching that game."

I said to him, "John, you've been involved in a lot of those games. What about the Boston-Phoenix triple-overtime play-off game in 1976? That had to be a very emotional game, very similar."

"Rick," he said, "I've been involved in a lot of those games, and have seen a lot of games since I retired. Our game with Phoenix was not as well played. It was emotional. But your game with Duke was the most exciting game I've ever seen."

"John," I said, "I'm biased, but hearing you say that makes me think you might be right."

I never stayed in Minneapolis long enough to watch Duke defeat Michigan, 71–51, to win its second straight NCAA title. I left Sunday and was back in Lexington in plenty of time to watch the championship game on TV. It was a little anti-climactic.

Apparently Cawood felt the same way.

Cawood did his final broadcast that night. Everyone was coming up, congratulating him on his brilliant career. "How could I tell them my season ended last week," he said wistfully.


I knew I'd never forget our four seniors.

C.M. didn't want the fans to forget what they had done for Kentucky, either. He told me he had a surprise planned for John, Deron, Sean, and Richie at a special awards ceremony at Rupp Arena the following Tuesday night.

C.M. invited the general public, free of charge, to the celebration. Some started to arrive early. Robert Vallandingham and his son Donald, who had been first in line for Big Blue Madness, were there at eight the night before and ended up sleeping overnight at Rupp. By the time the doors opened at six the next night, a line had spread halfway around the Civic Center complex. When the music started, there were over 13,000 in the seats. Many had never been inside Rupp before. Many had never seen the team that close, so they brought cameras to record the moment. Hundreds of flashbulbs went off as the lights went down and the spotlight shown on each member of the team as they paraded onto the floor during introductions.

I've never been big on awards banquets, where they charge $100 a plate and only the affluent can attend. This would be different. This night was for the grassroots fans. This was their team.

Our fans witnessed one of the most inspirational moments in Kentucky history. Jamal had collected his MVP award. Sean had received the Reggie Hanson sacrifice award. The other honors had been given out. Then C.M. called the four seniors and their families to center court.

"Many have scored more points than you have," he said. "They have won many more individual honors. But no one can match what you've given us by putting your heart into the wearing of the Kentucky jersey. Look to the ceiling."

Up there, sandwiched between Jackie Givens and Adolph Rupp, hung replicas of the jerseys of John Pelphrey, Sean Woods, Deron Feldhaus, and Richie Farmer. Their jerseys— Pelphrey's No. 34, Sean's 11, Deron's 12, and Richie's 32—will be retired in the rafters of Rupp Arena forever.

When C.M. told me they were going to retire their jerseys, I thought the school was going to put all four names on one jersey. They were such a team.

I watched their expressions when C.M. made the announcement. It was one of the most moving experiences I'd had in coaching.

The players appeared stunned, especially Richie. "I can't believe it," he said to his parents.

John was at a loss for words. "It's a big one," he said. "Something you don't dare dream about. I've seen a lot of great players who aren't up there."

"It's kind of scary," Feldhaus said. "You know Kentucky history. I guess, now, we're going to be a bigger part of it."

"Hey, out of all my years here, this is the most special night in my UK history," Sean said. "In my wildest dreams, I never dreamed my jersey would be retired."

C.M. wanted to make a statement about where this program

had come in three years, and he did. "The players up there are All-Americas," he said. "The players here contributed in a different way."

Some people missed the boat on why these players' jerseys were retired. The negative people will scream that, statistically, they don't deserve it. But they're not being honored because of their stats.

"In the last three years people have grown to appreciate a great effort and attitude, and that winning is not a bottom-line thing," C.M. added. "Can you imagine the despair, the second-guessing that would have taken place coming out of the Duke game? I sensed none of that."

I can still remember that first day I met them. I was saying to myself, you left Mark Jackson, Patrick Ewing, and Kiki Vandeweghe and the rest of the Knicks for this?

One was a skinny kid with red hair. One was an overweight guy who just wanted to talk about fishing. One never looked me in the eye and wanted to leave the meeting. And one was trying to sell me a couple of watches. But I saw John, Richie, Deron, and Sean in a different light after three years. It could get bigger at Kentucky. We could go further. But it couldn't be any better.

When we got back into the locker room, I called the team together for a few last words.

"They didn't wait for you to get old and gray," I told the seniors. "They honored you while you're still in your prime."

Then, I looked at the rest of the team.

"These guys showed you the way. They showed you how to achieve greatness," I said.

John wanted to take one more memory with him as he left Rupp. A bed sheet had been hanging from the upper right corner of the building. It read, "Pelphrey is God."

John shook his head at first. Then he figured, what the heck, and retrieved it.

"I'm going to put it on my bed," he said.

After all, it's only 210 days until the start of basketball practice.

# Epilogue

$\mathbf{E}$very spring, our seniors conduct an independent barnstorming tour in which they play exhibition games against local teams throughout the state.

It is a rite of passage.

It was also one final victory lap for Deron, John, Richie, and Sean.

Van Florence helped organize this year's tour. Then, Van hit the road with the seniors, Reggie Hanson, and two of our managers, Spence Tatum and Jeff Morrow. Rex Chapman also played in some of the games. They appeared in 25 towns in six weeks, playing before crowds of close to 5,000 in packed high school gyms. The players gave $10,000 from their earnings to the UK Library Fund, $5,000 to Big Brothers, and another $5,000 to AIDS Research. Twenty percent of the money went back to the communities that they played in.

I originally planned to play a couple of games myself, but

the NCAA put a stop to that because some of the towns planned to use high school athletes.

For the most part, it was a lot of fun. Deron got a chance to play against his brothers Allen and Willie when the seniors played in Maysville. John scored 50 points in a game at Hazard.

And the Richie Farmer legend took another quantum leap. When the touring team played in Manchester, Richie scored 110 points as the seniors defeated a Clay County all-star team, 179–176. Richie hit 30 three-pointers. He scored 68 first-half points and 42 in the second half. He even played for both teams. He scored 107 for the seniors before switching late in the game and getting his last 3 for Clay County.

John hit a three with 25 seconds left to put the seniors ahead by three points. Clay County set up a play to free Richie up for a three. But the seniors triple-teamed him and wouldn't let him get it off.

Richie will always remember that night when he writes his autobiography and goes into the insurance business with his father. Deron signed a contract to play in Japan. He will be joined there by Reggie Hanson, who still has an itch he has to scratch. Guess I'll be looking for a new strength coach. John and Sean are going to give the NBA a shot.

This spring someone else is having a rite of passage, too. Kentucky said a final farewell to the 66-year-old Cawood Ledford. Rupp Arena was the site of a dinner that raised $135,000 for the Cawood Ledford Scholarship Fund at UK. The fund is intended to help athletes work on their degrees after their eligibility expires.

I meant it when I told Cawood I couldn't have a better friend in 50 years than I'd had in the past three.

As for our program, Dick Vitale was already starting to beat the drums for next season. He had us ranked in his preseason Top 5 again, and had Mash rated among his Top 5 players in the country.

Replacing our seniors won't be easy. But Mash, Gimel, Dale, Jeff, Travis, Andrew, and Aminu should give us a solid nucleus. Jeff and Travis are both almost 100 percent again. Jeff's knee has been responding well to rehabilitation, and Travis should be much more effective following off-season surgery to repair a partially fractured kneecap. Carlos Toomer, sensing it would be difficult earning playing time, transferred to St. Louis, giving us an extra scholarship.

Help was on the way, too.

Rodrick Rhodes and Tony Delk both played in the McDonald's All-America game at Atlanta on Easter Sunday. Walter McCarty, Jarett Prickett, and Delk played in the Derby Classic in Louisville. Immediately after the McDonald's game, there was a wild rumor circulating that Othella Harrington, who had scored 19 points, grabbed 21 rebounds, and was selected MVP at the McDonald's game, was ready to sign at Kentucky.

I didn't know anything about it. But a story to that effect had actually moved on the AP wire and had been picked up in *The New York Times*. As it turned out, Harrington said he was interested in Kentucky because he felt I could help him get to the NBA. The next week, he held a press conference and claimed his top three schools were Georgetown, LSU, and Mississippi State.

He eventually signed at Georgetown. At least, we don't have to play against him in the SEC.

I still felt we had a better recruiting year at Kentucky than Michigan did in 1991 when they signed their Fab Five. The reason? I don't think Chris Webber and Jalen Rose will be around for four years. Our four incoming freshmen will be. I expect Rodney Dent, our junior college transfer, to be around for the next two years.

Dent finally sent off his letter of intent April 19. We received it at 12 noon via fax. I was relieved. Dent, who had committed to us in December, was originally supposed to have sent it by Federal Express four days earlier, but it never arrived. When Herb went to call him at his girlfriend's house in Dallas, the phone was off the hook. When Herb finally got through, his girlfriend said Rodney had gone to Atlanta to visit his mother's grave.

The next thing we knew he was spending the weekend on the Louisville campus. I was livid. His guardian Warren Heagy told us the trip was a spur-of-the-moment thing and that Rodney made the trip to Louisville out of friendship with assistant coach Larry Gay. According to Heagy, Dent had known Gay since he was a sophomore in high school.

It was most bizarre. I know one thing, if Rodney had signed with Louisville, I would have recommended we stop playing them in the interstate rivalry. Denny Crum and I both belong to the same golf club, but I don't think we'll be playing any rounds together in the near future.

The Kentucky-Louisville feud will never go away completely. But I put it out of mind for the moment. I had more important things to think about. Joanne was seven months pregnant. I was anticipating the birth of our baby daughter, Jaclyn. Herb was getting married. My brother Ronnie was continuing to improve. He was at a hospital in Westchester County, where he was trying to regain mobility in his legs and his arms.

Ralph had a chance to leave Western Kentucky for the head coaching job at Baylor. But, he decided to stay in Bowling Green for the time being.

The Kentucky Derby was coming up. I went over to Louisville to watch Rail run at Churchill Downs the Thursday before the big race. He was second coming around the turn, but the jockey lost the reins and he finished fourth.

I didn't have much more luck at the Derby. I loved Arazi, but he never finished with the same burst of speed he showed in the stretch run last November at the Breeder's Cup. I wasn't the only one disappointed; Arazi finished eighth before a crowd of 132,543. Lil E. Tee, who went off at 16–1, won the race and paid $36.50 to win.

Pat Day, the leading winner in the history of Churchill Downs, broke his nine-year Derby jinx by riding the horse to the winner's circle, where the three-year-old colt was presented with the traditional horseshoe of roses.

For Kentucky, it truly was a year for local heroes.

# --22--

## *TAKING THE NEXT STEP—THE 1992-1993 SEASON*

This time, Christian Laettner wasn't around to spoil the fun.

This time, we didn't leave anything to chance.

Kentucky was going back to the Final Four for the first time since 1984. We had defeated Florida State, 106–81, to win the Southeast Regional Finals at the Charlotte Coliseum. The predominately pro-Kentucky crowd, which had bought up most of the tickets, was going wild, chanting, "SEC, SEC" in the heart of ACC country.

After our senior walk-on center Todd Svoboda put the finishing touches on our victory with a three-pointer at the buzzer, he jumped into Jeff Brassow's outstretched arms and the celebration started in earnest.

Joanne and the boys made their way through the security guards to join me at center court. I motioned to John Pelphrey and Richie Farmer—who had made the trip with us—and they bounded out of their seats behind our bench and leaped over the press table and onto the floor to join the current players as we cut down the nets.

John and Richie had come so close last year and I wanted them to experience this, even if it was twelve months later.

"I'd probably be a water cooler on this team," John said later.

"I'd probably be a manager," Richie chimed in. "I don't see where I'd play on this team."

This was the best college team I had ever been involved with, in terms of talent, depth, and athletic ability. We won thirty games. We turned Freedom Hall into Three-dom Hall the night in December when we routed Louisville, 88–68. That alone should have made Bill Keightley's season. Someone even sent him a Christmas card with a cartoon of Jock Sutherland reading a newspaper with the final score. He keeps it over his desk as a reminder. We won the ECAC Holiday Festival, defeating St. John's in the finals, and even found time to celebrate at the Carnegie Deli. We defeated national powers like Indiana, Georgia Tech, Vanderbilt, LSU, and Arkansas during the regular season and were actually ranked No. 1 for a week in January.

But we saved the best for last.

I've been lucky. All three of the NCAA tournament teams I've coached have come on strong in March. This one was no exception. For three straight weeks, we were untouchable, winning a second straight SEC tournament and then disposing of four NCAA opponents by an average of thirty-one points on the way to a spot in the national semifinals at the New Orleans Superdome.

The momentum that carried us to the Final Four actually began in Lexington at the SEC tournament. We were scheduled to play Tennessee in the first round. The Vols had just beaten us, 78–77, with a fluke four-point play in the final seconds in Knoxville two weeks earlier and were looking to string together some late victories in hopes of stealing an NCAA bid.

We had been in the driver's seat against Tennessee, leading 77–74 with four seconds remaining when Allan Houston stepped to the line. Houston sank the first, then missed intentionally. The Vols grabbed the rebound after the miss and Corey Allen laid it in and was fouled. He sank the free throw to give Tennessee a storybook victory.

The unexpected loss really bothered our fans. You should have heard the callers to the talk shows. "What's wrong with Kentucky?" They were panicking.

But we weren't. We told the players not to worry about losses like that. They played hard. Luck just wasn't on their side. The important thing was to win the next game and execute better. They did. That started us on an uptick. We squeezed by Auburn on Senior night, scored 98 points on Ole Miss, beat Florida, at Gainesville, 85–77, on ABC-TV. Then we defeated Tennessee—by 61 points.

The final score was 101–40.

We got off to a 14–0 start and went on to hand Tennessee their worst loss ever. It was 41–13 at half. We completely shut down Allan Houston. Houston, the SEC's leading scorer, had burned us for 58 points in the two previous games. But this time Dale Brown did a great job on him. Houston was 0-for-6 in the first half and did not score his first and only field goal until 4:52 remained in the game.

Our fans like to point out that Todd Svoboda, who entered the game with 7:32 to go, actually outscored Alan that night, 4–3. Svoboda has been our human victory cigar all year. He transferred to Kentucky from Northern Kentucky, a Division II school near Cincinnati. Todd was a star at Northern, averaging 18.1 points and 10.1 rebounds as a junior. But he forsook his senior year at Northern to pursue the dream of playing for a national power. Under a dual degree program, Northern and Kentucky allow students to pursue a degree in chemical engineering with three years at NKYU and two at Kentucky.

When Todd contacted us about walking on, we informed him upfront he would not receive much playing time. But he didn't seem to mind being a practice player. He has since become a cult hero.

We didn't have much time to savor the victory. The game, the last of a quarterfinal quadrupleheader, didn't start until after 9:30 and didn't end until after midnight. And we had a big game the next afternoon with Arkansas. The SEC has a rule about keeping the locker rooms open for thirty minutes after the game so the media can interview the players. But we immediately shepherded them onto the bus so they could get some sleep.

When our players woke up the next morning, they found the city had been covered by a deep blanket of snow. Nine inches of the white stuff had fallen, closing I-64 east of Winchester and I-75 south of Richmond. Some areas had as much as twenty inches, making this the worst storm to hit the state since 1978. We had to send a four-wheel-drive over to pick up Joanne at the house.

That did not stop the fans from showing up. A crowd of 23,623 packed Rupp that afternoon for our SEC showdown with Arkansas. Arkansas had beaten us two straight times and almost five thousand of their fans traveled to Rupp to watch the game.

"You don't know Kentucky fans and Arkansas fans," Arkansas's coach Nolan Richardson said. "I know our fans didn't come to sit in hotel rooms or Winnebagos. And it would probably take two more feet of snow for Kentucky fans to stay home."

When the game started, it looked like we might bury Arkansas under an avalanche of our own. We got off to a 17–0 lead. But Arkansas came back and gave us quite a scare. With 15:23 remaining in the second half, Dale picked up his fourth foul. We were clinging to a 55–53 lead when Travis Ford left after picking up his fourth personal with 13:03 to play. But we never let Arkansas gain the lead. Nolan Richardson has always been one of my favorite coaches. His teams play hard and I enjoy their style of play.

Mash and four subs held on, building a 66–61 lead until Travis returned. We went on to win, 92–81. Travis finished with 26 points, making 6 of 9 three-pointers. This entire season was a coming out party for him. He had 29 in our big network-TV win over Indiana.

In just one year, Travis has changed from Eddie Haskell to Billy Donovan, Jr. He lost seventeen pounds and recuperated from a nagging knee injury. Shaun Brown and JoAnn Hauser pushed Travis through rehabilitation last summer. In the process, he gained some much needed quickness and became the leader we hoped for when he transferred from Missouri.

The fans here love him because he's one of their own. Travis was born to play for Kentucky. When he was five years old, his father Eddie, who was coaching Webster County High, taught Travis proper shooting form by having him lie on his back and flick his wrists as he shot the ball at the ceiling to develop the proper form. The only time Travis shot at a real basket, he was restricted to layups.

Some of that must have rubbed off.

Travis is truly one of the great shooters I've seen. Anyone who's ever seen Travis in one of our shooting drills knows he could win some of those NBA contests where you take the balls out of the rack and shoot three-pointers. He has put on some great exhibitions in practice. He once made two hundred straight from the free throw line and he rarely, if ever, makes less than sixty of seventy shots from the seven spots we use for individual instruction.

Travis made six three-pointers and scored 18 points during our 82–65 victory over LSU in the SEC finals. He made 14 of 22 threes in the three games and eventually went on to win MVP in the tournament. As effective as Travis was, Andre Riddick still stole the show in the finals against a team that had upset Vanderbilt, 72–62, in the other semifinal.

Andre scored 15 points, grabbed 10 rebounds and blocked 9 shots, playing his way onto the all-tournament team by outplaying LSU's 7' All-SEC center Geert Hammink. Riddick, who got a start after Rodney Dent injured his ankle against Arkansas, shut down Hammink, who shot just 2 for 20 and scored only 9 points.

You should have seen the proud look on the face of Andre's mother Lenora, who made her first visit to Rupp, along with her other son Adrian and Andre's adopted baby sister Rasheeda. When I recruited Andre, his high school coach told me it was a bad mix. I told Andre when he arrived that my job and his was to get him to love the game. I think he has a steady date now.

After the game, we made our way over to Da Shea's to eat and watch the NCAA selection show on CBS. The trip across the street was a lot easier than the trip to the TV studio where I do my weekly show on Saturday night. I drove over there with Jersey Red, who had come in for the weekend. Ours was the only car on the road and I couldn't believe it when we almost ran out of gas on the way back in a blizzard. We finally found a self-serve station that was open twenty-four hours. I was out there pumping gas and Jersey was inside, buying Kentucky lottery tickets.

Time for some fun in the sun. I really thought we were going to Orlando. I was hoping we would. So apparently was Commonwealth Travel, which began booking packages to the home of Disney World a week before the bids came out. But a half hour before the pairings were announced, C.M. Newton, who is a member of the tournament committee, called to inform me we were going to the No. 1 seed in the Southeast and would play in the subregional at Nashville.

C.M. said our first-round opponent would be Rider College. He told me the NCAA likes to reward a No. 1 seed by sending them to a site close to campus. Nashville is only a three and a half hour drive. I'm sure that pleased our fans, who had bought up most of the tickets at Memorial Coliseum as soon as they went on sale. Scalping is legal in Tennessee, so you can imagine the prices for two good courtside seats. Got change for a $500 bill?

Kentucky fans were getting fired up for the occasion. Two Lexington businessmen even wrote a parody of George Thoroughgood's "Bad to the Bone." It was entitled, "Blue to the Bone," and the first verse went something like this: "We're the wildest of all Cats, our reputation's well known. We're the bad of the baddest. We're Blue to the bone."

We felt good about ourselves going into the tournament. We were getting off to incredible starts. Even in the Arkansas game, we jumped out, 21–2. We were playing with great confidence. We had no fear of failure. Some people get into the tournament and turn conservative. We were more concerned with picking up the pace of the game.

A lot was made of the fact that we were going back to Memorial, where the benches are located along the baseline. We had lost to Vanderbilt there this season, but the problem that night was not the sight lines.

The fans who packed the arena Friday night got to see us put on another show. Andre came up big again with 16 points and we had 11 players score during a 96–52 victory. We led at halftime, 63–24, but we wanted to keep the score under 100. No need to embarrass a team that had worked hard to get here, winning their conference tournament on a shot at the buzzer.

I couldn't believe our opponent Sunday was Utah. Neither could Herb, who was almost suicidal. No one could believe Utah was an eight seed. They had been in the Top 10 part of the year and I thought they were one of the better teams in our regional. They were well coached, experienced, and had four good shooters, including forward Josh Grant, who was the WAC's best player.

We took a break from preparations Saturday to go out to dinner at the Warehouse Restaurant. While we were there, the TV in the lounge was showing Ralph Willard's second-round game between Western Kentucky and Seton Hall.

Ralph's success was one of my greatest treats of the season. I told Joe Iracane, the man who hired him at Western Kentucky, Ralph would put the school back on the map in two years. Ralph made a big splash in New York when he knocked off the Big East champions. Our players were going wild, jumping up and down. I was too. P.J.'s a great friend, but I've known Ralph almost my entire life.

Utah coach Rick Majeras set the stage for this one when he compared our team to the UNLV team his Utes had played against in the 1991 Western Regional semifinals. UNLV went on to reach the Final Four.

We took that as a compliment.

Our team jumped on Utah, taking a 27–8 lead and then cruising to a 82–63 victory. Just before we took the floor, we decided to start Jeff Brassow in place of Jared Prickett to stop Utah's small forward who was a great three-point shooter and force Utah to make defensive changes on Mash. Utah tried to alternate Grant and center Larry Cain on Mash. But Mash took Grant inside and center Larry Cain outside for 16 points and 10 rebounds in the first half. Mash finished with 19 points in just twenty-five minutes. We had ten players score. Nine had assists.

When we didn't play freshman forward Rodrick Rhodes for disciplinary reasons, speculation began to run wild in Jersey City he might transfer back home to Seton Hall after his freshman year. As it turned out, the rumors had started with his brother's telling people in Rex Chapman's club in Lexington that the two of them would sit down at the end of season and make a decision. I called Rodrick in and reminded him his sister asked me to guide him. Eventually, he owned up to the truth and didn't try to cast blame elsewhere. He told me he'd be crazy to transfer.

The worst thing that happened to him occurred when he got off to a fast start. Rodrick scored 27 points against Georgia Tech. He was the MVP in the Holiday Festival. He thought he had arrived. He had a lot of things to learn—that early success can turn into failure. He embraced success instead of managing it. He began getting outplayed in practice by both Jared Prickett and Jeff Brassow and ended up being the third best freshman on the team, behind Jared and Tony Delk.

As soon as the game ended, the hype began for the meeting with Wake Forest, specifically the matchup between Mash and Wake's powerful 6'7", 250-pound ACC Player of the Year Rodney Rogers.

Rogers, like Mash, was a potential high lottery pick and there was growing speculation he might also leave at the end of this, his junior season. When Mash was in high school, he seriously considered Wake. Both he and his mother Helen made a recruiting visit to the school and she seemed impressed. But Mash said he felt more comfortable with Kentucky.

Good thing.

Mash was the first Kentucky player since Kenny Walker in 1985–1986 to make consensus first team All America. I sat down with Mash prior to the start of the season and we decided it was in his best interest to declare for the draft at the end of the season. I just felt by dealing with it early, Mash wouldn't constantly be bugged by questions about whether he was going to leave or not. If you know, say so. Boom, it's over. I think it kind of diffused the pressure on Jamal because there was no debate.

Mash was going to be a high lottery pick in the draft, which means he should sign a contract worth more than $2 million a year. I believe in the whole Peter Pan thing—that for most people it's in their best interest to stay in school four years and walk on that stage with your classmates on graduation day. But you have to remember the family background in this case and the financial deals that will be available to him at season's end. The money is so incredible that you cannot be a risk-taker and say, "Okay, I'll go one more year."

For those irrational people who say you have to graduate, they should try to understand that for people like Mashburn, basketball is their vocation. Jamal is a bright young man who can come back in summer school and earn his degree if he so desires.

I'll miss him as a player and a friend. I didn't want Jamal to walk out the door at Kentucky without at least some recognition. So, two days before Senior night, we called a press conference so he could make his official announcement. We wound up honoring Junior, Dale, and Todd before the game, then held a special ceremony for Mash afterwards.

He ran through a hoop bearing his picture with the words, MONSTER MASH. JAMAL MASHBURN, printed on it. Mash was accompanied by his mother. He seemed very embarrassed by all the attention. He just wanted to get the heck out of there. Mash does not like being the center of attention. He doesn't mind stepping up, but he doesn't want all the glory for himself.

When Mash finally signs his pro contract, he says the first thing he wants to do is buy his mother, who is a bookkeeper for a Harlem River housing project, a new car and a house. "She's trying to decide between West Virginia, where she grew up, and North Carolina," Mash said. "She has a map now. She can live anywhere she wants."

I was studying the scouting report on Wake Forest on our flight to Charlotte. When I got to the page about Rogers, the lights went out. Lightning had hit the plane. It traveled the length of the plane and went right through the fuselage.

I had been trying to get my son Michael to sit down most of the flight. As soon as the lights ran out, he ran up the aisle and slid into the seat next to me.

"Dad," he said, "if I'm going to die, I want to be with my family."

We didn't find out until we landed that we had lost a piece of the tail.

That was not the first time we had experienced trouble flying. When we were flying to Georgia during the regular season, we were about to take off in that old charter aircraft we use and the engine caught on fire. We ended up making arrangements to fly two private jets and two commercial planes to Athens. We've since junked that fifty-year-old plane, sent it back to Casablanca, and got a beautiful new forty-seat jet. Every seat is first class.

Once on the ground in Charlotte, things went much smoother. Mash was the man the night we played Wake, scoring all 23 of his points in the first half as we went on to defeat them, 103–69. Wake's SID was so impressed, he looked over at Chris Cameron and said, "I feel like I'm watching Jordan in the finals."

The only part negative occurred when Florida State defeated Western in the first game. If Ralph and I had played each other, it could have been a tough situation. But when Western lost, Ralph stayed and helped us out with our scouting report on Florida State. If we had lost and he had won, I would have done the same thing.

Travis was selected MVP after we defeated Florida State. Mash and Jared Prickett also made the all-tournament team. Jared had the best game of his college career to date, scoring 22 points and grabbing 11 rebounds.

After the game, Florida State guard Sam Cassell had no idea who had done his team in, referring to Jared as "that guy—No. 32."

"That guy" has an old-fashioned Larry Bird work ethic ring to it. Jared's greatest challenge all year was that he had to work every day against Mash in practice. If you don't play hard, Mashburn will embarrass you. Jared's work ethic can be traced directly to Jared's roots. He comes from Fairmont, West Virginia, a coal mining town in the heart of a poor state. His father Don was a 6′ guard who played for Fairmont State, then went into the mines after graduation. He has since become a foreman.

Don Prickett taught his son how to survive in a hard-nosed world. Jared said the two used to play one-on-one all the time at the local middle school and it wasn't until Jared was a junior in high school that he actually beat him.

Jared chose Kentucky because he said our wide-open style

reminded him of his favorite NBA team, the Lakers. He was a perfect fit, running the floor and attacking the boards. And he has worked so hard to improve himself. Jared made just 39 percent of his free throws in high school. But we changed his form completely in individual instruction and he wound up shooting 67.1 percent from the line this year.

Three weeks before our trip to the Final Four, Joanne and I had made a trip to New Orleans for a speaking engagement. We arrived March 7, the day our son Daniel had died.

We both attended mass that day and the priest read from the Book of Daniel. "Rick," Joanne said to me, "It feels like an omen. I think we're destined to be here again at the end of the month."

She was right. We came back.

The last time I took a team to New Orleans for a Final Four, it was a very difficult time in our lives. I know I was preoccupied. This time, we decided to have a good time. We left on Wednesday and turned the players loose on Bourbon St. that night. Reporters and TV crews followed their every move. The streets in the French Quarter were already filled with Kentucky fans. I don't know how they got tickets. Kentucky was only given an allotment of 3,000, and only 500 went on sale to the students and general public. But our fans always seem to find a way.

While we were in the Quarter, we passed by a fortune teller. I jokingly told Billy Donovan to go in and ask who she thought was going to win our game with Michigan.

"Coach," he protested. "I've got on a Kentucky shirt. What do you think she's going to say?"

The next afternoon, we got down to business. We took a bus over to the University of New Orleans for a two-hour practice. Travis gave us all a scare during the scrimmage when he collided with Tony Delk, hitting his head on Tony's knee. Travis had to be helped to the bench, then blacked out. JoAnn Hauser thought it might be a concussion and we didn't take any chances.

Travis spent the night in his room with a severe headache. But he was back on the floor the next afternoon for our shoot-around at the Superdome. Some of the writers suggested the wide-open background might affect our shooting. I didn't bring it up. I don't believe in dwelling on the negative.

Mash and Travis did their most to dispel that notion when they staged a friendly game of H-O-R-S-E near the end of our hour long workout. Travis made two in a row from near half-court. Mash countered by making three in a row from twenty-five feet out on the left sideline near press row.

Mash finally put an end to the contest by driving the lane for a dunk. Travis just shrugged his shoulders and laughed. He knew he couldn't match that.

At the beginning of the tournament, the media focused most of its attention on Indiana, Michigan, and Duke. Kentucky was almost an afterthought. Once we got to New Orleans, the media jumped onto our bandwagon, calling us, "Killer Cats." Confidence must have been running high among the Kentucky faithful, too. Joe B. Hall was quoted in the New Orleans *Times–Picayune* as saying he felt Kentucky's players were in a class by themselves and that they would "humiliate Michigan." I can't believe Joe would make that statement. It had to be a joke!

For a team that had reached the Final Four two consecutive years, the Michigan players had been constantly criticized. Bill Walton even went so far as to call them the "biggest underachievers" in the history of the sport.

I'm sure Michigan carried the sting of those criticisms with them into the game. They played well during their 81–78 overtime victory against us, showing patience on offense, getting the ball inside to Chris Webber and Juwan Howard, making free throws and playing good defense.

We pretty much had had our way in the tournament. But this was an uphill battle. We played a good game, but Michigan took away some of the things we like to do. Travis had as good a tournament as a player can have. He fed off all the attention Jamal was getting on the floor.

In our game, Michigan chose not to pay as much attention to Mash. They stayed home on Travis and defended the three-point shot and it hurt. Travis did not score in the first half and finished with just 12 points. That game taught him what he has to worry about next year—to beat his man off the dribble.

We played the final moments without three starters. Dale Brown, who finished with 16 points and was having his best game as a Wildcat, suffered a bruised shoulder after crashing into a press table while diving after a loose ball with 6:13 left in regulation. Jared fouled out with 4:36 remaining in over-time.

Even though we shot only 41 percent, I still liked our chances. We thought Michigan was weary in the overtime. We were going to create motion and isolate Mash by spreading the offense. We wanted to take advantage and utilize his skills. Mash scored 26 points and helped us rally from an 11-point deficit to take a 76–72 lead. But after he fouled out with 3:23 left, we could manage only two more points—both free throws by Tony Delk. It wasn't enough.

Our fans filed from the dome in dead silence. Our players were very emotional, too. Dale was sobbing, realizing this may have been his last game ever and wondering what might have happened if he had not been injured. Travis was covering his eyes. I was upset, too. This loss hurt.

It was a tough night. I spoke to the team and we drove back to the hotel in silence. I went up to visit my mother, who had flown in from New York, and my uncle and aunt who had come over from Florida. But nobody felt like talking. Jersey told me he was leaving on the first flight out the next day. We originally planned to stay until Tuesday, but wound up flying back to Lexington on Monday. We never stuck around to watch the championship game between North Carolina and Michigan.

As a coach, you always want to win it all when you enter the tournament. I figure if you're in it long enough, you have a chance. But you have to keep things in perspective. Unless you win it all, there's bound to be some measure of disappointment. Michigan went away disappointed. So did Florida State. I did an interview with ESPN's Roy Firestone and he suggested I was the most talked about, respected coach who had never won it all. I'm the luckiest man in the world. I've coached three different tournament teams that had chances to do well. We've been to the Final Four, Elite Eight, and Final Four. I'm not greedy. I'm proud of what we've accomplished.

And the future looks bright.

Mash, Dale, Junior, and Todd may be gone, but we have Travis, Gimel, Rodney, Jeff, Jared, Andre, Rodrick and Tony back from our first ten, along with Chris Harrison and three new additions—Walter McCarty, Anthony Epps, and Jeff Sheppard.

Walter had to sit out as a Prop. 48 but should have a chance to move into Mash's spot. Jeff is a 6'4" guard from McIntosh High in Peachtree, Georgia, who has been compared by some to Rex Chapman because of his flying airing style. He even wears Rex's old number 3. Anthony is an All State guard from Marion County who was the MVP in the Kentucky State Tournament but will get a scholarship because of Aminu.

We underwent some changes in postseason, too. Aminu Timberlake announced his intentions to transfer to Southern Illinois. At the same time, we picked up a good one in 6'9" sophomore forward Mark Pope, who decided to leave the University of Washington after there was a coaching change there. Mark was the Pac-10 Rookie of the Year and figures to fit right in on our front line after sitting out for a year.

We also lost Herb Sendek to bigger and better things when he was chosen to be the head coach at Miami of Ohio. He became my tenth assistant to get a head coaching job. He interviewed Youngstown State, but he didn't think that was the right job for him. He was one of two finalists at Nevada-Reno, along with Pat Foster of Houston. Then the Miami of Ohio job opened up when Joby Wright went to Wyoming. It was a perfect job for him. Billy's time will come too.

I offered Herb's fulltime assistant's job to Bernadette. But she said she wanted to stay parttime. I think she'd like to have a family and pursue a career in athletic administration. So I moved Del Ray Brooks, one of my former players at Providence who had spent the year as our assistant strength coach, into Billy's spot, and Billy into Herb's position.

Next year, most of our talent will be in the sophomore class. Everett Case, the former coach of North Carolina State, used to have an old adage. Take sophomores and make your schedule difficult for them for that season—do a lot of scheduling on the road—and they'll be better off in the long run. This will be our toughest schedule in five years—we're going to Maui for the holiday classic there, playing UMass at the Meadowlands, Syracuse and Indiana on the road. We also play Louisville and Notre Dame at Rupp.

In the old days with Kentucky, the SEC schedule was a lightweight. Now our conference schedule is tough, so there will be no easy games.

I spent a couple of restless nights early in May when I was contacted by representatives of a few pro teams. If I had been thirty, I might have jumped at the chance at either job. But I'm forty now, and money is not the most important thing in my life. I'm not ready to move from Kentucky. My players are special young men. I've always felt there must be a motive to move. There certainly is no reason to leave; winning is the greatest vehicle for future opportunities. Kentucky offers me the true motive to stay: a chance to win.

At a press conference, I told the Kentucky media, "I have some good news and some bad news. The good news is I'm not going to the NBA. The bad news is that I've taken a job to coach the Silician national team. The pay is good, and my contract is for lifetime or until I lose."

To me, Kentucky is the best college coaching job in America. I really like this group of players and I want to stay around for a while to see how they develop. I guess I'm starting to bleed Blue.